The Dominion
of
Women

THE DOMINION
OF
WOMEN

The Personal and the Political
in
Canadian Women's
Literature

Wayne Fraser

CONTRIBUTIONS IN WOMEN'S STUDIES, NUMBER 116

Greenwood Press
New York • Westport, Connecticut • London

Library of Congress Cataloging-in-Publication Data

Fraser, Wayne.
   The dominion of women : the personal and the political in Canadian
women's literature / Wayne Fraser.
      p.   cm. — (Contributions in women's studies, ISSN
   0147-104X ; no. 116)
   Includes bibliographical references and index.
   ISBN 0-313-26749-9 (alk. paper)
   1. Canadian literature—Women authors—History and criticism.
   2. Women and literature—Canada.   3. Politics in literature.   4. Sex
   role in literature.   I. Title.   II. Series.
   PR9188.F7   1991
   810.9'9287—dc20   90-38417

British Library Cataloguing in Publication Data is available.

Library of Congress Catalog Card Number: 90-38417
ISBN: 0-313-26749-9
ISSN: 0147-104X

First published in 1991

Greenwood Press, 88 Post Road West, Westport, CT   06881
An imprint of Greenwood Publishing Group, Inc.

Printed in the United States of America

The paper used in this book complies with the
Permanent Paper Standard issued by the National
Information Standards Organization (Z39.48–1984).

10 9 8 7 6 5 4 3 2 1

For El

For Kate, John and Alexa

Contents

Preface

This book grew out of a love of reading. While reading, I noted the use of
the term "interior colonisation" to describe women's position in a male-
dominated society. Because the "colonial mentality" of Canadian literature
and culture was a well-accepted concept, I wondered if there could be any
literary relation between the two "colonies." I do not know how to convey
my surprise upon discovering, on the first page of Frances Brooke's *The
History of Emily Montague*, the hero stating his choice of Canada over New
York for the purpose of colonization because "the women are handsomer."
Could Brooke, I asked, a clergyman's daughter and a clergyman's wife, be
conscious of the innuendo in Rivers' talk of "cultivating" the *"human face
divine"*? Three pages later, with ribald humor, Rivers' friend uses the term
"colonisation" with just such sexual connotations. Two hundred years ago!
In the first Canadian novel! By a woman! In amazement, I proceeded to
examine the literature of Canadian women for what other female authors
did with—to use Brooke's phrase—"the politics of the little commonwealth
of woman." My discoveries, still ongoing, have, I suggest, implications for
historians and critics of women's literature.

I make my invitation to historians with some degree of humility, for I
realize that I could be a better historian, more knowledgeable about historical
facts and issues. Nevertheless, every stage of research revealed that each
author was confronting the events and issues of concern to historians. Frances
Brooks, Anna Jameson, Catharine Parr Traill and Susanna Moodie have been
long valued for their historical interest, that is, for the pictures of life they
recorded of their times. But such factual interest in these works overlooks
the personal dimension and thus misses the implicitly political. For instance,
in later editions of Jameson's journal, many personal references were edited

out in order to highlight the information deemed essential by historians; in so doing, the editors missed much of the original's political intent. As another example, Carl Berger concludes his *Sense of Power*, a study of imperialism, with two quotations from Sara Jeannette Duncan's *The Imperialist* to illustrate the imperialist fervor at the turn of the century. However, if Berger had realized the satiric intention of the romantic subplots, he would have seen that the novel fully supports his own contention that the imperial ideal "demanded too much of human nature." The title of Brooke's novel—*The History of Emily Montague*—provides the directive for historians: it is the history of a person, a woman, Emily Montague. I am not the first literary critic to suggest that history can be learned from literature, but I am arguing the nature and the value of women's literature to that field.

The operative words of my title, the relationship of the "personal and the political," moreover, provide a yardstick for measuring women's literature. The designation "woman's novel" is usually a disparaging term, denigrating the content of such "unimportant" matters as love, marriage and domesticity. Margaret Ann Jensen argues in her study of the Harlequin romance novel, *Love's Sweet Return*, that the woman's novel is avoided by academics, unlike westerns or thrillers, because it is associated with women, and is therefore automatically assumed inferior. Certainly reviewers of Margaret Laurence's *The Fire-Dwellers* dismissed its subject matter, a portrait of a middle-aged housewife, as unworthy of her talents. Even the protagonist cries out, "If I could only talk about it. But who wants to know and anyway, could I say?" Laurence knows, along with Bell Fermor in *The History of Emily Montague*, that "no politics is *worth attending to* [but] the little commonwealth of woman," that to attend to the feminine realm is to embrace the politics of the wider community. Denied active political power, throughout history, even to the present day, women writers employed "women's literature" as a venue for political analysis. Whatever we label it, the quality of each "woman's novel" can be measured by the political connotations of its personal contents.

I also recognize my temerity in publishing this examination of women's literature in light of the controversy surrounding "Men in Feminism." I recall Professor Elizabeth Waterston's gentle gibe at me during discussion of some of the formative ideas developed herein; she wanted to know why I was reducing issues important to women to mere matters of national politics. There could be a gem of truth in her joke, but I hasten to evoke Elaine Showalter's admonition not to "prejudge male feminist criticism, [to] refuse to give it a hearing. . . . [It] comes from friends rather than rivals." I write neither as a historian nor as a feminist, but as a literary critic; my focus is the text in its social and political context. While the universal theme of the novel concerns the individual in relation to community, the specific distinction of this study is that the individual protagonists and writers are women. It is hoped, again to quote Showalter, that the reader will find the analysis "genuinely exciting, serious and provocative, and that it has large and important cultural implications."

Having analyzed the perspective of the distaff, it would be useful to explore the spear side, the relationship between the feminine and the national in literature written by Canadian men. Unfortunately, the excessive length of this study would not allow consideration of male authors, but preliminary observations reveal that some men perceive a relation between the feminine and the Canadian psyche. The political connection is most straightforward when the author employs a female narrator. Sinclair Ross's depressed Mrs. Bentley in *As for Me and My House* is an apt objective correlative for the Great Depression. In Brian Moore's *I Am Mary Dunne*, the title character's confusion about which name to use, her own or her British husband's, reflects the identity crisis felt by many Canadians in the early 1960s. Robert Kroetsch in *Badlands* employs two narrators, William Dawe and his daughter, Anna, juxtaposing his and her stories; the female's is the more contemporary, the more hopeful. However, when a male novelist uses a male narrator, he presents women and the nation in a negative light. Mordecai Richler's Jake Hersch in *St. Urbain's Horseman* despises both his "Air-Canada promoting" mother and Canada. Robertson Davies' Dunstan Ramsay in *Fifth Business* discovers the rejuvenation of the feminine, but only through contact with women quite outside the Canadian landscape. The males in *Badlands* "light out for the territory" in true American fashion and Dawe fatally rejects the feminine realm.

The relation of gender-identity and national ethos raises some fascinating complexities for male writers. If a man perceives a feminine caste to the nation's identity, what happens to his masculine gender-identity? It is a commonplace to assert that men have reacted to the women's movement with some anxiety, that the advent of women's power threatens men's traditional position. In the above novels by male authors, there are some highly vulnerable male characters. What will happen, after all, to Mr. Bentley's art after he follows his wife to the city, away from his beloved prairies? If Hat Bell in Moore's novel is any model, he'll commit suicide at the loss of his talents. Or perhaps like Jake Hersch he'll be unable to take his own artistic ability seriously. Perhaps worse, he'll discover like Dunstan Ramsay that his books go unappreciated in his own country. Or like William Dawe will he "come to the end of words"? With the exception of Davies, these male writers were expatriates at the time of writing these particular novels. Sinclair Ross wrote his novel of Saskatchewan while working in Manitoba and he describes in an essay for *Mosaic* his entire writing career as a form of exile. Are male authors perhaps ambivalent about both nationalism and feminism? Whatever explorations in this field in the future, it will be important to keep in mind that when we are discussing feminine and masculine in writing, we are not defining rigid sexual barriers, but genres of gender. Literature as well as people must be liberated from sexual stereotyping.

How else could Laurence Ricou label *Badlands* one of Canada's most important feminist novels?

The political ramifications make the woman's novel instructive and important to men, as well as to women. In the novels I have examined, the authors recognize that the building of Canada, the maintenance of Canada, has required more of the feminine in us than we often care to admit. The phrases describing Canada—cultural mosaic, federal-provincial cooperation, community of communities, cooperative federalism—emphasize relatedness, the essence of femininity. The Canadian role as peace-keeper in international affairs, her gift for compromise, accommodation and conciliation—these strengths derive from our ability to work at relations among the various regions and ethnic groups of our nation. The tandem progress of the women's movement and of Canadian nationalism continues. In the Canadian Constitution of 1982, women were guaranteed equal rights in the Charter of Rights and Freedoms. As these rights are tested in the courts, the makeup of Canadian society will undergo change. As feminists in the 1990s redefine femininity, Canada too will rearticulate her identity as a nation. To understand the history and process of Canada's social and political evolution, it is advisable, this book argues, to continue to examine what women writers are saying.

Acknowledgments

Dr. Evelyn J. Hinz of the University of Manitoba English Department deserves my great appreciation for her encouragement and guidance throughout the course of this study of women's literature. Her faith in the project and her persistence led to its publication.

For their helpful comments on early drafts of this manuscript, I must acknowledge Dr. Elizabeth Waterston of Guelph University, and Drs. David Arnason, Robert Kroetsch and J. E. Rea of the University of Manitoba.

Finally, I want to thank my friend and colleague, Dr. Eleanor Johnston, who has helped immeasurably at every stage of the process—reading, talking, sharing ideas, editing and preparing the manuscript for publication. And as well, I thank our children, Katie, John and Alexa, for their patience and love.

Introduction

"Perhaps history would not be so lop-sided if we could hear *her* story as well." Following this directive from the Women's Liberation Movement, Susan Mann Trofimenkoff, in "Nationalism, Feminism and Canadian Intellectual History," argues that, by ignoring the role of women in Canadian intellectual history, historians—mostly male—have seriously limited their understanding of nationalism. She discovers many similarities, for example, in the "nationalism and feminism in French Canada at the turn of the twentieth century": "both . . . clearly stated a superiority to the Anglo-Saxon or male world around them . . . [and] promised to cleanse, purify and rectify society."[1] Trofimenkoff maintains that a new and valuable understanding of Canada's intellectual history might emerge from consideration of the relationship, in Canada, of nationalism and feminism. Yet she acknowledges that examination of the role of women in the development of nationalism is difficult because "until relatively recently women did not leave tracts for study, did not write, and therefore by implication did not think" (p. 16). In fact, there is such a "written record," for what Trofimenkoff overlooks is *literature* written by early Canadian women.

Other historians have not ignored this material but unfortunately, in making use of it, have discarded precisely that which is most valuable for a study of nationalism: namely, the personal element. Frances Brooke's *The History of Emily Montague* (1769), for example, has been valued by social historians essentially for its descriptive scenes of life in Quebec at the time of the Conquest. Anna Jameson's journals similarly have been appreciated mainly for their portraits of Indians and settlers in Upper Canada in 1836–37. Catharine Parr Traill and Susanna Moodie have been studied primarily for their contribution to our understanding of pioneer life in the backwoods of Canada.

Ignoring the distinctively feminine elements of this literature, these historians effectively transformed "her story" into history.

Moreover, in assuming that the personal dimension is irrelevant to his-
toriographical concerns, such researchers have failed to recognize the basic
contention of the women's movement: that "the personal *is* the political," a
contention which accounts for the more than purely metaphoric use of political language to describe and protest against the position of women. An
extremist version cries, "housewives are political prisoners."[2] A more rea-
soned approach is to be found in Betty Friedan's 1963 analysis, *The Feminine
Mystique*, which distinguishes the subject of her study—American housewives of the 1950s—from the women who "want careers, higher education,
political rights—the independence and the opportunities that the old-fashioned feminists fought for."[3] The very title of Kate Millet's *Sexual Politics*
(1969) emphasizes the political focus of her analysis of male-female relationships. And so subversive is Germaine Greer in 1970 that she hopes her
polemic, *The Female Eunuch*, will encourage women, "the true proletariat,
the truly oppressed majority . . . [to] revolution."[4]

Moreover, many analysts of woman's psychology and literature have used
the political language of colonialism to describe woman's position in a male-
dominated society. Karl Stern, in his 1965 *The Flight from Woman*, notes
that "for millennia women have suffered atrocious forms of social and legal
injustice. It is no exaggeration to say that they have been, and often still
are, the victims of a kind of interior colonialism."[5] Rosalind Miles too, in
her 1974 *Fiction of Sex*, concludes that nineteenth-century women writers
"embodied in their fiction the imposed social attitudes of the dominant sex.
Women writers were more influential even than men in keeping other
women in a carefully defined and rigidly restricted place. To borrow a metaphor from political philosophy, their colonization by male supremacists was
complete: they policed each other."[6]

If the colonial metaphor is apt for the condition of women in general, it
is particularly appropriate for Canadian women—for their country has struggled under the bondage of imperialism. Canada was established as a colony
of Great Britain and her parliamentary government, with the Crown of
England at its head, retains traces of colonialism to the present day. Canada
as an economic colony of the United States is an equally accepted concept
which has been much discussed since World War II, during the pipeline
debate of 1955 and, more recently, during debates over the Free Trade
Agreement. In the former discussions, the effect of our political and economic
structures on our culture may not have been noticed by Canadians at large,
but, as early as 1943, Northrop Frye reviewed Canadian literature and found
that it suffered from what he defined as "the colonial in Canadian life," the
artist's compulsion "to seek a conventional or commonplace expression of
an idea."[7] As well, W. P. Wilgar in 1944 discussed what he concluded was
the "Divided Mind in Canada": in order for artistic production to emerge

in Canada, the artist "must begin to evaluate actualities, to find a personal integrity, and to decide what he wishes to preserve from the culture of the Old World and from the strong movements of the New."[8] During debates over the Free Trade Agreement, however, heated concern was expressed over the effect of the agreement on Canadian cultural industries.

The colonial mentality of Canada has for some time been known to have shaped Canadian literature. Not surprisingly, therefore, there is a special immediacy to Margaret Laurence's use of the colonialist metaphor in her contribution to a collection of essays entitled A Political Art (1978). In addressing the implicit question of whether her novels are "political," Laurence maintains that "writers of serious fiction are almost always . . . consciously or unconsciously, expressing their own times"; by creating individualized characters who live in a specified time and place, the novelist provides "social commentary at a grassroots level."[9] Giving examples from her own experience, Laurence compares the struggles of Canadian and African writers to find their own "voices," to articulate their own experiences, rather than expressing the cultural norms of ascendant imperialist powers: "I was from a land . . . which in some ways was still colonial. My people's standards of correctness and validity and excellence were still largely derived from external and imposed values; our view of ourselves was still struggling against two other cultures' definition of us" (pp. 22–23). Laurence then connects her developing understanding of Canada as a Third World nation, a colony, with her growing awareness of "the dilemma and powerlessness of women [within Canadian society], the tendency of women to accept male definition of ourselves, to be self-deprecating and uncertain"; "to me the parallels seem undeniable" (pp. 23–24). Laurence's very "political" response to her analysis of these two forms of colonization was to choose, for her novels, "the theme of independence which was both political and inner" (p. 22).

Literary critics have begun to explore this colonialist metaphor in women writers. Barbara Hill Rigney, for example, in her 1978 study Madness and Sexual Politics in the Feminist Novel, notes that the protagonist of Margaret Atwood's Surfacing (1972) "like the exploited wilderness, represents Canada itself and its predicament as a political victim."[10] Lorna Irvine, in Sub/ Version: Canadian Fiction by Women (1986), analyzes contemporary women writers with the premise that "her story, the story of feminism, can, on one level, be perceived as another version of the colonial story. But it can also articulate a female voice that politically and culturally personifies Canada."[11] Finally, Coral Ann Howells, in the introductory essay to her Private and Fictional Words: Canadian Women Novelists of the 1970s and 1980s (1987), "Canadianness and Women's Fiction," notes that "the colonial mentality and Canada's recent emergence from it, have close affinities with women's gendered perceptions of themselves . . . as they struggle to find their own voices through which to challenge traditions which have . . . excluded them from power."[12] Only Howells explores the "best known nineteenth century records of English women's pioneer experience . . . as they rewrite male pioneer myths from the woman's point of view" (p. 14), but she offers only generalized conclusions. In the specific chapters on Laurence and Atwood, Howells does not develop the political dimension to any great extent. Irvine and Rigney, as well, are primarily concerned with psychological readings of the novels in an attempt to articulate the feminist voices of contemporary women writers. Their emphasis lies more on the "personal" than the "political."

Following Laurence's lead, then, my purpose in this study is to examine the connection between the twin forms of colonialism expressed by the Canadian woman writer throughout Canada's history. Specifically, I want to explore the interrelationship between the various reflections by women writers on the political development of the country and on the state of women in their times. The study focuses on eighteen major works written by ten women over the course of the history of English Canada, 1766 to 1988. The texts have been chosen partly on the basis of their literary sophistication and recognized cultural significance and partly on the basis of their coincidence with or treatment of important historical periods or events. Thus the study begins with an examination of Brooke's *The History of Emily Montague*, which is set at the time of the Conquest and is the first novel to be written about Canada. Jameson's *Winter Studies and Summer Rambles in Canada* (1838), Traill's *The Backwoods of Canada* (1836), and Moodie's *Roughing It in the Bush* (1852), which frequently have been discussed by both literary critics and historians, all comment on the 1837 Mackenzie rebellion. The conjunction, at the turn of the century, of imperialism and the women's suffrage movement is examined by Sara Jeannette Duncan's *The Imperialist* (1904), Nellie McClung's *Purple Springs* (1921) and Martha Ostenso's *Wild Geese* (1925). Ethel Wilson's *Hetty Dorval* (1947) and *Swamp Angel* (1954) take place in the depression and the post–World War II era. The impact of the new nationalism of the 1960s and 1970s and of the Women's Liberation Movement are explored by Laurence in *The Stone Angel* (1964), *The Fire-Dwellers* (1969) and *The Diviners* (1972) and by Margaret Atwood in *The Edible Woman* (1969), *Surfacing* (1972) and *Lady Oracle* (1976). Finally, Margaret Atwood's novels of the 1980s, *Bodily Harm* (1981), *The Handmaid's Tale* (1985) and *Cat's Eye* (1988), reveal the extent to which the relation of the personal and the political has become openly, and unabashedly, the focus of women's literature and criticism.

The chronological structure of the study reflects my concern with the way the rise of feminism parallels and contributes to the growth of nationalism. Accordingly, secondary sources include socio-psychological and feminist studies, on the one hand, and political-historical commentary, on the other. At the same time, it should be emphasized that my objective is to provide neither a history of the development of nationalism nor a comprehensive study of the emergence of feminism. My concern is with what the primary texts in question have to say on these two matters and with the way the authors of these works read from the personal to the political and vice versa. Shirley Neuman and Smaro Kamboureli note in the preface to their *A Mazing Space: Writing Canadian Women Writing* (1986) that study of women writers over the past decade has been "altering our sense of Canadian literary history. It delineates a specifically female tradition within that history and it also enlarges the confines of what has been seen as a dominantly male tradition in order to include women's text."[13] What should become evident to the reader of this study is that Canadian women have always been addressing political issues, providing commentary and reflection, some quite overtly, others more subtly. Moreover, I hope it will become clear why Canada has such a great proportion of distinguished women writers—why in many ways the Canadian literary domain has become "the dominion of women."

NOTES

1. Susan Mann Trofimenkoff, "Nationalism, Feminism and Canadian Intellectual History," *Canadian Literature* 83 (Winter 1969), 8.

2. Jerry Rubin, *We Are Everywhere* (New York, 1971), p. 109.

3. Betty Friedan, *The Feminine Mystique* (New York, 1963), p. 11.

4. Germaine Greer, *The Female Eunuch* (London, 1970), p. 22.

5. Karl Stern, *The Flight from Woman* (New York, 1965), p. 14.

6. Rosalind Miles, *Fiction of Sex* (London, 1974), p. 62. Miles repeats this observation in her more recent *The Female Form* (London, 1987), pp. 46–47.

7. Northrop Frye, *The Bush Garden* (1943; Toronto, 1971), p. 134.

8. W. P. Wilgar, "Poetry and the Divided Mind in Canada," in *The Evolution of Canadian Literature in English, 1914–1945*, ed. George L. Parker (Toronto, 1973), p. 317.

9. Margaret Laurence, "Ivory Tower or Grassroots?: The Novelist As Sociopolitical Being," in *A Political Art*, ed. W. H. New (Vancouver, 1978), pp. 15, 16.

10. Barbara Hill Rigney, *Madness and Sexual Politics in the Feminist Novel* (Madison, 1978), p. 100.

11. Lorna Irvine, *Sub/Version: Canadian Fiction by Women* (Toronto, 1986), p. 11.

12. Coral Ann Howells, *Private and Fictional Words: Canadian Women Novelists of the 1970s and 1980s* (London, 1987), p. 3.

13. Shirley Neuman and Smaro Kamboureli, *A Mazing Space: Writing Canadian Women Writing* (Edmonton, 1986), p. x.

The Dominion
of
Women

1

"A Husbandman As Far As Theory Goes": The Distaff View of Colonization

In the first Canadian novel, Frances Brooke's *The History of Emily Montague* (1769), land and women are connected from the outset as areas open for male colonization. Thus, Ed Rivers, the male protagonist, informs his friend in England, John Temple, that he has chosen Lower Canada over New York for his new home because he has heard that "it is wilder and . . . the women are handsomer." He hopes in Canada to become "lord of a principality which will put our large-acred men in England out of countenance. My subjects indeed at present will be only bears and elks, but in time I hope to see the *human face divine* multiplying around me; and in thus cultivating . . . I shall taste one of the greatest of all pleasures, that of creation, and see order and beauty gradually rise from chaos."[1] His language reveals that beneath his central position in the creation of "order and beauty" lies the assumption that the "divine" is masculine. Nor are the sexual connotations of colonization and "cultivation" missed by his licentious friend who responds to his letter with ribald humor: "Indeed! gone to people the wilds of America, Ned, and multiply the *human face divine*? 'tis a project worthy a tall handsome colonel of twenty-seven . . . excellent . . . for colonization: *prenez garde, mes cheres dames*" (p. 20).

Frances Brooke was well acquainted with men such as Rivers. When she published her novel, Canada was politically a colony, indeed only the northern part of the vast holdings of British North America, newly won after the Seven Years' War with France. The Treaty of Paris in 1763 had transferred the "St. Lawrence Colony" of New France to British control, and "Quebec," as it was renamed, was officially a British colony under military rule. Brooke came to Quebec City in 1763 to join her husband, John Brooke, who was chaplain of the garrison and who also held a political post, deputy of the

auditor general of Quebec. They remained five years and Brooke was acquainted with officers of the occupying army and members of the colonial
administration. Their stay in Quebec overlapped the governorship of General
James Murray and his successor, Guy Carleton. Recent archival research
has discovered that the Brookes were not popular with Murray, but seemed
to be so with Carleton. Murray found them "meddlesome"; Lorraine
McMullen has demonstrated that the differences with Murray were political.[2]

There was a good deal of political tension during Murray's time as governor. The policy at the time of Conquest called for the anglicization of
Quebec: the Royal Proclamation of 1763 had instructed Murray to establish
institutions of law and government "as near as may be agreeable to the Laws
of England."[3] Such intentions also included the replacement by the Church
of England of the existing Roman Catholic. Governor Murray, however, had
become sympathetic to the French Canadians' desire to maintain their religion, language and civil code of law; his sympathy was in part a reaction
against the pressures put upon him by English traders who had entered
Quebec from the American colonies with the hope of gaining control of the
new markets. The traders wanted British laws and customs in operation in
order to give themselves an economic advantage. They petitioned the king,
charging that Murray was not "acting agreeable to that confidence reposed
in by your Majesty" by encouraging the French "to apply for Judges of their
own National Language."[4] Murray for his part called them "Licentious Fan-
aticks" in his report and urged that the Canadians, "who are perhaps the
bravest and the best race upon the Globe," be granted "priveledges" [sic]
of religion.[5] It was his feeling that safeguarding French institutions would
ensure loyalty to the Crown, especially if there was rebellion from the
American colonies. Murray was recalled, however, and Carleton was dis-
patched to implement the orders of the Royal Proclamation.

History seems to place Frances Brooke squarely on the side of the English
traders. Mary Jane Edwards, for example, in her introduction to *The Evolution of Canadian Literature in English: Beginnings to 1867* (1973), notes
that interest in the new colony in England contributed to the novel's success
and that "views about Quebec expressed in the novel are important...
because they catch some typical eighteenth-century British thinking about
the future of this North American colony."[6] Edwards sees these views en-
dorsed by Brooke herself, just as in a more recent article she states that
Brooke "earnestly hoped that Carleton would encourage [the] establishment
[of English law, religion and language] and win the Canadians to their use."[7]
Moreover, McMullen, in a more extensive study of Brooke's life and works,
points out that the Brookes were of "the English Party" and she advances
the convincing case that John Brooke himself was the model for the character
of William Fermor, whose letters in the novel are the most descriptive and
political, presenting clearly the case for anglicization. McMullen concludes

that Brooke, "as the daughter and wife of Anglican clergymen," would have been "in accord with the [religious] views expressed by Fermor."[8] Closer examination of the novel reveals, however, that Brooke was sharply critical of the prevalent attitudes of the day.

She had been so earlier in her career. W. H. New has examined Brooke's "first publishing enterprise, a 37-issue weekly periodical called *The Old Maid* (1755–56)"; under a nom de plume, "Mary Singleton, Spinster," Brooke created fictitious correspondence between Singleton and other "old maids."[9] Through this format, New observes, she was able to use "sentimental literary conventions to argue wryly with certain social conventions," and having analyzed her techniques of characterization and her "social analysis and comment," he concludes:

By taking the province of love and the commonwealth of women as her overt topic, Mrs. Brooke does not abandon all discussion of her politics and ideas; instead, she uses what was in her own day a conventional sentimental subject and format to explore social and political attitudes that would otherwise not have been regarded as within her jurisdiction . . . *The Old Maid* shares with *The History of Emily Montague* a concern for political commentary and a commitment to female independence. (p. 11)

The overt subject matter of the novel is love. Written in the "new" form of the epistolary novel, *The History of Emily Montague* consists of letters among the principal characters who live in Quebec, as well as friends and family in England. The primary plot concerns Col. Ed Rivers' courtship of the young lady of the title who first must extricate herself from a promise of marriage to George Clayton. There are two romantic subplots: Emily's coquettish friend, Bell Fermor, pursues the attentions of many men, but finally settles on Officer Fitzgerald; Rivers' licentious friend, John Temple, is reformed through his association with Rivers' tender sister, Lucy. As befits a romantic comedy, there are obstacles to be overcome before the marriages of the principal characters can take place. In Brooke's novel, the barriers to the marriage of Rivers and Emily are broken after they return to England; all three couples marry and settle down in England.

The novel, throughout its history, has been valued primarily for the characters' descriptions of garrison life in Lower Canada.[10] But as New has suggested, this novel of sensibility has ironic and political undertones. Bell Fermor, socialite friend of the title character, notes that "the politics of Canada are . . . complex and . . . difficult" and dismisses them with the assertion that "no politics [are] worth attending to but those of the little commonwealth of woman" (pp. 86–87). Carl F. Klinck, in his introduction to the New Canadian Library edition, makes the mistake of equating Bell's opinion with that of Brooke,[11] but Brooke knows that the two dominions are intimately connected. The language of Rivers' first letter betrays the attitude of an imperial conqueror. The vanity and avarice behind this male attitude to colonization are exploded by Brooke, and in the process the domestic plot of the work is raised to the level of political commentary.

That the attitude of the men in power is inadequate becomes clear in Brooke's ironic characterization of Rivers. Enamored by his first meeting with Emily Montague, Rivers rhapsodizes on her beauty and sensibilities, and in his letter to Temple pronounces: "I am a philosopher in these matters, and have made the heart my study" (p. 30). Critics, like Ann Boutelle, who try to see Rivers as Brooke's characterization of an ideal man of sensibility who even advocates that marriage should be between equal partners, overlook the novel's irony.[12] Rivers' tendency to philosophize about matters of the heart was earlier deflated by Temple himself in response to Rivers: "on the subject of friendship . . . I deny that it gives life to the moral world; a gallant man, like you, might have found a more animating principle[:] *O Venus! O Mere de l'Amour!*" (p. 21). Rivers might well describe his "lovely Emily like Venus amongst the Graces" (p. 31), but he is too obtuse even to recognize that Emily loves him. Watching Emily in company with her fiancé Clayton, he interprets her behavior as a sign of love for this man; he writes his sister, "she loves him; I observed her when we entered the room: she blushed, she turned pale, she trembled, her voice faltered. . . . I hate this man for having the happiness to please her" (p. 53). Months later, as her marriage to Rivers draws near, Emily is still trying to convince him that she was flustered because of his presence, not the presence of her former fiancé (p. 254).

Rivers' questionable understanding of the heart is paralleled by his unsuitability as a successful settler in Canada. During the early stages of his enterprise he reports to his sister his "pleasure of cultivating lands here" and declares that he is not "ill-qualified for this agreeable task: I have studied the Georgicks [*sic*], and am a pretty enough kind of a husbandman as far as theory goes: nay, I am not sure I shall not be, even in practice, the best *gentleman* farmer in the province" (p. 32). At first Rivers' reference to the pastoral poem of Virgil seems to be a little joke on Brooke's part: a Latin poem written in 29 B.C. describing agricultural techniques suitable for Italy is a very inadequate manual for "cultivating" the Canadian wilderness.

When one considers the political origins of the *Georgics* and their portrayal of women, Brooke's ironic intent takes on wider implications. The *Georgics* were written, following a succession of civil wars, in order to help rebuild the country by enhancing the role of the farming peasants. The text was addressed, however, not to the people who would actually do the farming, but to the landowners themselves, the educated classes. As J. W. Mackail explains in his *Virgil and His Meaning to the World of Today* (1963), to approach "the *Georgics* as though they were a technical treatise on husbandry, a handbook for farmers, is to miss their whole meaning. . . . What they were designed to do . . . was to embody . . . an ideal, an imaginative vision, that of a life at peace with itself and in harmony with nature."[13] Furthermore, the *Georgics* were first translated into English by John Ogilby in 1649, the year ending the Civil War in England: thus Brooke's mention of them in a narrative dealing with the end of the Seven Years' War becomes more applicable. Further, when one considers that in the story of the *Georgics* the rape and death of a woman caused the infertility of the land, the reader can begin to see Brooke's feminine and political colors. The British attitude, epitomized by Rivers, cares only for the consolidation of power, and thus ignores both feminine sensibility and the reality of the Quebec landscape. Rivers' misunderstanding of Virgil is an early indication of his inappropriate approach to farming in colonial Canada.

In this light, the connotations both of marriage and of agriculture in Rivers' choice of the word "husbandman" suggest that he is inadequate as a farmer and as a lover; in other words, he is "a husbandman [only] as far as theory goes." Rivers' ideals of colonization are out of touch with the world around him, whether that world is North America or England or the "empire" of women (p. 23). New correctly argues in his "Frances Brooke's Chequered Gardens" that Rivers lacks self-identity and an awareness of reality: "He is a gentleman farmer . . . but by being the gentleman foremost he always stops short of the real thing."[14]

In addition to her ironic qualifications of Rivers' perceptions and postures, Brooke extends her discussion of imperialism in her characterization of the two major women in the novel, Emily Montague and her friend Bell Fermor. Emily is the fitting object of Rivers' adoration, for she is strictly conventional in attitude and behavior, acting always with precise propriety and excessive sensibility. In love with Rivers from "the moment I saw [him]" (p. 249), she is totally submissive to his will. Her only demonstration of a spirit of independence is early in the novel when she decides to break her engagement to the boring, condescending Clayton, despite social pressure to fulfill the obligations of her engagement. We have here that policing of women and interior colonization noted by Miles and Stern. In the social world of the British garrison, Major Melmoth's wife, at whose country home the principal characters often gather, virtually attempts to imprison Emily within the rules of propriety. She reproves "with pain" that Emily is more "quicksighted to [Clayton's] failings than is quite consistent with that tenderness, which . . . he has a right to expect" (p. 87). Mrs. Melmoth comments on Emily's reasons for breaking the engagement: "Though I approve your contempt of the false glitter of the world, yet I think it a little strained at your time of life: did I not know you as well as I do, I should say that philosophy in a young and especially a female mind, is so out of season as to be extremely suspicious." Emily defends herself against this pressure by asserting that "no one but myself can be a judge" (p. 88). However, once free from her engagement to Clayton, she becomes completely subservient to Rivers; she repeatedly tells him, "I have no will but yours" (pp. 179, 259). The extent of her "interior

colonization" is measured by her willingness to give up all personal considerations, even of marriage to him, to ensure Rivers' happiness and good
fortune: "my tenderness for you fills my whole soul, and leaves no room for
any other idea. Rank, fortune, my native country, my friends, all are nothing
in the balance with my Rivers" (p. 108).

The characterization of Emily acts, in the scope of the novel, as a mirror
of Canada under British domination; consideration of Emily's "history" suggests that Brooke intends it so. Emily was raised by her uncle for seven
years in France, taken to England for the remainder of her childhood, and
finally to Canada, whereupon her uncle died. At the novel's close her long-
lost and presumed dead British father appears to reward her not only with
a fortune, but also with a husband, by coincidence Rivers. She is thus,
throughout her four-year stay in Canada, *between fathers*. Rivers early in
the novel reported that there was no society in the colonies, "it being a kind
of interregnum of government" (p. 19). Edwards and McMullen have perceptively deduced that Rivers is specifically referring to the end of Governor
Murray's time in Canada and the advent of the new governor, Guy Carleton.[15] But considering that the Seven Years' War had ended in 1759, and
that the "Most Christian Majesty" of France "cedes and guarantees to his
said Britannick Majesty, in full right, Canada" by the Treaty of Paris in
1763,[16] the wider implications of Rivers' remark and of Emily's portrait
become clear. During Emily's brief four years in Canada, she is in hiatus,
awaiting confirmation of her engagement to a British gentleman; during the
period of the novel's action, the land of Canada is likewise in hiatus, awaiting
consolidation of British rule.

Brooke does not intend, however, that Emily's final self-effacement should
be the paradigm of future political arrangements. She criticizes the attitude
of both the colonial and the colonized through the comments of Emily's
friend, Bell Fermor. As others have noted, it is Bell who gives life and
vitality to the world of the novel and who functions as "a foil for the extreme
sensibility of the principal characters."[17] Her name, echoing as it does her
quip that she has "become an excellent farmeress" (p. 61), places her in
definite contrast to the "pretty . . . husbandman," Rivers. She continually
mocks both Rivers and Emily for their conventionality and foolish idealism.
Emily declares her love for Rivers in terms of self-negation: "I love him—
no words can speak how much I love him. My passion for him is the first
and shall be the last of my life. . . . I have no pleasure but in Rivers' conversation, nor do I count the hours of his absence in my existence" (pp. 153–
54). Bell, in contrast, denies such sentiments for herself: "I love, at least I
think I do; but, thanks to my stars, not in the manner you do. I prefer
Fitzgerald to all the rest of his sex; but *I count the hours of his absence in
my existence*; and contrive sometimes to pass them pleasantly enough"
(p. 154). At the novel's end, when both couples marry in England, it is Bell's
skeptical comments on Emily's marriage which overshadow Rivers' final

remarks concerning their blissful future: "It is your great fault, my dear Emily, to suppose your love a phoenix, whereas he is only an agreeable, worthy, handsome fellow, *comme un autre*. . . . beauty is in the lover's eye . . . however highly you may think of Rivers, every woman breathing has the same idea of *the dear man*. . . . Our romantic adventures being at an end, my dear; and we being all degenerated into sober people, who marry and *settle*; we seem in great danger of sinking into vegetation . . . " (p. 313). The first two phrases which Bell emphasizes mark her keen sense of irony, just as the third correlates marital and geographical settlement. Bell's diction implies that this particular colonial male and his colonized female, who were originally going to settle in the backwoods of Canada, are suited at best for a life in the old country, not the new. Edwards concludes that "Brooke removes her characters from Canada and presents an essentially ambiguous view of its politics" because "she feared [Carleton] wouldn't—possibly knew he couldn't"—establish British social codes in Quebec.[18] The comments of Bell Fermor suggest rather that Brooke doubted he should.

Bell's viewpoint is given further credence in the novel by her changing reaction to the landscape of Canada. McMullen speaks, in "Frances Brooke," of "the alarm with which [Brooke's] protagonists view the coming of winter" but cites only Bell's responses as examples (pp. 41–42); McMullen leaves the impression, even in *An Odd Attempt in a Woman* (1983), that all of the characters change their attitudes as Bell does. Bell's reaction is actually and definitely contrasted to those of the protagonists. Emily seems oblivious to the natural world around her, so caught up is she in her own sensibility and her love for *her* Rivers, rather than the natural rivers. For his part, Rivers sees the country only as a means of satisfying his pride and avarice: "This colony is a rich mine yet unopen'd; I do not mean of gold or silver, but of what are of much more real value, corn and cattle. Nothing is wanting but encouragement and cultivation. . . . I rejoice to find such admirable capabilities where I propose to fix my dominion" (p. 33). Nor through the course of the novel does he ever alter in his colonial attitude to the country. In contrast, as New has correctly argued in his "Chequered Gardens," Bell "throughout the book cultivates her landscape and . . . recognizes Canada for what it was—a wilderness garden with its own pleasures, its own advantages, its own prospect of danger and development, not a simple balance to cultivated civilization, nor a few acres of snow to be summarily dismissed" (p. 35). Not only is Bell lively and open in matters of the heart—unlike Rivers and Emily—but also she is free enough to learn to appreciate the Canadian landscape and French society for what they are. On her departure for England, she alone of the major characters expresses "regret which I had no idea I should have felt, at leaving the scenes of a thousand past pleasures" (p. 235).

In the last third of the novel, which stands in ponderous contrast to the lively Canadian section, the difference between Bell and the other trans-

planted characters demonstrates that all is not well in the conventional world
of England. There, all obstacles to the marriage of Rivers and Emily are
slowly but finally resolved. Still doubting that Emily loves him, Rivers, with
her, in their marriage and subsequent housekeeping arrangements, creates
and artificially maintains a contrived social world; Emily will make, she
declares, a "wilderness" of flowers on the estate and, dependent on his
father-in-law's money, Rivers trusts that his "dear groupe [sic] of friends
[will] have nothing to wish, but a continuance of [their] present happiness"
(p. 316). New perceptively observes in "Chequered Gardens" that the mas-
querade party at the novel's end signifies that the major characters "in happily
accepting the life they are living as the best of all possible worlds are living
with masks across their eyes, while Bell [who does not attend], living in the
same community, remains conscious of the rigours they choose to ignore"
(p. 36). As already noted above, Bell's fear of marital boredom undercuts
Rivers' final hopes of social happiness. His jest to Bell, "I must teach you
to love rural pleasures" (p. 314), suggests his own discomfort and points out
his ignorance of nature in contrast to Bell's acquired knowledge in Canada
about love and society. He and Emily will live in a world of their own
creation, supported by the conventions of their society; Bell lives in the
same society but acknowledges its artificiality. That they are settling in
"Bellfield" gives further weight to Bell's viewpoint.

The novel unmasks conventional views of nature and human nature and
shows how they do not transfer well to the harsher world of the North
American continent. A colonial, accepting the conventions of British society,
is inadequately prepared for the experience of life in Canada. The attitude
of domination seen in Rivers and the response of total submission made by
Emily are not positive bases for marriage, or for the British takeover of New
France. Historically, of course, exposure to the situation in Quebec did force
the questioning of those accepted colonial standards. The Quebec Act of
1774 actually reversed the policy set forth by the Royal Proclamation of 1763
and instituted in great part the very recommendations of Governor Murray
for the maintenance of French language and religious rights. Although historical evidence seems to suggest that Brooke supported the anglicization
of Canada along with her husband, the evidence of the novel implies that
perhaps, like Bell, Brooke was less than convinced by conventional opinions.
At any rate, the novel provided her with a forum in which to question those
issues.

Another British woman who came to Canada with just such criticism in
mind was Anna Brownell Jameson. She came for a nine-month stay in December 1836, out of a sense of duty to her estranged husband, the current
attorney general of Upper Canada, in order to help him further his political
career. Clara Thomas has done extensive, invaluable research on Jameson,
pointing out that she "was a respected authoress with a large circle of friends

and acquaintances, very much a part of the literary life [in England] of her day."[19] In 1838 she published in England a three-volume diary of her stay, *Winter Studies and Summer Rambles in Canada*.

Marian Fowler's more extensive biographical exploration, *The Embroidered Tent* (1982), expands our picture of Jameson's literary life by considering the nature of her marriage. Her relationship with Robert Jameson had always been difficult; after only five days of marriage, they went their separate ways.[20] Both Thomas and Fowler maintain that Jameson came to Canada not just out of a sense of duty to her husband, since married men gained political preferment more readily than separated men, but in the hope of "settling their marriage" one way or another.[21] She gave up much by coming. She had seven books to her credit, two of which were feminist in intent; before her voyage to Canada, she had lived independently in Europe for two years. In the opening entry of her journal, she records her "regret for what I have left and lost."[22] Her husband, on the other hand, seems to have gained the benefit of her visit: in the spring of 1837, he became Canadian vicechancellor. In a letter to a friend, Jameson comments that "he has much power."[23] Both Fowler and Thomas have noted that Jameson's unhappiness with her husband is "externalized" in her writings.[24] Fowler, in particular, advances the thesis that the gloom of the "Winter Studies" is in part caused by the misery of life with Robert, whereas the exhilaration of the "Summer Rambles" stems from her decision to leave the marriage (p. 159). What neither biographer has noted, however, is that Jameson projects her marital tensions onto her portrait of the political situation in Upper Canada.

Her book was well-received in England, primarily because of its timely publication; in 1838, there was great interest in the state of the colonies because of the recent rebellions in 1837 in both Upper and Lower Canada. Jameson quite probably capitalized on this interest, for she mentions in the opening sentence of her preface the "difference of opinion" and "animosity of feeling" surrounding "the country to which [the journal] partly refers" (I, p. v) and offers no convincing reason why the book has been rushed into print by its London publisher. Furthermore, the time span of the diary is significant and consciously determined by Jameson: it is dated December 1836 to late September 1837. The rebellion in Upper Canada, led by William Lyon Mackenzie, occurred on December 4, 1837. Jameson had left Canada in the autumn of 1837, but had been in New York until January of 1838 awaiting her separation papers from Robert, so she had been in North America at the time of the rebellion and she does refer to "the late revolt" in her preface.

Jameson's journal coincides, then, with the political tensions rising toward the violent confrontation, and she summarizes the salient features in volume I. In the spring of 1836, the autocratic governor, Sir Francis Bond Head, had clashed with the Reformers of the Executive Council and they resigned (I, pp. 146–48); Bond dissolved the elected legislature. In the ensuing election, Bond actively campaigned on the Tory side, which won resoundingly. During the time of Jameson's stay in Canada, the reform movement was frustrated in its inability to effect any change in the administration of the colony. The main thrust of its platform was that the governor should follow the advice of the elected representatives of the people, especially in matters of local concern, a principle to which Jameson coyly gives support when she concludes her summary: "as far as I can understand . . . the government of this province is not derived from the people who inhabit it, nor responsible to them or their delegates" (I, p. 148).

Throughout this turbulent period, Jameson's husband was deeply involved in the colonial administration, rising to the head of the judiciary. If Frances Brooke had been acquainted with the British authorities at the time of the Conquest because of her husband's position, Anna Jameson was even more so, as she was a prominent and important social figure, "the Chancellor's Lady." Indeed, she reports that she has "seen both sides" of the political argument (I, p. viii). One can only conjecture whether Jameson had read *The History of Emily Montague*, but comparison is certainly possible between the political intent of this work of fiction and Jameson's diary. In *Emily Montague*, Brooke brought into question many of the assumptions and values of colonial rule, even using her husband as a model for a character who advocates anglicization. Jameson's husband, in *Winter Studies and Summer Rambles*, is noticeably absent; Jameson was under pressure to do or say nothing which would embarrass or endanger Robert's position (I, pp. 35–36). But, unlike Bell Fermor who declares that "no politics is worth attending to, but the little commonwealth of woman," Jameson forthrightly states: "I am not one of those who opine sagely, that women have nothing to do with politics" (I, p. 104). Fowler's conjecture that Jameson felt much jealousy of her husband's position, particularly in light of all she sacrificed to come to Canada, is validated by her outspoken views in the published diary.

Despite her disclaimer in the preface that she has "abstained generally from politics and personalities," Jameson gives a damning summary of the administration's abuse of the colony (I, p. xi). Frances Brooke used the coyness of a coquette in her characterization of Bell Fermor in order to introduce an ironic viewpoint into her novel; Jameson employs in her journal similar self-effacing irony. By asserting that politics "are foreign to my turn of mind and above my capacity" (I, p. xi), she is able to make the following contradictory statement: "these notes . . . written in Upper Canada . . . have little reference to the politics . . . of that unhappy and mismanaged . . . country" (I, p. viii). She draws attention to the fact that the "breaking out of the late revolt" has "abruptly and painfully awakened" some "sympathy *now*," but concludes that neglect "has too long existed" (I, p. ix). With such an indictment serving as the introduction to her book, it is little wonder she could report in a letter to a friend that her husband was "much displeased."[25]

Certainly the bulk of her journal avoids direct reference to "politics and personalities," but she does describe the political parties in volume I, as well as the Prorogation of the House by Governor Bond Head in March of 1837, adding her own commentary on certain acts of the legislature. She concludes her summary with the comment that she was "never able to make out . . . to my own satisfaction . . . whether I am Whig or Tory or Radical" (I, pp. 104–5). The overall focus of the journal, however, suggests where her sympathies lie.

Her position as "Chancellor's Lady" is the focal point of her questioning. Thomas has made clear in *Love and Work Enough* (1967) that Jameson's prominent social status was founded on a false marriage and that she felt conscious of playing a definite role for the sake of her husband's career (p. 126). To be her husband's "lady" required her to give up independence and literary fame. Colonized as she was by the dominant power of her husband, she astutely analyzed the colonial tensions of Upper Canada. In the first volume, she pictures herself hemmed in by "domestic matters" (I, p. 259) and "this relentless climate" (I, p. 171); but "while imprisoned" she is unable to "seek the companionship and sympathy which stand aloof" (I, p. 172). Fowler has documented how Jameson's husband ignored her and treated her coldly once she arrived in Toronto. Jameson writes her father: "Mr. Jameson is just the same and . . . therefore we are . . . as hopelessly separated as ever. . . . He has done nothing to make the time tolerable to me, but this not from absolute unkindness, but mere absence of feeling."[26] She uses similar language of separation and frustration when describing the relationship of the colony to the British administration: "Upper Canada [is] resentful and repining under the sense of injury, and suffering from the total absence of all sympathy on the part of the English government with the condition, the wants, the feelings, the capabilities of the people and country" (I, pp. viii–ix). She postulates that separation of the provinces may "render more secure the subjection . . . to the British crown," but may also perpetuate "jealousies . . . divided interests, narrowed . . . resources, [and poor] improvement" (I, p. 104). Her feminine interest in relationships, painfully sharpened by her estrangement from her husband, made her conscious of political manipulation.

With several ironic phrases, she reveals her awareness of and disdain for the dominant position of the men in power. When describing the Prorogation of the House, she points out that "my proper place was . . . among the wives of the officials" (I, p. 152). In advocating a bill to make "women solely answerable for the consequences of their own misconduct—misconduct, into which, in nine cases out of ten, they are betrayed by the conventional license granted to the other sex," she argues that "our masters and legislators" should make this "first step towards our moral emancipation" (I, pp. 155—56). Finally, she reinforces the parallel between colony and lady by remarking that "the legislative council thanked his majesty's government humbly and gratefully for [its] . . . paternal regard" (I, p. 158). She characterizes the political relationship as that between kept woman and master.

On one occasion, for example, she tries to "rouse [herself] to occupation" despite the climate and her enforced idleness by involving herself in the important issue of the clergy reserves. Land was held by the Crown for the maintenance of the clergy, but there was continual agitation over whether the money raised was to maintain the Church of England or to be divided proportionally among the several leading denominations. Jameson details for her readers the various sides to the issue, "a question momentous for the future welfare of the colony, and interesting to every thinking mind" (I, p. 30). Her position on the matter demonstrates her concern for education and her personal satisfaction that she could be useful in the situation: "The strange, crude, ignorant, vague opinions I heard in conversation, and read in debates and the provincial papers, excited my astonishment. It struck me that if I could get the English preface to Victor Cousin's report (of which I had a copy) printed in a cheap form, and circulated with the newspapers, adding some of the statistical calculations . . . it might do some good—it might assist the people to some general principles on which to form opinions" (I, p. 35). However, in an oblique reference to her husband and his fellow officials, she notes that "cold water was thrown upon me from every side"; her involvement is seen as "interference" and deemed "visibly distasteful." She abandons "my project," but feels "more good-for-nothing than ever—more dejected" (I, p. 36). Open involvement in political and social matters is denied her by the propriety of her social position.

Consequently, her journal becomes her outlet, her forum for reform. She makes social and political commentary, primarily by focussing on the position of women as she perceives it in her personal explorations of the country. "The condition of women in any community," she maintains, "is a test of the advance of moral and intellectual cultivation in that community" (III, p. 300). Her frustrations in the role of "Chancellor's Lady" cause her to lash out against the "petty colonial oligarchy" (I, p. 98) which dominates the society and produces "conventionalism in its most oppressive and ridiculous forms" (I, p. 106). Her stay in Canada sharpens her appetite for independence and, consequently, her feminist views. Jameson's argument that "women need in these times" to be "self-governed" is a political challenge to those in power—the "men" whom she sarcastically labels "our natural protectors, our lawgivers, our masters"—for it is they who "cultivate" these "qualities which they pretend to admire in us" and "make them . . . the staple of the womanly character" (I, p. 203). This diction echoes that of Brooke's novel when Rivers sets out to "cultivate" both the wilderness and its women, and it emphasizes that, like Brooke, Jameson poses an alternate perspective to that of the colonizing male. "It is dangerous . . . [and] wicked," she asserts, "to bring up women to be 'happy wives and mothers' . . . as if for women there existed only one destiny." Since "thousands of women are not happy" in their colonized position as "wives and mothers," women must cultivate instead the "active energies of . . . the intellectual faculties" which will "enable [them] to find content and independence when denied love and happiness" (I, pp. 206–7). The last phrase suggests the personal anguish which fires Jameson's political stance.

Jameson's travels in Canada and observations of the positions of pioneer and Indian women provide further evidence for her arguments. During her "Summer Rambles" she spends some time in the company of Indian women. When she compares their "hard . . . lot" with that of civilized women, she nevertheless concludes that Indian women are "in no false position" (III, p. 303). When Jameson lists the advantages of Indian women, she implies not only the unjust treatment of women in Christian society, but also the unkind attitude of her own husband: "she is sure of protection . . . sure that she will never have her children taken from her . . . sees none better off than herself" (III, pp. 302–3). Furthermore, the hardships and degradation pioneer women face as settlers' wives are the results of the unrealistic expectations of their men. "In deference to the pride of man," she complains, "a want of cheerful self-dependence, a cherished physical delicacy, a weakness of temperament [are] falsely deemed . . . essential to feminine grace and refinement." Such socially inculcated characteristics are "altogether unfitting . . . for . . . the active out-of-door life in which she must share and sympathise." "A woman who cannot perform for herself and others all household offices, has no business here," declares Jameson. But the settlers themselves "declare that they cannot endure to see women eat, and . . . speak of brilliant health and strength in young girls as being rude and vulgar" (II, pp. 153–54). Throughout Jameson's studies of the position of women in the colonial world, she develops the theme that "there is no salvation for women but in ourselves: in self-knowledge, self-reliance, self-respect, and in mutual help and pity" (I, p. 118); in much the same way, the Reformers of the time were calling for "Home-rule" and "responsible government" for Upper Canada.

Jameson's identification with the political aspirations of the colony are manifested in her erotic description of the Canadian landscape. As Fowler notes, "men destroy the wilderness, and Anna, seeing the land as female, mourns the ravishment of its beauty" (p. 169). Although Fowler asserts that "Anna Jameson is the first Canadian . . . to eroticize" the land, Frances Brooke had already drawn attention to the sexual implications of man's cultivation of the Canadian wilderness. But Jameson's language is more direct. "A Canadian settler *hates* a tree," she notes, and then compares the "two principal methods of killing trees in this country" with the "two ways in which a woman's heart may be killed in this world of ours" (I., pp. 96–97). She likens the education of women to the process of dwarfing a tree "into an ornament for the . . . drawing-room" (II, p. 157). Just as Bell Fermor in Brooke's novel learned about natural behavior by her contact with Canada, so too does Jameson come to realize that "we have gone away from nature, and we must . . . substitute another nature" (I, p. 203). "Better the wilderness . . . that forest, that rock yonder, with creeping weeds around it," she cries, than the artificial conventions of colonial society (II, pp. 156–57).

Her forthright statements on the "Woman Question," as Thomas has argued in *Love and Work Enough*, "overstepped the fine-drawn line between permissible criticisms of the education of and role assigned to her sex and the highly suspect field of feminist propaganda. . . . She had dared to compare the lot of the European and the savage woman and to find the latter, in some cases, occupying the more honest and honoured position. Such radicalism could not be ignored" (p. 141). That it was not ignored is indicated by one male reviewer of the time:

No one reading these "Winter Studies and Summer Rambles" can possibly disentangle the outbreakings of the journalist's disappointed hopes and wounded feelings . . . from the enthusiast's constant resolution to represent any arrangement of the position and duties of her sex what-so-ever,—even that where the Squaw is the Red Man's drudge in field and wigwam . . . as more equitable and to be desired than that existing according to the present system of European civilization. Mrs. Jameson has thus rendered it impossible for anyone answering her in her capacity of advocate, to refrain from also inquiring into her personal stake in the cause she pleads so warmly.[27]

The reviewer recognized both the political implications of the journal and the personal dimensions of these "outbreakings" for a "more equitable" position than woman has in "the present system." The feminist and political "causes" which Jameson "advocates" in the journal actually do derive from and express her frustrations with the restrictions of matrimony; her call for social reforms for women stems from her personal desire for independence and freedom. That the reviewer should criticize Jameson's views by employing phrases alluding to the "outbreak" of 1837—led by the editor of *The Colonial Advocate*—reveals just how threatening Jameson's journal was to her male-dominated, imperialistic society.

Like Frances Brooke, Jameson offers a feminine perspective on social and political issues to counter the prevailing views of the men in power. Essentially, this feminine approach is personal, or individual. She begins her journal by asserting that she "know[s] no better way of coming at the truth, than by observing and recording faithfully the impressions made by objects and characters on my own mind—or, rather, the impress they *receive* from my own mind" (I, p. 3). Her preface explains that the "original character" of the "journal form of writing" requires as its structural principle "personal feeling, on which the whole series of action and observation" depends. She defends in essence a feminine way of writing, in contrast to a "flat, heavy, didactic" masculine style (I, p. vii). The masculine attitude which would dismiss the personal tone of the journal, demonstrated by the reviewer quoted above, prevailed in later editions. The editors of the 1943 Nelson text, for instance, explain that "*Winter Studies and Summer Rambles*, as originally published, contained much material irrelevant to her travels." They astutely hypothesize that "her unhappy marriage may have contributed to the extensive moralizing in which she indulged," but ignore the importance of this motivation and eliminate "such portions," while preserving "the real meat of the volume." Indeed, they produce what they want, "an excellent combination of readability and historical value,"[28] but in favoring the "historical," the editors have missed the central focus of the journal, and, ironically, the more profound political implications.

Fowler interprets *Winter Studies and Summer Rambles* as a record of the ending of Jameson's marriage and her embarkation into independence. In fact, Jameson's rhetorical question, "can you imagine the position of a fretful, frivolous woman, strong neither in mind nor frame, abandoned to her own resources in the wilds of Upper Canada?" (II, p. 134), contrasts her own position, for she displays both intellectual and physical strength and she uses the resources at hand to come to know Canada and herself. With the springtime, she journeys for two months, learning to appreciate the land and its people. Indeed, the record of her first view of Niagara Falls in the "Winter Studies" volume, when she was depressed and lonely, conveys her great disappointment at the scene (I, p. 86); when she records her second sighting in the "Summer Rambles" she is so impressed by the vitality mirrored in Niagara that she "could have . . . joined the dancing billows in their glorious . . . mirth" (II, pp. 53–54). Her "rambles" end abruptly with her return to "my own house in Toronto"; the pride of the possessive, in addition to her quiet pride upon completing her "wild expedition," contrasts sharply with her sense of imprisonment in Robert's house after her arrival in Canada.

Jameson was to leave Canada and her marriage almost immediately after the end of these "Rambles." She returned to her independent life in Europe, becoming an outspoken advocate of women's rights. At the same time, in Canadian politics, the brief rebellion in December made Britain aware of the problems to be addressed in the colonies. Some measure of self-government was granted, ending the "petty colonial oligarchy" which held power in the country. Over the next decade, the goal of "responsible government" was gradually realized. Thus Jameson's stay in Canada coincided with the rising resistance to and reform of the political abuses of the Colonial Office. Sensitive to her own lack of power in relation to her husband's position in both the administration and their marriage, she was able to offer subtle and accurate analysis of the colony's desire for the right to control its own affairs. Her journal records her movement away from her restricted position as the wife of the vice-chancellor toward an identification with the aspirations of the people of Canada. When, near the end of her overland journey she hears of the accession of Queen Victoria, Jameson declares that the monarch's "youth and sex are... in *our* favour"; Canada, "young like herself—a land of hopes," will mature, Jameson prays, under the "quick perceptions and pure kind instincts of the woman" (III, p. 263). She sees hope for the Reformers in Canada, for she expects the young queen to provide the "knowledge . . . judgement . . . [and] sympathy" needed to prevent "the loss of one of her fairest provinces" (I, p. x). There is no way of knowing if Queen Victoria ever read Jameson's advice, but recent research has indicated that the young monarch, along with her consort, took interest in the affairs of Canada and was at great pains to receive the most accurate reports on political issues requiring her decisions.[29]

Jameson's rejection of the common assertion "that women have nothing to do with politics" (I, p. 10), then, takes a more public and radical stance than the ironic and indirect means by which Brooke criticized the politics of men. Jameson's artistic efforts, as well, extend some aspects of Brooke's creativity. As Brooke used scenic description for thematic development and characterization, Jameson too weaves her observations of Canada into her primary thematic concern with woman's place in society and displays, by her growing identification with the landscape, her acceptance of her own independence. Both Bell Fermor and Jameson respond positively to the freshness and liberty of the rugged, young, unformed country. But whereas Brooke works through her fictional characters and her plot to offer her criticism of politics and love, Jameson puts herself forward as the heroine of her narrative. The epistolary novel of Brooke finds its correspondence in Jameson's journalistic structure. The author, in other words, becomes both narrator and subject. Despite the difference in generic mode, both expose the falsity and cruelty beneath the colonial attitude while Jameson openly calls for reform in the colonial structure of society.

Commenting on pioneer settlers' wives, Anna Jameson mentioned in passing that she "never met with *one* woman recently settled here who considered herself happy in her new home and country"; but she qualified her castigation by adding that she had "*heard* of one, and doubtless there are others, but they are exceptions to the general rule" (II, p. 133). That exception might well have been Catharine Parr Traill, for in 1836 she published *The Backwoods of Canada*, a collection of letters, addressed mostly to her mother in England, which records her adaptation, over the course of her first three years in Upper Canada, to the rugged life demanded of settlers. Traill and her husband emigrated to Canada in 1832, as did her brother, Samuel Strickland, the year before and her sister, Susanna Moodie, shortly thereafter; they were part of the great wave of British immigrants in the 1830s who were to influence profoundly the political development of Canada. The unique contribution of Traill to our understanding of this period lies in her seemingly calm and rational adjustment to life in the backwoods while yet adhering to British codes of gentility.

From the War of 1812 on, but especially in the 1830s, a large number of

emigrants arrived in Canada, and Upper Canada in particular. Carl F. Klinck
notes in his article "Literary Activity in the Canadas, 1812–1841" that "when
that decade ended, the settlers from Britain would outnumber those of North
American origin, and the English-speaking residents of the combined Canadas would match the total of those who spoke French." In this way, he
concludes, "Upper Canada remained a unique island in the American 'Old
Northwest'—retaining British rule, keeping up cultural relationships with
the Old Land, and possessing a governmental system which would be ad-
justed (after a small rebellion) to provincial responsibility."[30] Although
Klinck's conclusion is correct, his parenthetical remark slides over the period
of unrest leading to the 1837 rebellion which was largely a clash of cultures,
of a British colonial perspective against American republicanism. Donald
Creighton explains in his historical account, *Dominion of the North* (1957),
how the "new colonists . . . were for the most part, poor . . . and completely
alien to [the] pioneer tradition" of North America. "The settlers of good
family and breeding," he also notes, did not fare much better in the "un-
familiar and hostile environment [where they were] surrounded by Amer-
icanized neighbours who robbed them and watched their misfortunes with
malevolent satisfaction."[31] One of the loudest voices of dissent came from
one of these emigrants, William Lyon Mackenzie, who turned to "the example of America in 1776 . . . [for] an excellent and salutary lesson to the
statesman . . . with regard to . . . irresponsible government"; Mackenzie
sought "the independence of Canada from the baneful domination of the
Colonial Office."[32] He saw in "the principles of the [American] Constitution"
the political solution to the control of Upper Canada by the Family Compact,
the very "colonial oligarchy" which Jameson had criticized. When the Reformers won the election in 1834, the Tory reaction of the next two years
created the climate for open rebellion.

The political struggle between the Radical and Tory extremes of American
independence and British colonialism is played out in the language and
themes of Traill's book. Traill is divided, as are many of her contemporaries,
between admiration for American ingenuity and loyalty to British conventions. For example, she praises "the Yankees, as they are termed," for being
"the most industrious and ingenious . . . never at a loss for an expedient."[33]
She notices that even the "old settlers . . . acquire" American resourcefulness. Nevertheless, she qualifies her admiration by adding that "if I dislike
them it is for a certain cold brevity of manner" (p. 293). When a citizen of
Ohio inquires why the Traills chose to settle in Canada rather than the more
prosperous and civilized regions of the United States, her response is that
"British subjects preferred the British government; and, besides, they were
averse to the manners of his countrymen" (p. 293).

Traill's loyalty to the British system and her gentility go hand in hand;
throughout the text she extols the advantages of adaptation to Canadian life,
even advocating the necessity of changing opinions and habits, yet she en-

deavors to demonstrate that "conforming to circumstances"—a phrase she repeats countless times—does not entail the abandonment of British standards. Clara Thomas in her introduction to the New Canadian Library edition concludes that *The Backwoods of Canada* "provides . . . a portrait and a record of the woman Catharine Parr Traill . . . wished to be—a pioneer gentlewoman."[34] Certainly Traill "wished to be . . . a pioneer gentlewoman," yet she is not like Ed Rivers in *The History of Emily Montague* who, in his desire to be a "*gentleman* farmer," places more emphasis on the role of the gentleman than on the practical activities demanded by the role of farmer. Thomas is correct to assert that Traill was "superbly equipped for her role [and] eminently successful in it" (pp. 41–42), but while Traill displays the resourcefulness and ingenuity she so admires in her "Yankee" neighbors, she is at pains to assert her class and national origins. "It is considered by no means derogatory," she assures her reader, for "the wife of an officer or gentleman to assist in the work of the house, or to perform its entire duties. . . . In these matters we bush-ladies have a wholesome disregard of what Mr. or Mrs. So-and-so thinks or says. We pride ourselves on conforming to circumstances: and . . . we repose quietly on that incontestable proof of our gentility, and can afford to be useful without injuring it" (pp. 270—71). Traill may structure her book to display her adaptation to life in North America, but she does not want to be mistaken—like some of the "old settlers"—for an American.

Jameson's journal covers the months just before the rebellion, and the sexual politics of her work demonstrate clearly that her sympathies lie with the calls for reform. At the same time, although the dates of Traill's letters cover July 1832 to May 1835, she makes no direct reference to politics, even though 1834 and 1835 were so full of unrest. The closest she allows herself is a brief summary of the benefits of building the Trent canal system in order "to open a market for inland produce." She notes that the "project has . . . been under the consideration of the Governor" and acknowledges that "it presents some difficulties and expense" (p. 258). The disinterest of the colonial government in "allowing the colonists the management of their internal concerns" was the chief point of contention between the government and both Reformers and Radicals.[35] Traill, however, refuses to enter the debate, leaving the matter "to abler persons than myself to discuss at large the policy and expediency of the measure" (p. 258). Those "abler persons" are undoubtedly male—she ends her discussion of the "progress" of the "settled townships" with the apology that "all this . . . might afford subject for a wise discussion between grave men, but will hardly amuse us women" (p. 259). Unlike Brooke or Jameson, Traill declines to enter the male realm of politics, especially to offer criticism.

When Brooke characterizes the "pretty . . . husbandman," Ed Rivers, she portrays the unsuitability of his colonial attitudes; Traill emphasizes successful and practical husbandry, completely embracing her role as pioneer

wife and finding fulfillment in "the routine of feminine duties and employment" (p. 1). She agrees with the description of the condition of pioneer
women which Jameson had provided: they are "always pining . . . discon-
tented and unhappy. Few enter with whole heart into a settler's life" (p. 105).
But unlike Jameson, who attributes woman's condition to the impractical
definition of femininity required by men, Traill "prefers honestly representing facts in their real and true light, that the female part of the emigrant's
family may be enabled to look them firmly in the face . . . and, by being
properly prepared, encounter the rest with . . . high-spirited cheerfulness"
(p. 2). The all-encompassing detail of the companion-piece to *Backwoods*,
The Canadian Settler's Guide, published twenty years later in 1854, underlines Traill's focus on practical housewifery as the means for successful husbandry in Canada. So much does Traill enter her role as settler's wife that,
as she explains in the preface to *The Settler's Guide*, she is willing "to abandon
the paths of literary fame" if she can "render a solid benefit" to women who
"through duty or necessity are about to become sojourners in the Western
Wilderness."[36] Traill eschews writing "a work of fiction" like Brooke's or "a
mass of personal adventure" like Jameson's in favor of "collating my instruction into the more homely but satisfactory form of a Manual of Canadian
housewifery." Jameson's rebellious statements on the position of women
stemmed largely from her own needs; Traill's works, on the other hand,
have a noticeably detached tone, a lack of personal feelings and details. Her
brief allusions in books published late in her life to "hours of loneliness, and
hours of sorrow and suffering"[37] suggest that she, too, wrote out of personal
necessity. But rebellion against her "lot" (p. 310) is not her solution; "occupation within-doors" (p. 105) becomes her means of surviving the demands
of settlement.

Traill's personal trials have been the subject of much speculation in Canadian criticism despite the near absence of emotional references in her
work.[38] Fowler speculates quite convincingly that Traill focuses her attention
on running the household because of her growing fears of her own emerging
strengths, especially in light of her husband's growing weaknesses (p. 76).
Literary critics have often mentioned the Traills' success as pioneers, at-
tributing Mrs. Traill's calm, rational tone to her positive experience of settlement in the backwoods.[39] The Traills were not as successful as earlier
scholars believed, however, nor, more importantly, as Traill herself implies.
Traill notes, for example, the growth of the "family assets," while omitting
the fact which Fowler discovered that "their existence was such a struggle
that by 1835 Thomas wanted to give up, advertising their property for sale
in the *Cobourg Star*" (p. 76).

Just as Robert Jameson was conspicuously absent from Jameson's journals,
so too is Thomas Traill from his wife's book. Moreover, the references to
him that do exist reflect his weaknesses and poor adaptation to life in the
backwoods. On board the ship to Canada, Traill admits the "monotony" of

the voyage, but suddenly says: "I really do pity men who are not actively employed: women have always their needle as a resource against the over-whelming weariness of an idle life; but where a man is confined to a small space, such as the deck and cabin of a trading vessel, with nothing to see, nothing to hear, nothing to do, and nothing to read, he is really," she concludes, "a very pitiable creature" (p. 9). Shortly after their arrival, when Traill is "struggling with mortal agony" against cholera, she receives the care she needs "from the females of the house," who must as well "soothe the anguish of my poor afflicted partner" who is healthy but helpless (p. 43). Again, two years later, when the entire family is "confined to our beds with ague," Traill and her baby recover "in a fortnight's time"; on Thomas Traill, however, the illness hangs "during the whole of the summer, and [throws] a damp upon his exertions and gloom upon his spirits" (p. 300). In contrast to such examples of masculine weakness, the "prompt assistance" of Traill's sister and sister-in-law during their illness points out the nurturing strength of women. In the book as a whole, Traill distorts the portrait of her husband, both obscuring and indirectly suggesting his weaknesses. Her concluding remark, that her "husband is becoming more reconciled to the country" (p. 311), glosses over the fact that he has been unreconciled and obfuscates the fact, which Fowler records, of his steady decline in fortune and in health until "in 1857, when a fire completely destroyed [their farm], Thomas went into a deep depression from which he never recovered, dying the following year" (p. 84).

If *The Backwoods of Canada* reflects male weakness, it nevertheless re-veals female strengths. The "prospect" of the "loneliness of the backwoods . . . does not discourage [me, for] I know I shall find plenty of occupation within-doors, and I have sources of enjoyment when I walk abroad that will keep me from being dull" (p. 105). In addition to her own portrait, the book is filled with example after example of women who display not only courage and strength but also kindness. During her travels to the backwoods, she repeatedly divides the women she meets into those who nurture and those who do not, giving high praise to the former. For example, she notes how some servant girls in taverns give aid to weary travellers far beyond the requirements of their duties. She notes "the accomplished daughters and wives . . . milking their own cows, making their own butter, and performing tasks of household work that few [British] farmers' wives would . . . conde-scend to take part in" (p. 182). *The Canadian Settler's Guide* offers several examples of "female heroism": women whose husbands are ill or dead carry on the work of the farm in addition to running the home and caring for the children.[40] Finally, near the end of *The Backwoods of Canada*, Traill de-scribes a model family. The woman is the source of its health, peace and prosperity: the "neatly dressed matron, of lady-like appearance" is working at the "large spinning-wheel . . . [which] occupied the centre of the room." All of the children's clothing was "the produce of the farm and their mother's praiseworthy industry." The "good sense, industry, and order" of the "little household" are attributed by Traill to the woman's "prudence" (pp. 272–73). The woman in this family portrait, symbolically located at the heart[h] of the scene, stands as an icon of Traill's theme of "good housewifery" as the solution both for the loneliness and despair experienced by so many immigrant women and for the welfare of settlers' families.

The Backwoods of Canada was written, Traill says in the preface to *The Canadian Settler's Guide*, "with the view of preparing females of my own class more particularly, for the changes that awaited them in the life of the Canadian emigrant's wife" (p. xviii). There is, however, tremendous irony in her method of "preparing females." Her contention that women had the strength and ingenuity—if they willed—to accomplish numerous practical tasks, certainly released women from some of the restrictions of genteel femininity which Jameson criticized. She was able to declare that "I prize and enjoy my present liberty in this country" from "the fetters that etiquette and fashion are wont to impose" upon women in England (p. 269). But having thus on the one hand celebrated freedom for women to participate in the enterprise of settlement, she then confines their activity to the sphere of the home.

She "policies" other women, to recall Miles' observation, by employing rhetoric which enforces the wife's subservience to her husband. She describes the "qualifications of a settler's wife" by evoking biblical, imperial and patriarchal ideals: "Like the pattern of all good housewives described by the prudent mother of King Lemuel, it should be said of the emigrant's wife, 'She layeth her hands to the spindle, and her hands hold the distaff.' . . . 'She looketh well to the ways of her household, and eateth not the bread of idleness' " (pp. 181–82). The emigrant's wife should practice "a cheerful conformity to circumstances" and do "her duty in the state of life unto which it may have pleased God to call her" (p. 182). Traill repeats such pious admonitions in her "introductory remarks" to *The Canadian Settler's Guide* (pp. 4, 12). Inevitably, submission to God involves submission to one's husband. In a passage wherein Traill expresses the need for a book such as *The Backwoods*, she summarizes her main theme, which is to emphasize "our duties and the folly of repining at following and sharing the fortunes of our spouses, whom we have vowed . . . to love 'in riches and in poverty, in sickness and in health.' " "Too many [women] pronounce these words," continues Traill, "without heeding their importance"; "their faithfulness" may be put to the "severe test" of "quitting home, kindred, and country . . . but the truly attached wife will do this, and more also, if required by the husband of her choice" (p. 284). And Traill reinforces her prescription for other women with her own example. In a sentence which alludes to Thomas Traill's discontent, Traill asks rhetorically, "have I not a right to be cheerful and contented for the sake of my beloved partner? The change is not greater for me than him; and if for his sake I have voluntarily left home, and friends,

and country, shall I therefore sadden him by useless regrets?" (p. 105). Both
Jameson and Traill address the position of women on the basis of their marital
relations, but whereas Jameson advocates independence for women because
she desires it personally, Traill insists on the subservience of women to
counteract her own husband's loss of stature.

The sexual politics underlying Traill's "good housewifery" suggest the
wider political ramifications of *The Backwoods of Canada*. The very strengths
she manifests and which she calls on other women to display, "ingenuity
and expediency," are the ones she admires in the "Yankee" settlers. Several
times in her book she praises Canada as a "country where independence is
inseparable from industry" (p. 271); the emigrant comes "with the view of
realizing an independence . . . that he had not the means of settling in life
in the home country" (p. 269). Consequently the very qualities and motivations needed for settlement in Canada cause the settler to emulate those
Yankee qualities which guarantee success. But because Traill does not wish
to be mistaken for an American, she places heavy emphasis on her British
roots, and her genteel British manners, both of which distinguish her from
Americans. And, perhaps because her circumstances in the backwoods call
up her strengths and reveal—despite her half-hearted protestations to the
contrary—the weaknesses of her husband, Traill, conservative as she is in
international politics, calls also for the subservience of woman in the settler's
life. Traill fears the very qualities of independence which she so clearly
exemplifies and advocates, and she represses her fears beneath her conventional sexual and political views.

In the light of Traill's personal motivations, it is not surprising to learn
that she vehemently supported the Loyalists during the Mackenzie rebellion.
To a later edition of *The Backwoods of Canada* (1842) Traill added two final
chapters, one of which is entitled "The Mackenzie Rebellion." In this penultimate chapter, Traill recounts the events of the rebellion and its effects
on her family during the month of December 1837. She also reveals her
political position. The "men of all ages and degree" who answered the "sum-
mons" of the government "from every part of the country" are, in Traill's
assessment, "anxious to prove their attachment to their Queen," and as well
to "the established government, by whose laws they were protected."[41] Upon
hearing that "the party of rebels under their chief leader is . . . flying before
the loyal militia," Traill praises God, "who has confounded the malice of the
enemies of our adopted country" (p. 329). The rebellion was "uncalled for"
(p. 341). Most of *The Backwoods*, as already noted, is dominated by a cool,
rational tone, so it is important to remark the vehemence of her invective
against Mackenzie's attempt "to stir up the Americans . . . to tear from us
our Government and laws, and force us to become a free and independent
people." She continues sarcastically: "Surely our freedom would be a blessed
gift so obtained!! And with the traitor Mackenzie for our President our
independence were most honourable and admirable!! God forbid we should

change our dependence on a gracious Sovereign to become the tools and victims of the most despicable of rebels" (p. 335). She emphasizes that "the Canadian population . . . [is] opposed to change," and content with "our dependence" on "the Mother Country": "shall we like ungrateful children, while yet dependent on her for support, withdraw ourselves from her arms?" (p. 339). Her fierce assertions of national dependence indicate that Traill was ambivalent about the political, as well as the personal, independence to be found in Canada.

That tension is evident in her description of her family during the days following the rebellion. Although the subheading for the chapter mentions that "Mr. Moodie [her brother-in-law] and Mr. Traill Join the Forces to oppose Mackenzie" (p. 320), her description of these two "gallant volunteers" (p. 331) intimates, with the irony that characterizes her ambivalence toward men, that Mackenzie had nothing to fear from them. Each time Traill mentions her brother-in-law, she refers to his "lameness from a recent fracture of the small bone of his leg" (p. 326); despite the fact that he is "unfit for moving," he is stubbornly "resolved" to "join the rest of his brothers in arms" (p. 328). Little is said of her husband, except for her worry for his safety; but while Traill assumes the two of them are in Toronto, her husband arrives unexpectedly at the door, explaining that he had proceeded no farther than Port Hope. He departs the next day for another "meeting of the Volunteers," but having "fallen and sprained his ankle, so severely as to be unable to get farther on his way home," he sends for someone to come and fetch him. He is "so hurt as to require assistance to dismount from his horse" (p. 333). In contrast to these two ineffectual men, she and her sister, Susanna, cope with the homesteads and children. Despite her statements of worry for the absent men, Traill and her sister "made a merry party . . . [as they] chatted merrily away" in the oxsleigh, "not a whit less happy than if we had been rolling along in a carriage with a splendid pair of bays" (pp. 229–30). Such a sleigh-ride "through the thick woods after a heavy snowfall," continues Traill, "is one of the greatest treats this country affords me" (p. 330). "Enjoying quiet day[s]," "preparing for . . . tea," Traill presents herself as a composed and content lady awaiting the return of her "gallant" (p. 331).

One can conclude only that Catharine Parr Traill was unwilling to acknowledge the total implications of her own "facts." She retreats into the sanctity of home and country rather than declare herself independent of her husband or of England. Following the passionate outburst against Mackenzie and his rebels quoted above, Traill offers up a prayer of thanksgiving to the male Deity of Christianity for the prospect of the new year and prays to "be contented with our lot whatever it may be" (p. 336). Only symbolically does Traill come close to voicing her complex feelings regarding independence. She describes a "great American hawk . . . in pursuit of one of my geese"; "painfully interested for the safety of my goose, I could not help admiring the graceful evolutions of her assailant . . . rising slowly again higher and

higher." She admires the hawk for being "calm and collected as though he
disdained to exhibit fear or annoyance" (pp. 336–37). The hawk is, of course,
both American and male; the goose, female. Traill will admire, but not allow
her masculine strength to assert itself at the expense of her femininity; in
fact, she uses it to control her emotions and to rationalize her subservient
dependence. She quashes any thoughts of independence as severely as she
castigates the rebels of 1837.

Traill's control of her feminine impulses manifests itself, finally, in her
response to the Canadian wilderness. In her 1985 study of *The Wacousta
Syndrome: Explorations in the Canadian Landscape*, Gaile McGregor notes
that Traill's initial entry into the backwoods is described "in terms reminiscent of nightmare" and henceforth "Traill takes refuge in the cheerful, short-
range, domesticated view of the wilderness that dominates the tone of the
rest of the book."[42] Oddly, though, McGregor sees this shift in vision as
evidence of "an evolving rather than a static personality," so much so that
she typifies Traill's "encounter with the wilderness and subsequent change
of attitude . . . [as] a paradigm for the national experience." McGregor cites
Brooke's *History of Emily Montague* and Anna Jameson's journals as
"straightforward negative responses to the Canadian landscape" (pp. 28–29),
overlooking the fact that Traill evolves significantly less than do either of
these women. Bell Fermor, in *The History of Emily Montague*, sees the
possibility of a more natural basis in human relationships through her contact
with the Canadian landscape. Jameson, too, from her journey through the
Canadian wilderness and her contact with Indians, gained the courage to
leave her marriage for an independent existence. Traill, however, responds
to the natural world around her with the rational eye of a scientist. "As much
of the botany of these unsettled portions of the country is unknown to the
naturalist, and the plants are quite nameless," she remarks, "I take the
liberty of bestowing names upon them according to inclination or fancy"
(p. 120).

The power of naming is, of course, a traditionally masculine attribute; it
declares man's dominion over nature. To the same effect, it affords Traill a
means of controlling the unknown about her, just as she controls her feminine
nature and political impulses. In later life, Traill published botanical texts,
on the flora and fauna of Canada, for which she gained public recognition
and official commendation. Carl P. A. Ballstadt notes in Traill's later essays
"a degree of ambivalence about the impact of settlement and cultivation on
the Canadian forest. . . . [She laments] the disappearance of the flora and
fauna that settlement destroys."[43] It was, nevertheless, a settlement she
helped to accomplish. Like Jameson, Traill remarks that "man appears to
contend with the trees of the forest as though they were his most obnoxious
enemies" (p. 197); but unlike Jameson, Traill does not condemn masculine
destructiveness nor identify with the ravaged landscape. Her feminine intuition perhaps expresses itself in the first months of settlement as she pleads

with "the choppers to spare . . . a few pretty sapling beech-trees." The out-come is revealing: "only one . . . was saved from destruction in the chopping" and it is burnt by the heat of the sun. "It now stands," concludes Traill, "a melancholy monument of the impossibility of preserving trees thus left." Thereafter, Traill abandons such delicacy and bows to the dictates of the "useful" expediency of "preserving a grove of trees" on their land in order to "draw out the old timbers for fire-wood" (p. 199). This movement from what could be called a feminine to a masculine perspective reflects the intensification of repressive and conservative responses to sexual and political issues and to the landscape. Recognition of this shift, nevertheless, remains less central to an understanding of Traill than the observation of her am-bivalence and her apparent ignorance of her own contradictions.

Susanna Moodie followed her sister, Catharine Parr Traill, to the back-woods of Canada with her husband, J. W. Dunbar Moodie, to take up the land granted him as a half-pay officer. Although the sisters settled at the same time and in the same area, Moodie's published account in 1852 of her settlement, *Roughing It in the Bush*, records an experience and tempera-ment very different from Traill's. Moodie's stated purpose in writing the book is the opposite: Moodie, in contrast to Traill who wishes her book to be "a handbook for emigrating," hopes that "these sketches should prove the means of deterring one family [at least] from sinking their property, and shipwrecking all their hopes, by going to reside in the backwoods of Can-ada."[44] Moodie's account bristles with rage and indignation at her "lot" in Canada. Consequently, Moodie's writing style is emotional, personal and histrionic, as opposed to the sure, measured pace and impersonal manner of Traill's history.

The differences in style derive from two very different personalities and experiences. Previous scholars have attributed Moodie's attitude to the fact that the Moodies failed miserably at farming while the Traills succeeded.[45] We now know that the Traills were not as successful as *The Backwoods of Canada* implies. Nevertheless, evidence indicates that the Moodies were spectacular failures; bad management of finances, ill luck, natural disasters and mounting debt reduced them to a hopeless situation. The two women held different perspectives on their roles on the family farms. Moodie learned the tasks of practical housewifery quite unwillingly and often only out of necessity. Although she managed well when she eventually did labor in the home and on the farm, she was slow to adapt, to accept the change from her former genteel station in life. Moodie in no way followed Traill's example or instruction; however, if McGregor had examined Moodie's text as closely as she did Traill's, she might have perceived an even more striking evolution of personality and an alternative national paradigm.

That *Roughing It in the Bush* was written with her sister's book in mind cannot be doubted. As Carl F. Klinck points out in his introduction to the

New Canadian Library edition, "thousands of readers in England knew the farm life of the Otonabee woods before Mrs. Moodie wrote about it, because her sister's *Backwoods* was so popular as to be a handbook for emigrating gentlewomen."[46] In her introduction to the first edition, Moodie deliberately alludes to the title of her sister's book, addresses its audience and counters its theme: "what the Backwoods of Canada are . . . these simple sketches will endeavour to portray."[47] The uncapitalized phrase, "backwoods of Canada," is repeated often throughout her book, but most pointedly in Moodie's concluding remarks which contain some of her most critical comments about the life of a settler in Canada. "I have given you a faithful picture of a life in the backwoods of Canada, and I leave you to draw from it your own conclusions," she claims, and then continues by stating concisely her conclusion: "To the poor, industrious workingman it presents many advantages; to the poor gentleman, *none!*" (p. 562). There is only one explicit reference to Traill as "the author of *The Backwoods of Canada*" (p. 514). However, in an earlier scene, just after the Moodies first arrive in the backwoods, Traill appears "to escort [Moodie] through the wood." "Timid . . . with only my female companion in the vast forest," Moodie nevertheless feels it necessary to keep "my fears to myself, lest I should be laughed at." Traill, "who had resided for nearly twelve months in the woods," is wearing "Indian moccasins"; Moodie, on the other hand, new to the backwoods and no doubt dressed according to British fashion, "stumbled at every step" (p. 292). Throughout her time in the backwoods Moodie indeed "stumbled at every step" and, perhaps out of her bitterness toward her life in Canada, she harbored some jealousy toward her sister who adapted so well to that same life. Her inclusion of an anecdote which ridicules a botanist's interest in "lichens . . . [and] all sorts of rubbish . . . insignificant plants that everybody else passes by without noticing" would seem to be a deliberate attempt to belittle her sister's interest and fame as a botanist (p. 236). Despite the closeness between Moodie and Traill revealed in their correspondence, collected in *Susanna Moodie: Letters of a Lifetime* (1985), it is significant that Moodie chose to "assist . . . the work's public reception"[48] by dedicating the book to her other famous sister, Agnes Strickland, "Author of the *Lives of the Queens of England*."

In her preface and throughout her book Moodie makes clear that her emigration to Canada is "determined" by her husband (p. 88). She rather stresses "the hurry and bustle of a sudden preparation to depart" (p. 88). Only one month before their departure, her husband goes to a lecture about emigration to Canada; one of her sisters suggests that he "is possessed with the . . . mania" to emigrate. "Little dreaming that I and mine should share in the strange adventures" of emigration, Moodie replies to her sister: "Nay, God forbid! . . . I am certain [he] will return quite sickened with the Canadian project" (p. 77). In a later, more reflective passage, she explains that on "the last night . . . at home" she would not have emigrated "had it still been in my power" (p. 242). Instead, she had "bowed to a superior mandate, the command of duty." She explains that her husband's "half-pay . . . is too small to supply the wants of a family and . . . maintain his original standing in society" (pp. 242–43). She acknowledges his economic point of view, that the "inclination" to marriage is "an act of imprudence in over-populated England" and "emigration must be the result" (p. 243). "My dear wife," she recalls him saying, "I feel confident that you will respond to the call of duty; and hand-in-hand and heart-in-heart we will go forth to meet difficulties" (p. 244). Moodie hides from him that she is "reluctant to respond to my husband's call."

Part of her reluctance stems from her family's "energy and strength" which had led them to use their "literary attainments" to overcome the loss of their father's wealth, "without losing aught of their former position in society" (pp. 244–45). Moodie implies that her husband is too proud to do as she and her family had; her account of their departure stresses that he lacks the "self-denial" and "high resolve" which would enable him to provide for his family in England.

These weaknesses also rendered him quite unfit for the task of emigration. Fowler points out that Mr. Moodie "didn't suffer from [Thomas] Traill's deep depressions, but he had a physical handicap: his left arm was partially paralyzed from an old wound and almost useless. . . . [As well] Moodie was quite as inept as Traill in financial matters" (p. 122). Mrs. Moodie expresses her frustration at his pronounced failure in the backwoods of Canada in comments about the inadequacies of the "gentleman farmer" as a settler, comments which are not at all flattering to her husband. She describes him as the "lover of ease . . . the poet, the author, the musician, the man of books, of refined taste and gentlemanly habits" (p. 244). Frances Brooke's theme that the gentleman is unfit for Canada, reinforced by Traill's narrative, is furthered by Moodie's concluding statement:

The gentleman can neither work so hard, live so coarsely, nor endure so many privations as his poorer but more fortunate neighbour. Unaccustomed to manual labour, his services in the field are not of a nature to secure for him a profitable return. The task is new to him, he knows not how to perform it well; and, conscious of his deficiency, he expends his little means in hiring labour, which his bush-farm can never repay. Difficulties increase, debts grow upon him, he struggles in vain to extricate himself, and finally sees his family sink into hopeless ruin (p. 563).

Moodie had a much more critical perspective than did her sister, and her refusal to gloss over difficulties led her to other forms of rebellion.

The narrative of *Roughing It in the Bush* unfolds within a political framework, as do the works of Brooke, Jameson and Traill. Its time span corresponds to the dates of Moodie's arrival to and departure from the backwoods,

1832 to 1839; unlike her sister, she not only covered the time of the 1837 rebellion but also incorporated the uprising into the structure of her story, and, like Jameson, identified with the rebellious spirit of 1837. Moodie writes, of course, with the benefit of hindsight, so that although at the beginning of the chapter, "Outbreak," she remarks that "buried in the obscurity of those woods, we knew nothing, heard nothing of the political state of the country," subsequent events make her realize "the abuses that had led to the . . . position of things" (pp. 467, 472). In his study of the publication dates of Moodie's patriotic poetry, Carl Ballstadt concludes that, contrary to such claims of ignorance, Moodie knew of "the stir of discontent and the rebellious mood preceding the uprisings."[49] Her preface to the 1871 edition of *Roughing It* reveals the extent of her political awareness: "the insurrection of 1837 . . . gave freedom to Canada. . . . It drew the attention of the Home Government to the many abuses then practised in the colony, and . . . ultimately led to all our great national improvements."[50] At the time of the rebellion, she castigates Mackenzie in one of her poems, "On Reading the Proclamation Delivered by William Lyon Mackenzie, on Navy Island" but later, in the companion volume to *Roughing It*, concerning her life in Belleville, *Life in the Clearings* (1853), she defends Mackenzie and his followers, pointing out that they rebelled "not without severe provocation . . . towards the colonial government and the abuses it fostered."[51] Michael A. Peterman, in his biographical article on Moodie, has concluded that the Moodies were "progressive and reformist" in their politics, as is indicated by the fact that they named one of their sons Robert Baldwin in honor of the Reform politician who was the principal architect of the responsible government instituted in 1848.[52] Although Moodie "own[s] that [in 1837] my British spirit was fairly aroused," so much so that she composed some "loyal staves" in order to "serve the good cause" (p. 472), she becomes after "that great day of the outbreak" (p. 468) an advocate of reformist politics, very unlike her sister who in 1842 was to add her loyalist and repressive views of the rebellion to the text of *The Backwoods of Canada*.

Consequently, what is important to note in the chapter "Outbreak" is that it records how Moodie becomes politicized. Most of the chapter on the 1837 rebellion which Traill added to her book relates the facts of the conflict and reveals her passionate loyalty to England. In contrast, Moodie mentions few facts about the rebellion; instead, she focuses on how she "breaks out" in order to gain independence from her oppressive poverty: "To remain much longer in the woods was impossible, for the returns from the farm scarcely fed us, and but for the clothing sent us by our friends from home, who were not aware of our real difficulties, we should have been badly off indeed" (p. 484). It is ironic that the only way Mr. Moodie is "enabled to liquidate many pressing debts and to send home from time to time sums of money to procure necessaries" is to abandon farming and reenter the military; he joins the "regiments of militia . . . formed to defend the colony," after the rebellion, against attack from the United States (p. 474). During his absence of several months, Mrs. Moodie displays a notable development; she and her old servant, Nellie, run the farm successfully. In the early stages of her experience of "bush life," she had great difficulty with her servants; now, "the good old Jenny" is a friend (p. 486). Unlike her husband who was swindled by several business arrangements, Moodie makes satisfactory deals with her neighbors: "by lending my oxen for two days' work, I got Wittals, who had no oxen, to drag me in a few acres of oats, and to prepare the land for potatoes and corn" (p. 480). "Our garden was well dug and plentifully manured," Moodie brags, because she and Nellie bring the manure, "which had lain for several years at the barn door, down to the plot in a large Indian basket placed upon a hand-sleigh." Presumably, her husband had been too gentlemanly all those years to see to this mundane task. Since they "did not know how to use" the guns in the house, Moodie utilizes her female talents to invent a trap for ducks "by braiding" strips of bark. During the summer there is even an incident when Moodie borrows a kettle—a reverse of the borrowing episodes of earlier chapters—and, though the pot breaks, the situation turns to her advantage when she sells her daughter's toy to mend the broken pot and to purchase a new one: "in exchange for the useless piece of finery, we had now two kettles at work" (p. 477). After her husband returns in August, Moodie proudly points out that "the harvest was the happiest we ever spent in the bush. We had enough of the common necessaries of life. A spirit of peace and harmony pervaded our little dwelling" (p. 486). "Outbreak," then, tells little about the colony's rebellion, but a great deal about her temporary freedom from patriarchal authority.

She also puts her feminine, genteel talents to work to gain financial independence. It is "just at this period [that] I received a letter from a gentleman, requesting me to write for a magazine [the *Literary Garland*], just started in Montreal, with promise to remunerate me for my labours" (p. 475). Before this time, ironically, she had been too fatigued "to turn my thoughts toward literature." Now, even though she is running the farm as well as the house, she "no longer retired to bed when the labours of the day were over [but] sat up and wrote" (p. 476). The "new era in my existence" which has "opened up" repeats her family's use of literary talents to overcome financial difficulties. She also adapts another genteel feminine talent to her purpose: "Besides gaining a little money with my pen, I practised a method of painting birds and butterflies upon the white, velvety surface of the large fungi, that grow plentifully upon the bark of the sugar-maple. . . . These, at one shilling each, enabled me to buy shoes for the children" (p. 479). "I actually shed tears of joy," she exclaims, "over the first twenty-dollar bill I received from Montreal. It was my own; I had earned it with my own hand; and it seemed . . . to form the nucleus out of which a future independence for my family might arise" (p. 476). She gains confidence and strength over the course of this chapter as she usurps her husband's role as breadwinner.

The most significant act of independence, if not rebellion, in the chapter is Moodie's letter to the lieutenant-governor explaining their situation and asking "him to continue my husband in the militia service, in the same regiment in which he now held the rank of captain, which by enabling him to pay our debts, would rescue us from our present misery" (p. 485). She knows that "the act I had just done would be displeasing to . . . my husband." Nevertheless, she "felt resolutely determined to send it." Her confession, "the first secret I ever had from my husband was the writing of that letter," implies that this secret was not the last. It is, after all, successful: from this covert action comes her husband's appointment as sheriff of Hastings County and their removal from the bush to Belleville. Mr. Moodie remains ignorant of the source of his good fortune; he "looked upon it as a gift sent from heaven" (p. 544). When Moodie "return[s] thanks to God that night for all His mercies to us," and adds that "Sir George Arthur [the lieutenant-governor] was not forgotten in those prayers," she is clearly aware that her rising power is in contrast to his ineffectual bumbling.

From reluctant but dutiful wife of an emigrant, Susanna Moodie developed into a resourceful, independent settler. She overcame the limitations of genteel femininity and social prejudices to run effectively both home and farm and to establish a literary career. But the most significant aspect of the record of her experience in *Roughing It* was her political evolution. Through her own rebellion in 1837 against male domination, she succeeded in extricating herself and her family from debt in the backwoods. Moodie, moreover, recognized the connection between her personal development and that of the country, for she incorporated the political rebellion into the very thematic and structural climax of the book. In doing so, Moodie openly dissented from the conservative and reactionary views represented by her sister. Like her sister, she "conform[ed] to circumstances" in the backwoods, and, again like Traill, maintained her monarchical ties to England. But very much unlike Traill, her voice became, as Robert L. McDougall has noted, that of the Moderate Reformers, "those who sympathized with Mackenzie's quarrel but refused to back the extreme republican measures he eventually proposed."[53] One of the few passages of emotional intensity in Traill's book was directed against Mackenzie and his followers; Moodie's *Roughing It*, on the other hand, in the chapter on the Mackenzie rebellion, exuded the kind of spirit of action and independence which would lead Canada toward "Home-rule." Contrary to David Jackel's attempt to see "the real strengths of our British inheritance" in Traill[54] and to Gaile McGregor's description of Traill's experience as "a paradigm for the national experience," it is Moodie's *Roughing It* which best mirrors the unique adaptation of the British political tradition to the backwoods of Canada.

NOTES

1. Frances Brooke, *The History of Emily Montague* (1769; Toronto, 1961), p. 17.
2. See Mary Jane Edwards, "*The History of Emily Montague:* A Political Novel,"

in *The Canadian Novel: Beginnings*, ed. John Moss (Toronto, 1980), p. 25; Lorraine McMullen, "Frances Brooke," in *Canadian Writers and Their Works*, ed. Robert Lecker, Jack David and Ellen Quigley (Toronto, 1983), p. 26. For a fuller account, see McMullen's biography, *An Odd Attempt in a Woman: The Literary Life of Frances Brooke* (Vancouver, 1983), particularly the chapter "The Brookes in Canada," pp. 67–83.

3. "The Royal Proclamation 1763," in *A Source-book of Canadian History: Selected Documents and Personal Papers*, ed. J. H. Stewart Reid, Kenneth McNaught and Harry S. Crowe (Toronto, 1959), p. 49.

4. "Petition of the Quebec Traders, 1764," in *Pre-Confederation: Canadian Historical Documents Series*, ed. P. B. Waite (Scarborough, 1965), p. 50.

5. "Murray to the Board of Trade, October 29, 1764," in *Pre-Confederation*, p. 50.

6. Mary Jane Edwards, Introduction, *The Evolution of Canadian Literature in English: Beginnings to 1867*, ed. Mary Jane Edwards, Paul Denham and George Parker (Toronto, 1973), p. 2.

7. Edwards, "*Emily Montague*: A Political Novel," p. 23.

8. McMullen, *An Odd Attempt in a Woman*, p. 92; cf. as well her similar statement in "Frances Brooke," p. 40.

9. W. H. New, "*The Old Maid*: Frances Brooke's Apprentice Feminism," *Journal of Canadian Fiction* 2 (Summer 1973), 9.

10. McMullen gives a critical overview of Brooke in *Canadian Writers and Their Works*, ed. Lecker, David and Quigley, and notes that from the nineteenth century until the early 1960s, "Canadian critics saw the novel's portrayal of Canadian life as its main value, dismissing it artistically." Not until the 1961 publication of the New Canadian Library edition with its introduction by Carl F. Klinck do we get "our first critically perceptive evaluation" (p. 32). As pointed out in the text of my study, New first introduces a study of Brooke's feminism in 1973.

11. Klinck, Introduction, *The History of Emily Montague*, p. viii.

12. Ann Edwards Boutelle, "Brooke's Emily Montague: Canada and Woman's Rights," *Women's Studies* 12 (Winter 1986), 7–16.

13. J. W. Mackail, *Virgil and His Meaning to the World of Today* (New York, 1963), p. 63. See also T. F. Royds, Introduction, in *The Eclogues and Georgics of Virgil*, trans. and introduction by T. F. Royds (London, 1907), pp. vii–xv, and Jacques Perret, "*The Georgics*," in *Virgil: A Collection of Critical Essays*, ed. Steele Commager (Englewood Cliffs, 1966), pp. 28–40.

14. W. H. New, "Frances Brooke's Chequered Gardens," *Canadian Literature* 52 (Spring 1972), 36.

15. Edwards, "*Emily Montague*: A Political Novel," p. 22; McMullen, *Odd Attempt*, p. 105.

16. "The Treaty of Paris, 1763," in *Pre-Confederation*, ed. Waite, p. 48.

17. Hazel Mews, *Frail Vessels* (London, 1969), p. 73. New, especially, develops Bell's ironic function in his "Frances Brooke's Chequered Gardens."

18. Edwards, "*Emily Montague*: A Political Novel," p. 23.

19. Clara Thomas, *Our Nature, Our Voices* (Toronto, 1972), p. 11.

20. Marian Fowler, *The Embroidered Tent* (Toronto, 1982), p. 143.

21. Clara Thomas, "Journeys to Freedom," *Canadian Literature* 51 (Winter 1972), 13; Fowler, *The Embroidered Tent*, p. 146.

22. Anna Jameson, *Winter Studies and Summer Rambles in Canada* (1838; Toronto: Coles facsimile edition, 1972), pp. 2–3.

23. Fowler, *The Embroidered Tent*, p. 153.

24. Cf. Fowler, *The Embroidered Tent*, p. 145, and Clara Thomas, *Love and Work Enough* (Toronto, 1967), p. 130.

25. Thomas, *Love and Work Enough*, p. 128.

26. Quoted in Fowler, *The Embroidered Tent*, p. 150.

27. *"Winter Studies and Summer Rambles in Canada," British and Foreign Review* 8 (1839), 134–35. This unnamed review is quoted in Thomas' *Love and Work Enough*, p. 140, but Thomas stresses that the editor of the *Review* at the time was John Kemble.

28. Anna Jameson, *Winter Studies and Summer Rambles in Canada*, ed. James Talman and Elsie Murray (Toronto, 1943), pp. vii-viii.

29. Ged Martin, "Queen Victoria and Canada," *American Review of Canadian Studies* 13 (Spring 1983), 215–33.

30. Carl F. Klinck, "Literary Activity in the Canadas, 1812–1841," in *Literary History of Canada*, gen. ed. Carl F. Klinck, 3 vols. (Toronto, 1976), 1, 151.

31. Donald Creighton, *Dominion of the North* (Toronto, 1957), p. 217.

32. William Lyon Mackenzie, *The Selected Writings of William Lyon Mackenzie*, ed. Margaret Fairley (Toronto, 1960), pp. 340, 351.

33. Catharine Parr Traill, *The Backwoods of Canada* (1836; Toronto: Coles facsimile ed., 1980), p. 292.

34. Clara Thomas, Introduction, C. P. Traill, *The Backwoods of Canada* (Toronto, 1966), p. 7.

35. Mackenzie, *Selected Writings*, p. 341.

36. Traill, Preface, *The Canadian Settler's Guide* (1854; Toronto, 1969), p. xviii.

37. Catharine Parr Traill, *Studies of Plant Life in Canada* (Ottawa, 1885), p. 2.

38. Thomas devotes only three brief paragraphs to Traill after lengthier discussions of Jameson and Moodie in her "Journeys to Freedom." She comments that Traill "simply walked past—or through—the dragons which beset the others" (19). Thomas' qualification hints at depths in Traill's persona which other critics have explored. William D. Gairdner ("Traill and Moodie: The Two Realities," *Journal of Canadian Fiction* 1 [Spring 1972], 35–42) is led to ask "how, for a woman dependent on reason, the paradoxes so apparent to others ... were resolved" (p. 37). Gairdner comes to "regard these searchings for botanical justification a result of her wish to evade" (p. 36).

39. Clara Thomas is the chief perpetrator of this distinction in her early biographical article "The Strickland Sisters," in *The Clear Spirit: Twenty Canadian Women and Their Times*, ed. Mary Quayle Innis (Toronto, 1966), pp. 42–73.

40. Traill, *Settler's Guide*, pp. 24, 114–15.

41. Catharine Parr Traill, *The Backwoods of Canada* (1842; Toronto, 1929), p. 332.

42. Gaile McGregor, *The Wacousta Syndrome: Explorations in the Canadian Landscape* (Toronto, 1985), p. 41.

43. Carl P. A. Ballstadt, "Catharine Parr Traill," in *Canadian Writers and Their Works*, ed. Lecker, David and Quigley, p. 181.

44. Susanna Moodie, *Roughing It in the Bush* (1852; Toronto: Coles facsimile ed., 1980), p. 563.

45. This difference has its roots in the portrait Traill presents of her family's

increasing prosperity and the repetition of calamities found in Moodie's account. However, T. D. MacLulich, for example, compares the two sisters and reaches a conclusion opposite to what I propose in this study. "Mrs. Traill sees that the genteel ideal must be modified," says MacLulich, "but Mrs. Moodie holds fast . . . to her concept of social class. . . . [There is no] indication that Mrs. Moodie has herself become a changed person" ["Crusoe in the Backwoods: A Canadian Fable?" *Mosaic* 9 [Winter 1976], 124).

46. Carl F. Klinck, Introduction, Susanna Moodie, *Roughing It in the Bush* (Toronto, 1966), p. xii.

47. Moodie, Introduction to the First Edition, *Roughing It in the Bush* (Toronto, 1966), p. xviii.

48. Moodie, *Susanna Moodie: Letters of a Lifetime*, ed. Carl Ballstadt, Elizabeth Hopkins and Michael Peterman (Toronto, 1985), p. 111.

49. Carl P. A. Ballstadt, "Secure in Conscious Worth: Susanna Moodie and the Rebellion of 1837," *Canadian Poetry* 18 (Spring-Summer 1986), 89.

50. Moodie, "Canada: a Contrast," *Roughing It in the Bush* (Toronto, 1980), p. 9.

51. Susanna Moodie, *Life in the Clearings* (1853; Toronto, 1959), p. 35.

52. Michael A. Peterman, "Susanna Moodie," in *Canadian Writers and Their Works*, ed. Lecker, David and Quigley, pp. 89, 91.

53. Robert L. McDougall, Introduction, *Life in the Clearings*, p. xix.

54. David Jackel, "Mrs. Moodie and Mrs. Traill, and the Fabrication of a Canadian Tradition," *The Compass* 6 (Spring 1979), 20.

2

"The Home Has Expanded Until It Has Become the Whole State": Imperialism to Emancipation

"You cannot mean to tell me," asks Hugh Finlay, the young Scots Presbyterian minister in Sara Jeannette Duncan's *The Imperialist* (1904), "that . . . my sincere and devoted friendship for Miss Murchison has been in any way prejudicial—." Dr. Drummond, his senior colleague, understands and completes his sentence: "To her in the ordinary sense? To her prospects of marriage and her standing in the eyes of the community? No, Finlay. No."[1] The conflict between Mr. Finlay's and Miss Murchison's "friendship" and "the ordinary sense" of relationships between the sexes acts as the romantic subplot in Duncan's novel of imperial and colonial politics. As such it highlights the attempts of many Canadian women in the first two decades of the twentieth century to redefine the partnership between men and women. Adelaide Hoodlis founded the First Women's Institute in Brantford, Ontario, in 1897, dedicated to educating women in matters of food and hygiene. The Women's Christian Temperance Union crusaded not just for temperance but also for the moral reform of society and was an early advocate of women's suffrage as a means to achieve their ends. Involvement in "the Woman Question" naturally led to political campaigning for the rights of female enfranchisement and the right for women to hold public office. Women openly challenged their position in Canadian society, and with it, conventional relationships with men.

During the same period, the young Dominion of Canada was evolving its position within the British Empire. From the 1890s onward, Canada strove to resist Great Britain's rising desire to tighten its imperialistic holdings into a stronger, centralized federation. Joseph Chamberlain, secretary of state for the colonies in 1895, was for the next decade an enthusiastic proponent of the concept of imperialism. The country's twentieth-century prime ministers, Sir Wilfrid Laurier and Sir Robert Laird Borden, however, each in his own way slowly moved the nation away from its colonial status and onto the road of national independence. Robert Craig Brown and Ramsay Cook note in their study *Canada 1896–1921: A Nation Transformed* (1974) that when Chamberlain proposed "something in the nature of an Imperial Council, sitting permanently in London and acting as permanent advisers to the Secretary of State for the colonies," Laurier remained wary of "any detailed plan of. . . organization which would impose on the Colonies fixed. . . obligations."[2] Donald Creighton concludes in his *Dominion of the North* (1957) that "Laurier supported, and often led, the other colonial prime ministers in their defence of colonial autonomy against imperial centralization."[3] From the turn of the century to World War I, Canada steadily declared her intention to remain detached from but concerned with England's international affairs.

Sara Jeannette Duncan in *The Imperialist* directly addresses this political issue, and there is some significance in the very fact that a woman at the turn of the century chose to write on such a decidedly political theme. Women were certainly changing their image during the last two decades of the nineteenth century; the New Woman, what William Wasserstrom defines as "independent, assertive young ladies. . . competent in love,"[4] at first shocked society, then came to represent the best the West had to offer. Duncan aspired to be one such liberated woman; her early career in journalism and her popularity as a novelist, playwright and travel writer attest to the degree of her success. Born in Brantford, Ontario, in 1861, she was a journalist with the *Washington Post* in 1885, and became the first woman hired in the editorial department of the *Toronto Globe* in 1886. While in Washington, she covered the Suffragist Convention; her report not only revealed her sympathies for female suffrage, but also her impatience with conventional women who are content with their present subservient position in society. "It is a supreme moment in a woman's existence," she claims, "when she commits herself to suffrage for her sex. It marks the temporary and hard-won victory of her intelligence over her instinct."[5] But Duncan gave up her journalistic career in 1891 to marry Everard Cotes, a British civil servant living in India. In her biography of Duncan, *Redney* (1983), Marian Fowler dramatizes the damaging effect of the marriage on Duncan's spirit and art.[6] The pull between "intelligence" and "instinct" became a significant factor in Duncan's own life and in her portrait of women in *The Imperialist*. One can determine the psychological cost to Duncan of her marriage on the basis of *The Imperialist*, for in it she tries hard to reconcile the conflict between the aspirations of the New Woman and the traditional bonds of matrimony.

The novel focuses primarily, however, on the title character, Lorne Murchison, a young lawyer who enters politics as an advocate of closer ties between Canada and England. But unlike many of his fellow citizens, he is

not motivated by economics; rather, his vision is of "the moral advantage
. . . to keep[ing] up the relationship" with England. Canada in his estimation
is "young and thin and weedy," whereas "the very name [of England is]
great . . . rich with character and strong with conduct and hoary with ideals"
(p. 98). The reader early suspects Lorne's political and cultural colonialism
because of his choice of Dora Milburn as his fiancée: Dora, a proper young
lady with neither intelligence nor character, is rather reminiscent of Dickens'
character in *David Copperfield*. Duncan contrasts Dora, with her allegiance
to established forms of feminine behavior, to the independent-minded female
protagonist, Lorne's older sister Advena, whose very name suggests the New
Woman. "Bookish and unconventional" (p. 45), Advena eventually finds both
freedom and fulfillment with her love, Hugh Finlay, the young immigrant
Scots preacher who slowly rejects his old-country values and embraces the
new nation and the possibilities of forging new identities, both personal and
national. As the young Dominion rejects the colonial subservience implied
by the concept of imperialism, Lorne loses both his seat in Parliament and
Dora, while Advena and Hugh overcome the barriers to their love and move
to the Canadian West.

When introducing the various members of the Murchison family, the
narrator admonishes, "we must take this matter of names seriously" (p. 17).
The Murchison family, like the majority of the townspeople, are fervent
Liberals. The two younger sons are named after Alexander Mackenzie, federal Liberal leader in 1874, and his contemporary, Oliver Mowat, the Ontario
Liberal leader. Neither son, comments the narrator, "could very well grow
up into anything but a sound Liberal . . . without feeling himself an unen-
durable paradox." With no intended sense of paradox, on the other hand,
Lorne is named after Canada's governor general, the Marquis of Lorne, as
"a simple way of attesting loyal spirit." Lorne's mother has "more particular
motives" for his name: "The Marquis of Lorne . . . was the son-in-law of a
good woman, of whom Mrs. Murchison thought more . . . for being the
woman she was than for being twenty times a Queen" (pp. 16–17). In the
act of naming the sons after Canadian Liberals and "the Royal representative," the Murchisons expressed their divided sense of allegiance. Lorne's
naming presages his own passionate attachment to the principle of Empire
espoused in the novel by Wallingham, Duncan's thin disguise for Chamberlain. The Liberals in the novel, however, as in history, move slowly away
from the imperial cause in favor of national autonomy. And it is the clash of
these national and imperial forces which occupies the main plot of the novel.

Moreover, "this matter of names" points up the patriarchal nature of this
society. Great attention is given to the names of the sons in the hope of
"doing well" for them; their christening is described as a "rite" (p. 17).
"Politics were," after all, "accepted as a purely masculine interest" (p. 189);
only the male offspring are named after political figures. The insignificance
of the daughters' naming is suggested by the fact that the narrator deals with

the subject in one sentence. Mrs. Murchison dismisses the matter just as quickly; because Advena "was named after one grandmother," the next girl, "to make an end of the matter," was named after the other (p. 16). That they are named after female family "relations" emphasizes the social expectation that they continue to fill woman's place in the home. Abigail, the second-eldest daughter, "had taken no time at all to establish herself; she had almost immediately married" (p. 45). "Elgin society," comments the narrator, "shaping itself . . . to ultimate increase and prosperity, had this peculiarity, that the females of a family, in general acceptance, were apt to lag far behind the males. . . . the young men were more desirable than the young women [because] they forged ahead, carrying the family fortunes" (pp. 45–46). "Increase and prosperity," the economic basis of this patriarchal society, necessitate that the woman, even while she performs the biological and domestic functions to which she is restricted, is nevertheless less valued, less valuable, than the man.

The economic, political and sexist dimensions of Canadian society are likewise evoked by Duncan's use of Elgin as the name for the town. Not only was Lord Elgin a patriarchal figure and an efficient colonial administrator, but also his crowning achievement was the negotiation with the United States of the Reciprocity Treaty of 1854. It is precisely this economic factor which Lorne in his zealous idealism refuses to countenance. The election campaign allows Duncan to introduce various points of view on "the subject of the day." "Imperialism is intensely and supremely a national affair," says Lorne, summing up many an imperialist's belief that "the centre of the Empire must shift . . . to Canada" (p. 229).[7] He recalls that "the northern and strenuous half" of the continent did not "throw overboard" the "precious cargo [of] our heritage"—"the ideals of British government" (p. 230). The problems of American annexationist threats and of "trade relations" are accurately introduced: "The imperial trade idea has changed the attitude of our friends to the south. They have small liking for any scheme which will improve trade between Great Britain and Canada, because [such trade] must be improved at their expense" (p. 231). Carried away by his rhetoric, Lorne dismisses too glibly the wider population's interest in the "balance of trade." "We cannot calculate," he maintains, "in terms of pig-iron, or . . . any formula of consumption" (p. 232). "The whole stamp and character" of Canada, in Lorne's view, has been "acquired in the rugged discipline of our colonial youth, and [is to be] developed in the national usage of the British Empire" (p. 232).

As Alfred G. Bailey and Joseph M. Zezulka have both pointed out in their historical considerations of the novel, the political arguments in *The Imperialist* indicate that Duncan was thoroughly familiar with the various sides of the issue of her day expounded by men such as Sir George Parkin and Sir Andrew MacPhail; both Parkin and Goldwin Smith, the latter a powerful voice for stronger ties with the United States, are referred to in the novel

(p. 200).[8] Bailey and Zezulka conclude, on the basis of the historicity of the novel, that Duncan was an imperialist at heart. Bailey writes: "one can only suppose that while her reason and experience led her to conclude that [imperialism] was the embodiment of an impossible ideal, it was one to which her own heart was not altogether a stranger" (p. 140). Zezulka equates Duncan with a leading proponent of imperialism, Stephen Leacock, stating "both . . . [were] ardent nationalists" (p. 145). On the other hand, in book-length studies of Duncan's life and works, *Sara Jeannette Duncan: Novelist of Empire* (1980) and *Redney: A Life of Sara Jeannette Duncan*, Thomas E. Tausky and Fowler, respectively, more perceptively acknowledge that Duncan does not take sides in the novel on the question of imperialism. Tausky notes that "there are whole pages on the social structure of Elgin, but nary a sentence of authorial opinion about imperialism" (p. 161); Fowler agrees that Duncan is "consciously ambivalent about Imperialism" (p. 259). Tausky does conclude, however, that "the reader of *The Imperialist* does . . . gain the impression that Sara favours imperialism."[9] Duncan's political position, it would seem, cannot easily be defined.

All four critics ignore two important aspects of the novel: the narrative point of view and the satirical intent of the romantic subplots. Critics of *The Imperialist* seem to overlook the fact that life in Elgin is described through the eyes of an unidentified character, not of the author. For example, Zezulka refers to "Duncan's bemused and frequently astringent intrusions [which] are clearly intended to guide the reader's response to Elgin society" (p. 147). Tausky feels that "Duncan chooses to communicate information through an impersonal and omniscient narrator" in "the method of the great eighteenth and nineteenth century English novelists" (p. 84). The frequency with which Tausky interchanges the term "narrator" and the author's name reveals that he too does not differentiate between them.

Point of view is the central issue in the theory of fiction of Henry James, the literary leader whose novels and aesthetics influenced most turn-of-the-century authors.[10] Richard Chase notes in his study *The American Novel and Its Tradition* (1957) that for James "the great thing is to get into the novel not only setting but somebody's sense of the setting."[11] In order to capture in a novel an "air of reality," James wrote, it was necessary that the novel present not facts but someone's interpretation of facts: "A novel is in its broadest definition a personal, a direct impression of life."[12] It is important to realize that the narrator of *The Imperialist* who relates all the events and interprets the thoughts and actions of the characters seems to be an inhabitant of the fictional Elgin and is present at many but not all of the story's events; "There is a party at the Milburns' and some of *us* are going" (p. 46; emphasis mine). This person is clearly neither omniscient nor impersonal as she constantly reminds the reader that the novel is a report of what has been seen and heard. For example, the description of the Murchison home is punctuated by such phrases as "Mrs. Murchison often declared," and includes the interjection, "I

must, in this connection, continue to quote the mistress [of the house]"
(p. 29). Furthermore, when Lorne impulsively abandons his prepared campaign text to give an impassioned plea for the cause of imperialism, the narrator asks rhetorically, "Who knows at what suggestion, or even precisely at
what moment, the fabric of his sincere intention fell away?" and then offers in
answer the views of others who were present: "Bingham does not; Mr. Far-
quharson has the vaguest idea; Dr. Drummond declares that he expected it
from the beginning" (p. 228). "I can get nothing more out of them," she concludes, even at this climactic moment reminding the reader that the novel is
a personal impression of events and of opinions.

This use of a persona as the center of intelligence is essential for Duncan's
purpose which, as she explains in a letter to Lord Lansdowne, is "to present
the situation as it appears to the average Canadian of the average small
town."[13] The narrator, like a newspaper reporter—and one recalls Duncan's
beginnings as a journalist—polls the opinions of other citizens and consequently provides a spectrum of responses to the issue of imperialism. The
narrator is able to place each event, each character, within the context of
alternative perspectives. Unlike the English novelist who, as Chase explains,
absorbs "a wide range of experience into a moral centrality and equability
of judgement" (p. 2), Duncan explores "a wide range of experience," but,
by using the persona, imposes no ultimate authorial judgement. "My book
offers only a picture of life and opinion, and attempts no argument," claims
Duncan to Lansdowne.

However, as Duncan's narrator notes, "those who write . . . transcribe
themselves in spite of themselves" (p. 69). Duncan's political feelings are
not to be found by equating the author and the persona, but by examining
the structure of the novel. Critics miss the satirical intent of the romantic
subplots. Tausky discusses Lorne at great length and mentions Advena only
briefly; Fowler too focuses primarily on Lorne and devotes only a paragraph
to the manner in which Advena's "abstract idealism . . . capitulate[s] to emotion" in the relationship with Hugh (p. 260). They do not realize that, as
does Brooke in *The History of Emily Montague* (1769), Duncan raises the
love affairs to the level of political commentary. "Politics and love are thought
of at opposite poles," muses the narrator, but then goes on to reveal that
she does not hold to this popular assumption: in Lorne's case they are related
since his "exalted allegiance" to the cause of imperialism stemmed "in part
[from] a half-broken heart" (p. 261).

The extension of Lorne's misguided love for England is his foolhardy love
for Dora Milburn. Coming from a family which imitates British propriety,
Dora is the embodiment of colonial femininity: conventional and commonplace. Her reaction to Lorne's rising political fortunes is selfish and frivolous;
when he announces that he has been invited to join a trade delegation to
England, Dora is piqued that he should forget "the regatta coming off the
first week in June, and a whole crowd coming from Toronto for it" (p. 98).

She insists on keeping their proposed engagement a secret because "an engaged girl has the very worst time. She gets hardly any attention, and as to dances—well, it's a good thing for her if the person she's engaged to can dance" (pp. 145–46). While Dora "make[s] little tentative charges of extravagance in his purchase" of an engagement ring, the narrator comments that Lorne "did not stop to condone her weakness; rather he seized it in ecstasy [for] it was all part of the glad scheme to help the lover." As Lorne sits "elated and adoring," the narrator concludes the scene by calling him "the simple fellow" (p. 145). After Lorne loses his seat in Parliament, he learns that Dora has engaged herself to marry the arrogant, vacuous British gentleman, Hesketh. The narrator again wryly notes that "Mr. Hesketh's engagement to Miss Milburn was the most suitable thing that could be imagined or desired" (p. 268). Dora and her socially inculcated femininity are as unworthy of Lorne's devotion as the ideal of imperialism.

In direct contrast to Dora and her feminine behavior stands Lorne's sister, Advena; her characterization and complex, yet positive relationship with Hugh Finlay also counterpoint Lorne and his futile engagement. Advena is an independent-minded person who "would hide in the hayloft with a novel; she would go for walks in the rain on windy October twilights and be met kicking the wet leaves along in front of her 'in a dream' " (p. 45). Her mother cannot imagine how Advena will be "fit for the management of a house" (p. 32); Advena's disinterest in "good housewifery" renders her "[un]fit to be a wife" (p. 104). "By taking the university course for women at Toronto, and afterward teaching . . . to the junior forms in the Collegiate Institute," Advena "justified her existence [and] placed [herself] outside the sphere of domestic criticism" (pp. 32–33). But her interest in books and her position as teacher are termed "shortcomings" by her mother (p. 33). "She'd much better make up her mind," concludes Mrs. Murchison, "just to be a happy independent old maid" (p. 104). The characterization of Advena as a New Woman and her profession as a teacher are indicative of the changes taking place in Canadian society since the time of Jameson, Traill and Moodie with regard to the social position of women. Mrs. Murchison is the perfect embodiment of Traill's definition of the good housewife, but Advena resists any attempts by her mother to be "policed" into that role.

Nevertheless, despite Advena's independent status, women in 1904 had neither the franchise nor the legal status of equality with men, and Duncan uses the relationship which develops between Advena and the newly arrived Scots preacher, Hugh Finlay, to explore and challenge the traditional patriarchal relationship between the sexes. Coming as he does from the "old" country, Hugh has inherited patriarchal "ideals about women . . . he saw them . . . concerned with the preservation of society, the maintenance of the home, the noble devotion of motherhood" (p. 106). Whereas Mrs. Murchison has been unsuccessful in indoctrinating Advena, Hugh is well-trained by his "widowed and frugal and spare" Aunt Lizzie, who "had presided over his

childhood and represented the sex to his youth" so carefully that he is in "a
reasonable disposition to acquiesce" before leaving for Canada to her suggestion that he become engaged to the woman of her choice. Conditioned
as he is, it is a great surprise for Hugh that "the chief interest of his life [in
Elgin], the chief human interest, did lie in his relations with Advena Murchison." Advena, for her part, is attracted to him immediately; together,
they come to discover that "the steps they took together lead somehow to
freedom" (p. 70).

Influenced as she is by the writings of Henry James and William Dean
Howells, Duncan is aware of the political implications of her variation on
the international theme. "If anyone had told Mr. Hugh Finlay, while he
was pursuing his rigorous path to the ideals of the University of Edinburgh,
that the first notable interest of his life in the calling and the country to
which even then he had given his future would lie in his relations with any
woman, he would have treated the prediction as mere folly" (p. 106). Like
Ed Rivers, Hugh comes to Canada with set attitudes to the country and to
its women, but unlike Rivers, Hugh experiences, in his first conversation
with "the heiress of all the ages," a "sudden liberation" and, after Advena's
promptings, realizes his limitations as "a moralizer" (p. 71). In a later conversation, Hugh has dropped his old-world sense of destiny: "there is something in a fresh start: we're on the straight road as a nation. . . . England has
filled [her future] up" (p. 110). At the conclusion of their first conversation
Hugh takes "the road to the north which was still snowbound," while Advena
goes "into the chilly yellow west" (p. 71). Later, when Hugh persists in
honoring his ties to Scotland, when his pathway remains "snowbound" by
an arranged marriage, he contemplates going "to British Columbia" where
"those mining missions would give a man his chance against himself" (p. 184).
The significance of the western province of Canada for Hugh's venture is
deliberate on Duncan's part; Hugh, like the country of his adoption, will
seek a compromise of his old-world values in the new west.

Advena, however, asking him to stay in Elgin, is, in her own way, as
idealistic as her brother; but where Lorne's attachment is to conservative
values, Advena, in her attempt to continue her "companionship" with Hugh
not only outside marriage but also despite his pending marriage to another
woman, struggles with him to maintain a platonic friendship beyond "the
common type" (p. 181). Their relationship grows through "evenings together
. . . talking about . . . books and . . . authors" (p. 103); but after "they had
come to full knowledge" of their love for each other, they are reduced to
talking "like tried friends of every-day affairs" (p. 180). "One might think,"
comments the narrator, "that Nature, having made them her invitation upon
the higher plane, abandoned them in the very scorn of her success to . . .
human commonplaces" (pp. 180–81). Their domesticated evenings by the
fire—"he always brought [his pipe] with him, by her order, and Advena
usually sewed" (p. 181)—are comical, as they attempt to resist "the currents

from the heart" while developing a "friendship of ideas . . . a friendship of spirit" (pp. 183, 184). Only the humorous intervention of Dr. Drummond can release Hugh from his firm resolve to marry Miss Cameron, but not before Advena rushes "into the full blast of the veering, irresolute storm" (p. 248) to throw herself "at his feet in a torrent of weeping, clasping them and entreating": "I know now what is possible and what is not!" (p. 250). Unlike her brother, Advena comes to admit that "their struggle" had been an attempt "to establish the impossible," that "she had preferred an ideal to the desire of her heart" (p. 250).

Advena and Lorne are crucial to an understanding not only of the changing relationships between the sexes but also of the political theme of the novel. The narrator makes clear that they have vastly different ideals. Advena's intellectual development takes her "outside the domestic sphere," outside the conventional role of housewife played by her mother and sister. Consequently, her relationship with Hugh, initiated as it is by their mutual interest in literature, is one between equals, a "companionship." That she finally "pulled [her ideal of a platonic relationship] down to foolish ruin" (p. 250) does not diminish the heroic attempt she has made to forge a relationship with a man beyond the bounds of convention. Lorne, on the other hand, clings to his outmoded ideals in politics and love. It is instructive to note, as Zezulka correctly points out (p. 149), that Lorne and Dora always meet within-doors, whereas Hugh and Advena frequently meet out-of-doors. Lorne is walled in by convention, whereas Advena is "outside"; it is only when Advena and Hugh try to deny the consummation of their passion that their relationship becomes stale, "absorbed by homely matters" (p. 182). When they are free to marry, they accept "the charge of the . . . Mission" and take their companionship in love to the unformed west. Lorne remains locked in the imperial sphere; that he remains behind the times is indicated by the fact that his political colleagues force him to withdraw from the election because he "didn't get rid of that save-the-Empire-or-die scheme" (p. 262). The intransigence of his attitude is suggested by his curt reply, "I shall never get rid of it." Out of step with his countrymen, Lorne has no sense of progress: he has only the old ideal of British imperialism.

Duncan has developed her political theme, then, as Brooke did, by contrasting the love relationships in her novel. Duncan's concerns, however, are not limited to issues of Canadian politics and women. In her early journalism Duncan expressed her belief that a "national literature cannot be wholly evolved from within . . . but to give it growth, variety and comprehensive character, it has to be fed from without."[14] Consequently, Duncan incorporated in her novels techniques of the American school of realism. Wasserstrom explores the phenomenon of the many novels which followed James' lead in using an "American girl [to embody] her society" (p. 126). He concludes, moreover, that "James in the international plot showed how devotedness [as wife and mother] deprived [women] of the capacity for freedom" (p. 128). With the publication of her first novels, A *Social Depar-ture. How Orthodocia and I Went Round the World by Ourselves* (1890) and *An American Girl in London* (1891) to the later *Canadian Girl in London* (1908), Duncan explores her interest in James' "international theme." Like James, Duncan explores the international theme, the contrast of Old and New World cultures, by using a young woman as the focus of study. Duncan's writing is certainly influenced "from without," for not only does Duncan live with her husband in India during her writing years, but also only one of her novels is actually set in Canada. That one novel is *The Imperialist*, structured as we have seen according to the international theme of her other works. Using techniques of the American analytical school of realism, she is able to achieve her goal, which is, as she explains to Lord Lansdowne, to present the "colonial view" of the Empire question. The international theme, the study of women and the domestic setting allow her to articulate "Canadian sentiment."[15]

The new womanhood of Advena and Hugh's growth in the New World contrasted with Lorne's stagnation and the commonplace femininity of Dora establish Duncan's political, and by extension her literary, values. As long as old-world conventions, political or romantic, are imported to Canada, Duncan knows, the nation and its people will be as static and conventional, as colonial, as Lorne and Dora. "So long as Canada remains in political obscurity," she writes in the article "Colonialism and Literature," "so long will the leaves and blossoms of art and literature be scanty and stunted products of our national energy."[16] In her biographical consideration of the creation of *The Imperialist*, Fowler concludes that Duncan had come to perceive "how unsuitable, for any Canadian, are American and British [environments]. . . . Canada must not be imprinted with the 'stamp and character' of the American republic, but with Canada's own peculiar stamp and character. Nor must Canada slavishly follow British patterns" (p. 254). Canadians, in their politics and their literature, must break from the British pattern, just as Hugh liberates himself from his ties with Scotland and as Advena frees herself from society's expectations for young women.

Not only have recent scholars ignored the political implications of this love story but also, as Tausky reports, critics at the time offered "almost universally hostile reviews." Tausky concludes his survey: "a point of view that underlies all the . . . hostile comments [is that] politics and 'romance' should not be mixed, especially . . . by a lady author" (p. 267). The *Globe* reviewer dismisses the novel's "political passages" because "that half of the population which is disenfranchised takes but little interest in politics, and it is a rule to which there are few exceptions that even when our sisters and wives make a conscious effort to compass the mystery, their success is but partial. That is about all that could be said . . . of *The Imperialist*" (p. 270). It is perhaps instructive that only the *New York Times* perceived the satire of the "attitude of the ladies of Elgin" and of "the English imperial idea" (pp. 268–69), but even this favorable review persisted in keeping the two areas apart. Duncan's perceptions seem to have been ahead of their time.

The positive reception by an American, moreover, reminds us that Duncan employed the international theme of the American school of realism in *The Imperialist* in order to tackle the major national issue facing Canada in 1904, whether or not to draw closer her ties to Great Britain. By using American literary models, perhaps Duncan inadvertently touched a sore nerve among Canadian nationalists: the increasing fear of American domination of Canada. It was only after World War I that Canada came to recognize the continental concerns of her national interests; in 1904, there was distrust after the Alaska boundary dispute of American annexationist intentions. Fear of America became strong enough that when, in 1911, Laurier and his Liberals campaigned on a platform of increased reciprocity with the United States, they were soundly defeated. Although suggesting closer ties with the United States was far from her purpose, Duncan did reflect the coming shift of the nation's feelings toward increased independence—the imperialist of the title, contrasted to his forward-looking sister, is definitely at odds with his community. Introducing Advena as a "new woman" in her "novel of today," Duncan foreshadows the emancipation of Canadian nationalism from British imperialism; whether Canada could avoid American characteristics remained as problematic in her future as was the "new" relationship developing between men and women.

The controversy over imperialism and the question of Canada's national status found issue, between 1900 and the outbreak of World War I, in two international incidents, the war in South Africa and the Alaskan boundary dispute. Brown and Cook succinctly describe the way the Boer War polarized national opinions: "English-Canadian nationalists . . . wanted Canada to participate as an equal in the war, and to prove that equality by assuming full responsibility for Canadian troops in South Africa. French-Canadian nationalists wanted Canada to prove her equality of nationhood by refusing to participate at all" (p. 41). Canada did send troops to Africa in response to the will of the English-speaking majority, but Laurier appeased others by claiming that, "in future, Canada shall be at liberty to act or not to act . . . she shall reserve to herself the right to judge whether or not there is cause for her to act."[17] After the Alaska boundary was settled by a joint Anglo-American tribunal in favor of the United States' claim, Canadians saw themselves, in Creighton's words, as "the duped victims of American and British imperialist power politics"; Laurier began to press for "the treaty-making power . . . to dispose of our own affairs . . . in our own way, in our own fashion, according to the best light that we have" (p. 410). Before World War I, then, Canada began to redefine her relationship to the Empire and to the United States by pressing for greater autonomy in international politics.

At the same time Canada experienced tremendous internal expansion and prosperity. As Creighton notes, "the period from 1896 until the beginning of the war of 1914–18 saw the third and greatest migration of peoples which had ever come to British North America. . . . The most spectacular feature of this last migration was, of course, the peopling of the western prairies" (p. 410). In 1905 two new prairie provinces were created and "the centre of gravity of the Canadian population was moving rapidly westward" (p. 411). The constitution of the Canadian population also began to alter with this expansion, as the most recent immigrants came from Slavic and Scandinavian countries. These peoples brought with them no innate loyalty to the British system, but an intense desire for the right to maintain their own ways of life.

One political demand which stemmed from these two factors sought the extension of the franchise to women; Scandinavian women formed the first women's suffrage organization in Manitoba as early as the 1880s. Catherine L. Cleverdon notes in the preface to her pioneering study *The Woman Suffrage Movement in Canada* (1950) that the growth of the Canadian prairies was accompanied by the expansion of the suffrage movement. "Pioneer communities were invariably the first to enfranchise women," she notes. "On both sides of the border the feeling generally prevailed that women as well as men had opened up the country, had shared the experiences of settling a new land, and were therefore entitled to a voice in making the laws."[18] Nevertheless, while Manitoba was the first prairie province to grant female suffrage in 1916, the women there had to struggle, as did Canada against her traditional masters, in order to gain the rights of equality.

Nellie McClung must be included in any literary study of feminism and nationalism, for she was personally active in the suffrage movement in Manitoba and later in politics as a member of the Alberta legislature and as a Canadian delegate to many international conferences such as the League of Nations Conference of 1938. As well as two very readable autobiographies, four novels and several volumes of sketches, short stories and poems, she wrote a series of essays on feminism and social ills, *In Times Like These* (1915). Although McClung is well known for her first novel, *Sowing Seeds in Danny* (1908), her third novel in the Pearlie Watson series, *Purple Springs* (1921), is most relevant to this study for it presents a young woman's initiation into adulthood against the backdrop of the battle for suffrage in Manitoba, events which closely resemble those in which McClung took part.

Nellie McClung was an outspoken critic of many social ills, notably intemperance and the sufferings of women and children it caused. In one of her essays in *In Times Like These*, she attacks the government's lack of health care "on the border of civilization, where women are beyond the reach of nurses and doctors."[19] She couches this attack in political language, describing, for example, the "toll of colonization" paid by such "brave women" when "august bodies of men" can ignore "delegations of public-spirited women" yet "pour out money like water" when "a duke or prince comes to visit our country." Such imperial disregard could not exist, she argues, if women were allowed a greater part in the decision-making processes of the country: "Our national policy is the result of male statecraft" (p. 19), whereas women would avoid imperialism and war and use public funds for internal improvements.

Her futuristic fantasy of such female "statecraft" in *Purple Springs* dramatizes the way in which an entire province is revitalized through the heroine's nurturing justice and good sense. McClung describes the novel in her autobiography: "the struggle for the vote in Manitoba became the background for this, the third and last of my Pearlie Watson stories. It is a work of fiction, but the part relating to the Women's Parliament is substantially a matter of history, although the characters are imaginary, of course."[20] McClung's characterization of the men in power reflects the chauvinism and resistance to change of Premier Rodmond Roblin and his Conservative government, who in 1914 declared that "wifehood, motherhood and politics cannot be associated together with satisfactory results."[21] Such arguments enabled the men of Manitoba to retain social dominance and such specifically male customs, as McClung and the Women's Christian Temperance Union argued, as the maintenance of barroom drinking which was so detrimental to women and children. Set against the actual battle for suffrage in 1914, the novel's "imaginary" part rings a bell of emancipation.

The plot of *Purple Springs* centers on the political renewal brought about by Pearl Watson as, over the course of three months, she "grows up." Having been spurned in love by the local country doctor, Horace Clay, she finds self-expression in social involvement, first as a schoolteacher, then as a suffragette. In a Mock Parliament, wherein the women in power wait on a delegation of men petitioning for the right to vote, Pearl's satire of the premier stirs up public opinion in favor of the vote for women, and the ensuing election defeats the government and brings about the great promises of change. Furthermore, the blind arrogance of the premier himself is broken and, through Pearl, he is reunited with his estranged daughter-in-law and grandson. They move to Purple Springs, where the reformed premier stirs the community to a renewal of good fellowship. The community has matured wonderfully, as has Pearl, who is reunited, somewhat anticlimactically, with Dr. Clay. The plot, then, demonstrates the conflict between the masculine values engrained in social and political customs and the feminine desire for justice and equality.

These opposing forces in the novel are established by the chapter "The Innocent Disturber," in which Pearl, invited to speak to her community as its "favorite son" because of her successful year at the Normal School in the city, answers the chauvinistic comments of Mr. Steadman, the MLA (member of the Legislative Assembly) for the region. Mr. Steadman is characterized by the narrator's description as well as by his name: there is "a well-fed, complacent look about him . . . which left no doubt that he was satisfied with things as they were—and would be deeply resentful of change. There was still in his countenance some trace of his ancestors' belief in the Divine right of kings!"[22] Just as Ed Rivers assumed that divinity is masculine, the male antagonists in *Purple Springs* invoke religious authorities to support their argument for male domination. The premier of the province himself pronounces, "Women are weaker than men . . . God made them so. He intended them to be subject to men. . . . It sounds well to talk about equality—but there's no such thing. It did not exist in God's mind, so why should we try to bring it about? . . . women are subject to men, and always will be" (p. 222). The men use religion to keep women in their place, the "sacred precincts of home" (p. 97). In her role as "queen of the home," woman becomes "the bulwark of the nation"; "her very helplessness is her strength," for she supposedly can "influence her husband's vote—her son's vote" (p. 96). The "queen's" power is, in the society of this novel, inevitably determined and limited by that of the "king."

In response to the religious basis of the masculine argument for superiority, McClung laces Pearl's language with biblical and spiritual references, invoking Christian analogies to argue for equality for women. After the collapse of her romantic dream of becoming "queen" in a traditional, male-dominated marriage, Pearl fills the void with "a new sense of responsibility" based on her affirmation that "it is a good world . . . God made it, Christ lived in it—and when He went away, He left His Spirit. It can't go wrong and stay wrong. The only thing that is wrong with it is in people's hearts, and hearts can be changed by the Grace of God" (p. 74). Her status becomes that of a biblical prophet, as McClung alludes to "the vision which came to Elisha's servant at Dothan"; "the horses and the chariots of the Lord" presumably now support Pearl's mission. Referring to the Old Testament (Ezekiel 37:1–14), a newspaper reports that if Pearl Watson got into Parliament, "there would sure be . . . a rustling of dry bones" (p. 108). When she is urged by a desperate woman to eschew marriage in order to be free to "talk about . . . the vote," Pearl answers, "Wherever two or three gather, Pearl Watson will rise and make a few remarks" (p. 135). With this allusion to Christ's mission, the movement for female franchise is raised to the level of gospel truth. Finally, the protagonist's name itself suggests that her qualities and her battle for equality are "the pearl of great price."

Not only does McClung reverse the masculine religious argument in favor of enfranchisement, but also, with Pearl as her mouthpiece, she undercuts man's traditional sanctification of woman's domestic sphere as "the bulwark of the nation" by extending the boundaries of home-care into politics. Pearl argues that "one of the reasons that the world had so many sore spots in it was because women had kept too close to home" (p. 103). With their recently awakened "social consciousness," women now "were beginning to see that in order to keep their houses clean, they would have to clean up the streets." The vote would allow women "to do their share, outside as well as in." Pearl further extends this domestic metaphor when she envisions "Canada . . . like a great big, beautiful house that has been given to us to finish" (p. 104). In a 1914 speech, "The Social Responsibilities of Women," reprinted by Candace Savage in *Our Nell: A Scrapbook Biography* (1979), McClung argues that "politics is only public affairs. . . . [Women] are affected by what goes on outside of the four walls of home,—the home has expanded now until it has become the whole state. The work has gone out of the home and women have had to follow it."[23] Like many turn-of-the-century feminists, McClung asserted that motherhood is basic to woman's nature, but rather than being a criterion for the exclusion of women from politics, "organized motherhood," a term she used to describe the Women's Christian Temperance Movement, is the "agency whereby men are made better and Christ's kingdom extended."[24]

McClung was apparently more concerned with reform than aesthetics; her novel is political in purpose and consequently replete with political language which casts men as imperial powers and women as rebels. Thus the premier of the province is known as "the Chief" and a party bagman as "King-maker" (p. 156). George Steadman, with his "belief in the Divine right of kings," senses after his first encounter with Pearl that she is a "radical . . . a fire-brand, and incendiary" (p. 106). When news of his besting at her hands reaches the opposition newspaper, Steadman is "as quick to see the import of it as King James was to smell gunpowder on that fateful November day when the warning letter was read in Parliament" (p. 193). And in the forum of a homespun tableau, Pearl plays the role "of a foolish old king, who thought he could command the waves to stand still" (p. 195), foreshadowing her satirical portrait of the Premier in the Woman's Parliament. The tableau depicts the "arrogance and pride" of the king overcome by the "revolution . . . [of] wave after wave" (p. 196). The water imagery recalls Steadman's frightened reaction to Pearl's words: he "found his soul adrift on a wide sea, torn away from the harbor that had seemed so safe and landlocked" (p. 106). The revolutionary language of McClung's politics underlines Pearl's feminist challenge to "male statecraft."

The rising action of the novel is structured around the cases of two women whose situations are designed to illustrate the unjust treatment of women by men acting within their legal rights. Pearl's involvement with each woman brings her more intensely into battle with the government—male—forces. Mrs. Paine has no legal means to stop her husband from selling their home and forcing her and her children to live and work in a public house. Mr. Paine has the financial power to sell, for his profit, the farm which has prospered primarily because of his wife's efforts. Mrs. Paine's plight typifies the legal status of Manitoban women in McClung's time which Savage documents as that "of infants. . . . In theory (and sometimes in practice) the father could put his children up for adoption or assign them to guardians without his wife's consent. He might also sell the family home or will it away without a thought of his wife's well-being" (p. 78). McClung's rebellion against such "blatantly unjust" and old-world laws is perhaps reflected by her allusion through the woman's name to Thomas Paine, the American dissenter who at the time of the American Revolution combined political and religious language to advocate what Henry F. May has called, in his study *The Enlightenment in America* (1976), "a new and profoundly important interpretation of the colonial struggle."[25] At the moment when the farm transaction is about to take place, Pearl appears and gives a moving speech about the injustice and unkindness of Mr. Paine's action; all the men present are moved by both her arguments and the gentle manner of her presentation. The buyer refuses to purchase the farm and Mr. Paine's love for his wife is reawakened. Reform is possible, at least in McClung's fantasy, for this victim of "just" social structures.

The second woman Pearl is able to help is Annie Gray who, along with her ten-year-old son Jim, has been ostracized from the community of Purple Springs because of the unfounded rumor that the boy is illegitimate. McClung uses her story to illustrate the irony that "only the unmarried mother has the absolute right to her child" (p. 264). Annie Gray was married, but she suppresses this fact in order to regain custody of her child from her father-in-law, the premier, who has threatened to send the boy to school in England despite her objections: "He told me I had nothing to say about it, he was his grandson's guardian. Jim [her husband] had made a will before he left home, making his father executor of his estate. He told me the father was the only parent the child had in the eyes of the law, and I had no claim on my boy" (pp. 260–61). When Pearl publicly sides with Annie by lodging in her home, the parents of the community protest by keeping their children from school. Forced from her teaching post, Pearl refuses the bribe of a government job and accepts the request of the suffragettes that she take part in a Mock Parliament. Her political actions bring down the premier's government and persuade him that his daughter-in-law is one of the many "women who had suffered from the injustice of the law and men's prejudice" (p. 306). The "broken old man" confesses "the evil he has done" and is reconciled with his family; again, feminine justice triumphs simultaneously in the home and the political "house."

But the very ease with which Pearl achieves victory in the political world betrays the element of fantasy in her characterization. Pearl spurns such traditional female occupations as "tatting and . . . eyelet embroidery" in favor of "social duties . . . [and] leadership": "there were neighbourhoods to be awakened and citizens to be made" (pp. 101–2). Again, McClung interjects that "if Pearl Watson had not had a taste for political speeches and debates; if she had read the crochet patterns in the paper instead of the editorials, and had spent her leisure moments making butter-fly medallions for her camisoles, or in some other lady-like pursuit, instead of leaning over the well-worn railing around the gallery of the Legislative Assembly, in between classes at the Normal, she would have missed much" (p. 228). Having created a woman who, in her avoidance of "the Woman's Page" of the newspapers, is not "normal," McClung then invests her heroine with maternal strength; the oldest girl in the Watson family, she is "often left to mind the swarm of boys while her mother was out working" and she accomplishes the "strenuous task of keeping her young brothers . . . happy" through "the wealth of her quickened imagination" (p. 3). No household task is too difficult or onerous for Pearl, "she's that light-hearted and free from care" (p. 23). Duncan ridicules Dora's femininity in favor of Advena's; McClung, in rejecting conventional femininity, creates a prodigy of feminine power.

McClung endows her heroine not only with feminine nurturing powers but also with "brains" and, more significantly, the traditionally masculine weapon of wit. Pearl ridicules Mr. Steadman's views on the rights of women: "I am sorry Mr. Steadman is not in favour of women voting, or going to Parliament, and thinks it too hard for them. It does not look hard to me. Most of the members just sit and smoke all the time, and read the papers. . . . I have seen women do far harder work than this" (p. 100). Yet McClung repeats several times that Pearl's attack is delivered with "the friendliest motive," "in her guileless way" (p. 100). At the climax of the novel her fantastic ability enables Pearl to mimic the premier's physical gestures and rhetorical style so successfully that she becomes the toast of the town and guarantees the defeat of the government in the coming election. McClung is attempting to present Pearl as a complex and subtle combination of masculine and feminine strengths, but one might argue that the apparent necessity of reinforcing Pearl's feminine strengths with masculine ones undercuts the story's political themes.

The problems in Pearl's characterization are amplified by the structural inconsistencies of the novel. The political battle of the sexes takes place within the framework of a courtship novel. The first two chapters build up the romantic expectations of the young Pearl, and of the reader, as she awaits the appointed day, her eighteenth birthday, when Dr. Clay has indicated he will propose marriage. But because Clay learns he is seriously ill—the disease is never specified—he chivalrously sets Pearl free, but without explaining why. She understands intuitively that "he was suffering, there was a bar between them—for some reason, he could not marry her" (p. 57). The denouement of the novel resolves this dilemma, but it is an uneasy ending for a novel so stridently feminist in its statements. Having witnessed Pearl's strength in the male realms of wit and logic, it is disconcerting for the reader to see that Pearl "gets her man," mainly through conventional feminine wiles. She calls Dr. Clay to pull a sliver from her brother's foot when there is no real need for a doctor; operation completed, Pearl's sister arranges for Pearl to be alone with her beau. When Pearl assumes a masculine assertiveness and asks Clay directly to explain his failure to propose marriage, he confesses his love and his illness but nevertheless remains chivalrous and patronizing: "I cannot let you bind yourself to me until I am well again" (p. 331). Pearl continues in her masculine manner and takes the initiative of proposing: "I'll just marry you without being asked." She sanctions her behavior by once again using religious language to defend her equal status: "The covenant between you and me was made before the foundations of the world. You're my man. I knew you the moment I saw you. So when I say, 'I, Pearl, take you, Horace,' it's not a new contract—it's just a ratification of the old. It's just the way we have of letting the world know. You see, dear," she concludes forcefully, "you just can't help it—it's settled" (p. 331).

But McClung has not successfully realized a consistent characterization in Pearl for, resorting again to coquettish wile, she "rub[s] her cheek against his shoulder, like a well-pleased kitten" when Clay is threatened by her claims of independence: "These new women can get to be so independent— they are uncomfortable to live with" (p. 334). Pearl's coquettish response undercuts the image of her assertive, independent nature, just as she is cute and cloying as she submits herself to Clay's status as "breadwinner": "I'll let you pay every time—I'll just love spending your money" (p. 334). No doubt McClung was attempting in the happy resolution of the love story to answer the oft-repeated charge against the principle of sexual equality that, if women "were independent in the eyes of the law, independent economically . . . they would not marry" (p. 222). In order to demonstrate that equality does not threaten the homes of the nation, McClung gives Pearl love and marriage. But Pearl's coyness and subservience stand at odds with the forcefulness of her personality and convictions and therefore with the novel's central themes as well. The last chapter is entitled "Nothing Too Good to be True," as if McClung were acknowledging the improbability of her happy ending. The character of Pearl, who never makes a mistake, is likewise much "too good to be true."

The uncomfortable resolution to the story and the idealistic characterization of Pearl point out the problems not only of McClung's art but also of her feminism. The novel suffers from the unresolved conflict, quite understandable in such a time of change, between the propaganda for the cause of women and the belief that woman's nature is fulfilled in motherhood, hence in marriage. The suffrage movement strove for the right to vote, for legal equality with men; on this level, McClung's feminist heroine is developed as the rational proponent of the rights and powers of women, successful in the political arena because she can outwit the men in argument. Certainly enfranchisement altered the conventional sexual roles and relationships, just as Duncan had predicted in *The Imperialist*; women were no longer the legally held chattel of a male-dominated society. Still, even leaders such as McClung continued to comply with male expectations of the status of wife. Consequently, the fictional leader, Pearl, can and does act like a "kitten." *Purple Springs*, no doubt unwittingly, portrays some of the difficulties of liberation. Ultimately, the novel raises a question similar to Duncan's: how will the conventional relations between the sexes continue to function? In 1921, the answer is not known and the new alliance is uneasy.

Just as the relations between men and women underwent their awkward adjustments, Canada's international affairs also caused apprehension in the postwar years. Because of her tremendous contribution to the war effort, Canada demanded, and finally won, separate representation at the Peace Conference and the right to sign the treaty as an autonomous nation. Prime Minister Borden was led to comment sardonically, "Canada got nothing out of the war except recognition."[26] But the constitutional challenge of the Dominion's new status was postponed until the first postwar Imperial Conference in 1921, where the question of the feasibility of a common imperial foreign policy dominated discussions. Carl Berger sums up this development: "the First World War killed . . . the appeal of imperialism. . . . Canadian foreign policy after 1921 stressed status rather than responsibilities and guarded autonomy against any kind of imperial co-operation" (p. 264). But with her national status ratified only by membership in the newly founded League of Nations, Canada had to operate in an international arena before adequate redefinition of her relationship within the Empire could be clarified and before the social unrest and problems of a postwar society could be solved at home. Her turn-of-the-century status had definitely altered during the first two decades of the twentieth century, but her future course remained unclear.

While Duncan's assumptions about the direction Canadian nationalism should take were clearly presented, the structure of McClung's novel reveals the more common sense of ambivalence. The courtship plot which frames *Purple Springs* aligns the book with the British literary heritage. But the conventions of that plot are quickly abandoned and ignored through most of the novel and are only awkwardly resolved in the final chapter. Through the body of the novel, McClung plays with her reader's expectations of a sentimental love story; for example, chapter 11 is entitled "Engaged," but the engagement referred to is not of marriage but of Pearl's appointment as a teacher. As the chapter ends with Pearl trying to brave the heartaches of unrequited love and face her new public role with courage, McClung seems to imply that the reader must set aside traditional expectations of what constitutes both a novel and a young heroine.

Indeed, the central plot focuses on Pearl's fight against the political "machine." The propagandistic nature of this section derives from such novels of sentimental social protest as Harriet Beecher Stowe's *Uncle Tom's Cabin* (1852). As Leslie Fiedler notes in his seminal study of the American literary tradition, *Love and Death in the American Novel* (1975), "the spirit of social protest and the causes with which that movement occupied itself" offered fresh material for the sentimental novel in America: "The campaign against liquor is, of all reforming movements, the one most easily adapted to the demands of traditional Sentimentalism and the image of the Suffering

Woman."[27] Social activist as she was, McClung turned to this American genre to dramatize her cause, just as the Women's Equality League and other suffrage organizations turned to the example of American women in the fight for political equality. But if Pearl uses an American political slogan to call upon every "man or woman" to use "fair dealing" in order to make foreign-born citizens "think well of Canada," she also defines the task to be that of "a Master Builder in this Empire" (p. 104). McClung's use of the sentimental protest genre, the rhetoric of monarchical loyalty and the framing device of the courtship plot all suggest that she is fearful of the implications of what she is advocating.

The chief concern of both Duncan and McClung, one might conclude is the theme of political change, specifically, the increasingly prominent role of women in society. Both authors use the New Woman as a metaphor for a changing nation, a change both see as progressive. Nevertheless, neither author explores the psychological makeup of her heroine in any depth. *The Imperialist* focuses on the title figure, Lorne, while the heroine's movement to freedom is in a secondary position; Advena, kept as she is at a distance by the narrator, does not become a fully realized character. *Purple Springs*, on the other hand, brings a young woman to the forefront, but the author's propagandistic concerns make of Pearl a mouthpiece for women's rights; she becomes a caricature of the New Woman. And because her chief talent is argument and her venue politics, she is more convincingly masculine than feminine. This unconvincing portrait concludes with Pearl, having single-handedly overthrown a government and having won social equality for women, subjugating herself in marriage. Both Advena and Pearl end up in the subservient position of wife; neither writer has answered her own novel's challenge to the conventions of marriage. The ironic result is that the changes in status for these women, as for the nation, come about only partially. Each novel suggests that the relationship between the sexes should be one between equals, but the wider implications of that change, as with Canada's sudden elevation to autonomy within the Empire without constitutional amendment, are not adequately explored. In light of the times in which *Purple Springs* was written, the tension between the courtship framing device and the political themes reflects the unresolved conflicts, felt by many, between women's traditional subservience to men and their growing freedom after 1917 when they gained legal rights and a voice in the running of the country.

The novel reflects, as well, Canada's ambivalent relations with Britain and the United States. McClung saw in the United States not only a country which had successfully thrown off its colonial status and succeeded in altering society through its suffrage movement, but also, by the time she published *Purple Springs* in 1921, Canadians too viewed the relationship with the United States as increasingly more important than that with Great Britain. For example, Canada placed the continental concerns which she shared with the United States above the interests of her imperial allies during the 1921 discussion of the renewal of the Anglo-American alliance. And in 1923 she was to insist on negotiating and signing the Halibut Treaty with the United States without British representation. But it is possible that McClung had doubts about the growing partnership with the republic to the south. Certainly during World War I, as Savage reports, when the federal government passed a Wartime Election Act disenfranchising "most men who had come to Canada from 'enemy' countries," McClung supported the bill, because she had become "concerned about the 'moral tone' of the Canadian electorate . . . [since] the public-spirited English-speaking men had enlisted, leaving the indifferent 'foreign' element behind" (p. 134). Like her novel, then, McClung is divided between the past and the future, the British and the American.

There were many aspects of Canada's situation after World War I which called for intensive analysis. During the twenties, Canada experienced economic expansion and increased prosperity. Wheat, the primary product of the prairies, continued to be the staple of the national economy, but the twenties saw a widening exploitation of Canada's natural resources, namely in the areas of pulp and paper and mining. "Wheat had proved itself to be a force in favour of national unity," notes Creighton, "but the new staples almost seemed to encourage the unfortunate process of regional division" (p. 477). While the Imperial Conference of 1926 turned to the questions of constitutional definition of dominion status, many underlying problems of social and regional disparity were not addressed by Ottawa. Thus, by the end of the twenties, when the world depression of the 1930s began, Canada found herself unprepared to handle both economic and natural catastrophes. Even at the time it was apparent that poor farming techniques—inadequate crop rotation and the lack of mixed farming—existed in part because of the high price for wheat and the understandable but lamentable greed of farmers for higher profits.[28]

The appearance of Martha Ostenso's first novel, *Wild Geese* (1925), portraying as it does man's fundamental alienation from nature in pursuit of increased productivity, foreshadows the destruction to come unless he learns to respect the balance of the natural world. *Wild Geese* has as its primary conflict the battle between the sexes, but this battle becomes one of elemental forces, the domineering will of the male opposing the powerful passions of the female, what Mrs. Rix Weaver calls the struggle between the Logos and the Eros principles: "If an attempt is made by Logos to remodel Eros in his own image, feminine values fall into the limbo of the lost, and real feminine values look too much like nature with all its mysterious irrationalities and its dark forces."[29] Caleb Gare's domination of his wife, children and land is the action of a man who has been unable to come to terms with his own self, particularly his own Eros-ruled unconscious. Gare fears just

such irrationality in the world about him: "Disease—destruction—things
that he feared—things out of man's control."[30] The last phrase is doubly
significant, since the natural world is perceived to be not just out of control,
but out of mankind's and, more particularly, male control. Gare's fear of
chaos causes him to bind his family and his land to the will of his exploitive
greed. The imbalance enforced by Gare on his community is corrected
through the awakening to femininity first of his daughter, Judith, then of
his wife, Amelia.

To what extent Ostenso managed to reconcile, in her own life, the conflict
between Logos and Eros would be a fruitful area of biographical research.
It is interesting to speculate, on the basis of the limited information available
and the novel, that Ostenso herself was torn between her intellectual pro-
clivities and more instinctual desires. This interpretation of the novel is
invited by Ostenso's brief comments on the origins of the novel, quoted by
Clara Thomas in her article, "Martha Ostenso's Trial of Strength"; Ostenso
says that on "the frontier of that northern civilization" she witnessed the
"stark" quality of "human nature . . . unattired in the convention of a
smoother, softer life" with which she was more familiar.[31] If Lind Archer,
the schoolteacher in *Wild Geese*, is Ostenso, thinly disguised—as suggested
by Stanley S. Atherton's information in "Ostenso Revisited" that both author
and character taught for a summer in a one-room school in Hayland, Manitoba, and that Ostenso modelled the character Judith on the daughter of
the family with whom she boarded[32]—then the attraction of the educated
and conservative Lind for the sensual and strong Judith suggests the possibility of an author struggling with the two sides of her own nature. In
addition, one could also speculate that Ostenso's twenty-year relationship
to the man who would become her husband, Douglas Dirkin, reveals that
her life, along with *Wild Geese*, can be read as an intellectual young woman's
exploration of her instinctive self.

The conflict of male and female forces in a rural setting returns us to the
themes of the works examined in chapter 1. Jameson portrayed the land as
feminine in order to suggest the destructive consequences of masculine
misappropriation of power. Brooke too was critical of the selfish greed of
the colonizer. Traill and Moodie in their statements, echoing Jameson, regarding "how a settler hates a tree," delineated the masculine antipathy to
the natural world which he considered in the way of his material success.
These writers explored male attitudes to colonization at the very inception
of Canadian history. Ostenso's novel, it is important to realize, is set in a
Manitoban farming community which has emerged from the pioneer stage.
The farmers are established on their lands, have several fields cleared and
in production, and are planning more expansion for their operations. Ostenso
explores the psychological ramifications of the relationship between farmer
and landscape at this more advanced stage of settlement. Her characteri-

zation of Gare and of his attitude toward "his land" reveals the spiritual self-destruction of such determination for economic success.

Caleb Gare is presented throughout the novel as a man at war with all that is natural. One recalls the nineteenth-century writers' observations on the enmity between the settler and the tree which stands in the way of his plans for economic success. On one section of Gare's land stands "the muskeg and a dried lake-bottom . . . bottomless and foul" (p. 14); the area is a "sore to Caleb's eye" because he cannot control it, cannot bring it under his possession. His cultivated land is described in imagery which suggests wildness held in check by Gare's possession. His fields are "tame" but "the oats . . . stirring like a tawny sea . . . [and] the acres of narrow woodland stretching . . . like a dark mane upon the earth" (p. 13) represent the uncontrollable natural force lurking beneath the surface of the land. Ostenso emphasizes Gare's possessive attitude by the constant repetition of the phrase "his land." The most haunting image of the novel pictures Gare out at night, alone, prowling "to assure himself that his land was still all there": "Far out across the prairie a lantern was swinging low along the earth, and dimly visible was the squat, top-heavy form of a man. It was Caleb Gare. He walked like a man leaning forward against a strong wind." The darkness and the silhouetted figure suggest the eerie, primordial quality of his atavistic claims.

Gare struggles "against some invisible obstacle." The first description of him in the novel, emphasizing his "top-heavy form," implies that the obstacle is within his own soul. His "towering appearance," "his tremendous shoulders and massive head" (p. 5) suggest not only that Gare rules his world through force of will and brute strength, but also that he is psychologically disproportioned, for "the lower half of his body . . . seemed visibly to dwindle." Gare is perhaps sexually maimed, less than the man he should be. His fear of the irrational realm of Eros is appropriately the source of his control of his wife, "that little folly of hers . . . a son born out of wedlock" (p. 15). The knowledge of Amelia's illicit love maddens Gare with jealousy:

Amelia had loved the boy's father, that he knew. The knowledge had eaten bitterly into his being when he was a younger man and had sought to possess Amelia in a manner different from the way in which he possessed her now. In that earlier passion of the blood he had found himself eternally frustrated. The man who had been gored to death by a bull on his farm in the distant south had taken Amelia's soul with him, and had unwittingly left bearing in her body the weapon which Caleb now so adroitly used against her. His control over her, being one of the brain only, although it achieved his ends, also at moments galled him with the reminder that the spirit of her had ever eluded him. (p. 16)

Gare's inability to share erotic passion with Amelia and to accept her erotic past has driven him to his inhuman state. His response is to control, to possess, to negate the power of passion by subjugating it to his will.

Inevitably, Gare's relation with the land, which Ostenso portrays as feminine, is sensual: "Caleb would stand for long moments outside the fence beside the flax. Then he would turn quickly to see that no one was looking. He would creep between the wires and run his hand across the flowering, gentle tops of the growth. A stealthy caress—more intimate than any he had ever given to woman" (p. 171). But this feminine force is daemonic, sucking the very life-blood from Caleb, who "was absorbed with the process of growth on the land he owned, lending to it his own spirit like physical nourishment." He sees his relation to the land on the heroic level, but it is a masculine definition of heroic, for he tries to deny the natural life-cycle: "While he was raptly considering the tender field of flax—now in blue flower—Amelia did not exist to him. There was a transcendent power in this blue field of flax that lifted a man above the petty artifices of birth, life, and death. It was more exacting, even, than an invisible God. It demanded not only the good in him, but the evil, and the indifference" (p. 171). Gare's spiritual deficiency results from his inability to understand nature, represented not only by woman but also by the landscape as woman: his attempt to control feminine "nature" brings about his own destruction.

It is significant that the time period of the novel is not only after the first stages of prairie settlement, but also after World War I. Thomas points out that before the publication of *Wild Geese* Ostenso produced *A Far Land* (1924), a book of poems about "the death-in-life of the spirit of man and his terrible isolation" (p. 40). Thomas compares one of the poems to A.J.M. Smith's, but a more fruitful comparison of Ostenso's "Wasteland" would be with T. S. Eliot's postwar poem which shares the same name and similar themes and imagery. Atherton has made it clear that Ostenso was well-read as a young student of literature (p. 58), but whether she was influenced by Eliot or whether she produced from her own observations poetry and fiction dealing with the spiritual poverty of postwar society must remain speculation. What is safe to say is that Ostenso moves beyond the politics of Duncan and the didacticism of McClung to explore the "wasteland" of the modern Canadian psyche.

During the 1920s, with increased trade between Canada and the United States and an expansion of industry and mining operations financed by American investment in Canada, such social examination was even more appropriate. Berger in *Sense of Power* (1970) notes that imperialists at the turn of the century had become wary of the "industrial state" as witnessed by the example of the United States: "it stood as a warning of what Canada might become if men of conscience did not denounce the irresponsibility of business and correct the short-range views of politicians" (p. 174). World War I and its aftermath caused some Canadians to question "the definition of individual merit and national progress in terms of dollars and cents and the identification of government with the broker state mediating between . . . mainly economic interests" (p. 203). But the imperialist solution of closer ties with the Empire was no longer appreciated in postwar Canada; in the face of increased prosperity and the growth of national autonomy, such esoteric questions about the kind of society Canadians wished to build were largely ignored, until the economic and natural consequences became all too apparent in the 1930s.

In light of this economic mismanagement of natural resources, it is significant that Ostenso embodies the force working against the masculine abrogation of power in Caleb's "wild-locked" daughter, Judith. McClung had argued the equality of women on the basis of religion; Ostenso argues on the basis of nature. The imagery describing Judith echoes that presenting Caleb's untamed fields. Judith's wildness is barely under control: "Her hair . . . wild-locked and black . . . shone on top of her head with a bluish lustre" (p. 2); she is "strangely beautiful . . . like some fabled animal—a centauress, perhaps" (p. 9). Her "wild-locked" nature seeks freedom and expression in "something apart from the life" of her father's world (p. 216). And she extends her resistance to male domination to her affair with her neighbor, Sven Sandbo. Before she will allow Sven to kiss her, Judith wrestles with him: "Her limbs were long, sinewy, her body quick and lithe as a wild-cat's. . . . She slid through his arms and wound herself about his body, bringing them both to the earth. . . . Then something leaped in Sven. They were no longer unevenly matched, different in sex. They were two stark elements, striving for mastery over each other" (p. 117).

As this human relationship is discovered and expressed in terms of her interaction with nature, so too Judith finds her sense of femininity in the very wilderness Gare seeks to tame: "she threw herself upon the moss under the birches, grasping the slender trunks of the trees in her hands and straining her body against the earth . . . here was clarity undreamed of, such clarity as the soul should have, in desire and fulfillment. Judith held her breasts in ecstasy" (p. 216). Nature and what is clearly "natural" sexuality provide meaning and joy: Sven appears to her at this moment "as a god, out of space." They also free her from her father's "unnatural" oppression. The novel's original title, "The Passionate Flight," refers most certainly to the lovers' escape from Gare and Oeland; their passionate affair, out of wedlock, releases the natural forces against Gare, for after witnessing its consummation he begins the open persecution which leads to her rebellion. Judith, then, along with the fields, are Ostenso's symbols of nature, against which she defines male oppression.

Indeed, the climax of the novel records "nature's" resistance to and triumph over this "unnatural" man. When Judith announces her planned flight, Amelia, realizing her daughter's pregnancy, awakens to a consciousness from which she has long been dead: "a terrific, incognizable world had opened upon her" (p. 329). Judith represents "another, clear, brave world of true instincts" (p. 332). And Amelia, remembering her own youthful, sexual past, joins the rebellion of "nature": "Judith—Judith. Herself over

again. Judith must go. Enough to have one life ruined. Not Judith's, too"
(p. 334). Amelia determines to "outwit Caleb"(p. 331) and when he learns
of Judith's escape, Amelia's resistance breaks his power: "Cold realization
came upon him suddenly. . . . She had broken him. Broken him in the crisis.
Something crumbled within him, like an old wall, leaving bare his spirit"
(p. 345). The destruction of his male power, perhaps ironically, restores his
"natural" understanding: "His sanity came back to him, the cold clear sanity
that had been gone from him during the years of his hatred. . . . Shame and
self-loathing broke upon him over-poweringly" (pp. 345–46). Judith's and
Amelia's resistance is repeated as nature completes Gare's downfall. "Blind
with sight," he lunges out of doors where he sees the forest fire racing to
destroy his crops. In a mad, vain attempt to save his precious flax-field, he
meets his end in the quicksand of the muskeg. The earth, presented as it
has been throughout the book as female, reaches up to pull him into a final
embrace: "Now silky reeds were beginning to tangle themselves about Caleb's legs . . . something seemed to be tugging at his feet. . . . Water was ooz-
ing into his shoes and pushing up about his ankles . . . the strength of the
earth was irresistible . . . the insidious force in the earth drew him in deeper
. . . the over-strong embrace of the earth" (pp. 351–52).

Ostenso's novel demonstrates that Gare's fear of change, of "things out of
man's control," produces a spiritual, psychic crippling not just in himself,
but in the entire community within his power. Written as it was during a
time of shattering global change, when the old imperial organization of
England and the Empire was in the process of redefinition, when Canada
became acutely aware of the importance of her relations with the United
States in the development of her future, and when Canada moved from
reliance on agriculture as the basis of her economy to expansion and exploitation of her mineral resources, Wild Geese sounds a familiar warning
note about the destructiveness inherent in a male-dominated society's lust
for material gain. When the oppressive masculine power of Logos is brought
into balance with the feminine principle of Eros, "the world of true instincts"
could reshape the community. And in the restoration of the "natural" characters and the community, simplistic as it may be, Ostenso posits a hope of
psychic balance, very much needed in the postwar world.

However, there are some complexities, some unanswered questions posed
by the novel's denouement. Although Ostenso's themes are profoundly
deeper than the social status of women, the prime issue which inspires
McClung, she concludes her book, like McClung, on a simplistic and sentimental note: Amelia invites neighbors into her home for coffee and cake;
Gare's son, Martin, draws up "a plan for the New House" (p. 353); the
Bjarnassons invite the Gares to fish once again in their lake. Furthermore,
Ostenso only briefly explains in the closing chapter that Judith and Sven are
"in the city" and "very happy" (p. 353); nothing is mentioned of their do-
mestic arrangements, but the reader must pause to wonder, especially when

Judith's passionate longing had called out to Sven for them "to be different, not like people round here . . . or even in the town. . . . We're going away, across the ocean, maybe" (p. 217). That they move no further than Winnipeg suggests the problem of adjusting romantic passion to workaday reality, a problem encountered by Hugh and Advena, Pearl and Horace. Achieving a balance between passion and intellect in a domestic relationship is as problematic to Ostenso as it is to Duncan and McClung.

Moreover, Judith and Sven are not the only set of lovers. Lind Archer, who has come to the region as its schoolteacher, falls in love with Mark Jordan, Amelia's illegitimate son, who has been educated by priests away from this community. As the novel opens, one senses that the point of view through which the Gare family is presented is that of Lind; indeed, perhaps Ostenso's original intention was to focus on Lind and Mark as the major characters. But as the conflict between Gare and Judith develops, Ostenso leaves Lind and Mark in the background, bringing them to the fore only to facilitate plot development or to comment on the characters and action. These characters, educated and civilized as they are, stand in marked contrast to the more primitive major characters. Ostenso's presentation of this intellectual couple suggests the sterility in such rational, controlled relationships. For instance, Mark is in the community doing farm work as a means of relieving the "nervous disorder" brought on by "over-work" in his studies of architecture which he "had gone into . . . seriously after the war" (p. 16). Significantly, the only references which pinpoint the time period of the novel as post–World War I occur in the introduction of Mark Jordan to the novel. It is the war which has maimed him—like Gare he is "sick" (while all the women in the novel are strong). Jordan's relationship with Lind, which develops mainly through intellectual conversation, originates from their mutual loneliness for someone of like background. But their chaste love affair never manifests itself beyond hand-holding and gentle embraces. They are sentimental lovers: he is protective of Lind and she depends on his strength. Although their ordered, conventional love may seem in Judith's inexperienced eyes to represent "part of the thing to which she belonged" (p. 132), the outcome of the novel implies that the educated and urban Mark and Lind lack the strength of the others' "passionate flight." Indeed, it is Judith's rebellion which frees Mark and Lind, for with Caleb's death Amelia's secret that Mark is her son born out of wedlock will never be revealed—Mark and Lind may leave Oeland to be married in peace. Their marriage, one might suspect, would be threatened by the taint of the kind of out-of-wedlock, "natural" passion which Judith and Sven share. Not only are Mark and Lind unaware of the danger to which they were exposed, but also they remain ignorant of Mark's true, "natural," parentage.

Ostenso, then, has created two love affairs, neither of which is completely successful for the lovers nor entirely convincing to the reader. The plot of her third novel, *The Young May Moon* (1929), moreover, suggests that

Ostenso was never able to resolve the dilemma. Clara Thomas and Atherton, comparing *Wild Geese* with *The Young May Moon*, find Ostenso developing similar themes in both novels.[33] One important difference, however, is that the bulk of the later novel focuses on the efforts of Marcia Vorse to live independently, raising her child on her own after rebelling against both her husband, who refused to communicate with her or gratify her desires, and her mother-in-law, who embodies a harsh, life-denying religious code of behavior. Marcia succeeds, as did Hester Prynne before her, in achieving the esteem of the community for her nurturing services. This independent woman, however, quite unsatisfactorily reverts in the final chapter to her former subservient position as a wife when she accepts the profession of love given her by the aloof, demanding local doctor, who claims that they have been denying their mutual need for love with another human being. It seems that Ostenso, like Duncan and McClung, relies on a romantic solution for the dilemma of her heroine, rather than accepting the full implications of her revealed strengths of character. All these passionately strong female characters are forced to fall back on the traditional relationship with men. But with her two very different heroines in *Wild Geese*, Ostenso had at least approached alternatives.

If we recall that it was in a remote Manitoban community that Ostenso first recognized the primitivism which inspired her novel, then the setting of her novels may indicate how Ostenso pursued her topic. Thomas and Atherton both assert that *Wild Geese* and *The Young May Moon* are the only two of Ostenso's novels set in Canada,[34] but there is little in the settings of either novel to distinguish them from the northern plains of the United States, the settings of her other novels such as *The Mad Carews* (1927) or *O River, Remember!* (1943). Clara Thomas's speculation that the setting of *Young May Moon* is "a composite, but certainly Manitoban" (p. 50n) overlooks the obvious fact that Ostenso deliberately obscures any distinctively Canadian setting. Thomas asserts that *Young May Moon* draws on the "little towns" of Ostenso's childhood (p. 43); but if that is the case, the setting would be based on the six towns of her childhood years in Minnesota and South Dakota. Ostenso lived only six years in Canada, from age fifteen to twenty-one, after which time, in 1921, she returned to the United States. Her long publishing career was launched there; *Wild Geese* received the prestigious Dodd Mead, Famous Players–Lasky Award for "the best first novel by an American author." Ostenso's literary influences were American and it was the United States which provided the market for her romances. Ostenso and her work are, apparently, not Canadian.

How do both fit into this study then? After all, equality, on the basis of the "natural" claims of heroines and countries, challenges conventions, but the only literary solution Ostenso can offer is romantic, and this idealism, avoiding social realism as it does, limits her heroines to the awkwardly conventional. But Canada too, having developed her "natural" resources, did not easily achieve the status of nationhood. Her insistence on equal representation at the Paris peace talks, a right earned by her substantial war effort, caused, as Brown and Cook note, "problems within imperial circles and among the allies" (p. 286). Moreover, while constitutional questions dragged on through the 1920s, Canada's economic development and prosperity became more dependent on the American economy, further curtailing her traditional imperial links. Thus when Ostenso sounds an "international" note, suggesting that the prairie experiences on either side of the forty-ninth parallel have much in common, she gives artistic voice to the contemporary political claim that Canada must accept her "natural" alliance within the North American continent.

But if Canadians saw in the United States a nation which had successfully overcome colonial status, Canada was nevertheless wary of the repercussions of democratic republicanism, particularly, as Berger explains, the extension of the franchise not only to women, but also to "foreign" citizens (pp. 155–57). Ostenso's exploration of the political ramifications of settlement are in the tradition of Brooke and Jameson, but her resolution in American ideology is in contrast with Duncan and McClung. Duncan and McClung saw in American experience a political and literary mode for developing Canada's national identity while yet retaining her distinctive links with the Empire; Ostenso portrays no difference between the American and Canadian prairie experiences and even in her own career presages the growing absorption of Canada into the American political system. One wonders, however, when reading the novel published in the year of her marriage, *O River, Remember!*, filled as it is with nostalgia for the bygone days of the Red River caravans and developing as it does the portrait of a woman whose greed and lust for land corrupt her "natural" maternal affections, whether Ostenso came to despair of the possibility of establishing a "world of true instincts" within a system irrevocably founded on the economic exploitation of nature.

NOTES

1. Sara Jeannette Duncan, *The Imperialist* (1904; Toronto, 1971), p. 160.

2. Public Archives of Canada, Minto Papers, Chamberlain to Minto, March 2, 1900; Laurier memo, April 9, 1900, quoted in Robert Craig Brown and Ramsay Cook, *Canada 1896–1921: A Nation Transformed* (Toronto, 1974), p. 43.

3. Donald Creighton, *Dominion of the North* (Toronto, 1957), p. 396.

4. William Wasserstrom, *Heiress of All the Ages* (Minneapolis, 1959), p. 82.

5. Sara Jeannette Duncan, "Woman Suffragists in Council," in *The Evolution of Canadian Literature in English: 1867–1914*, ed. Mary Jane Edwards, Paul Denham, George Parker, 4 vols. (Toronto, 1973), 2, 181.

6. Marian Fowler, *Redney: A Life of Sara Jeannette Duncan* (Toronto, 1983), p. 211.

7. Carl Berger summarizes the imperialist contention that a federated empire

would naturally find its center in Canada in his *Sense of Power: Studies in the Ideas of Canadian Imperialism 1867–1914* (Toronto, 1970), pp. 61–66.

8. Alfred G. Bailey, "The Historical Setting of Sara Duncan's *The Imperialist*" and Joseph M. Zezulka, "*The Imperialist*: Imperialism, Provincialism and Point of View," both examine Duncan's references to leading figures in the imperialist debate. See *The Canadian Novel: Beginnings*, ed. John Moss (Toronto, 1980), pp. 139, 145.

9. Thomas E. Tausky, *Sara Jeannette Duncan: Novelist of Empire* (Port Credit, 1980), p. 161; Marian Fowler, *Redney*, p. 259.

10. Claude Bissell noted Duncan's indebtedness to James in his introduction to the 1971 New Canadian Library edition of *The Imperialist*. More recently, Francis Zichy's biographical article in *Profiles in Canadian Literature 1*, ed. Jeffrey M. Heath (Toronto, 1980), quotes pertinent passages from Duncan's journals on the modern novel. The opening sentence of Duncan's first novel, *A Social Departure. How Orthodiocia and I Went Round the World by Ourselves* (New York, 1890), refers directly to James.

11. Richard Chase, *The American Novel and Its Traditions* (New York, 1957), p. 23.

12. Henry James, "The Art of Fiction," in *The American Tradition in Literature*, ed. Sculley Bradley, Richard Croom Beatty and E. Hudson Long (New York, 1967), pp. 1279, 1267.

13. Letter to Lord Lansdowne, January 8, 1905, in Fowler, *Redney*, p. 269.

14. Duncan, *Sara Jeannette Duncan: Selected Journalism*, ed. Thomas E. Tausky (Ottawa, 1978), p. 102.

15. In Fowler, *Redney*, p. 269.

16. *Selected Journalism*, p. 109.

17. As quoted in Creighton, *Dominion of the North*, p. 402.

18. Catherine L. Cleverdon, *The Woman Suffrage Movement in Canada* (Toronto, 1950), p. 46.

19. Nellie McClung, *In Times Like These* (1915; Toronto, 1975), pp. 87–88.

20. Nellie McClung, *Clearing in the West* (Toronto, 1935), p. 45.

21. *Record of the Roblin Government, 1900–1914* (Winnipeg, 1914), pp. 168–70.

22. Nellie McClung, *Purple Springs* (Toronto, 1921), p. 93.

23. McClung, in Candace Savage, *Our Nell: A Scrapbook Biography* (Saskatoon, 1979), p. 82.

24. McClung, in Savage, p. 48.

25. Henry F. May, *The Enlightenment in America* (New York, 1976), p. 162.

26. Brown and Cook, *Canada 1896–1921*, p. 287.

27. Leslie Fiedler, *Love and Death in the American Novel* (New York, 1975), pp. 262, 263.

28. A. C. Stewart (Minister of Highways, Saskatchewan) in a letter to R. B. Bennett, May 26, 1931, stresses that the deplorable conditions of the land "would not be so bad" if the farmers had "engaged in mixed farming to any extent." Quoted in *The Dirty Thirties*, ed. Michael Horn (Toronto, 1972), p. 96.

29. Mrs. Rix Weaver, *The Old Wise Woman* (New York, 1973), p. 80.

30. Martha Ostenso, *Wild Geese* (Toronto, 1925), p. 76.

31. Clara Thomas, "Martha Ostenso's Trial of Strength," in *Writers of the Prairies*, ed. D. G. Stephens (Vancouver, 1973), p. 40.

32. Stanley S. Atherton, "Ostenso Revisited," in *The Canadian Novel: Modern Times*, ed. John Moss (Toronto, 1982), p. 58.

33. See Thomas, p. 48, and Atherton, pp. 63–64.

34. See Thomas, p. 43, and Atherton, p. 58.

3

"Nothing and No One Could Complicate Life Here": Isolationism in the Novels of Ethel Wilson

On her way to Buckingham Palace for an audience with her queen, Topaz Edgeworth, protagonist of Ethel Wilson's *The Innocent Traveller* (1949), is chided by her brother for her boisterous enthusiasm: "I do wish, Topaz . . . that you would try to control yourself, and—er, conform a little. You really sound very Colonial sometimes."[1] Topaz, who had emigrated to British Columbia twenty years earlier, defends herself: " 'Colonial!' You don't know what the word means! You say the word as if it were something to be ashamed of! . . . I'm Colonial and I'm proud of it. . . . those who left this country as colonists and established colonies in the New World have a deal more to be proud of than you who stayed at home and were comfortable . . . a deal too comfortable" (pp. 229–30). Despite Topaz's apparent challenge to accepted conventions, the narrator makes it clear that Topaz's image of the muscular and innovative colonial does not arise from personal experience: "You would have thought that [Topaz] had hewn down the forest and raised the home . . . and planted the garden herself" (p. 230). What is ironic about Topaz's fiery defence of her Canadian experience is her thorough acceptance of colonial values; this chapter, titled "Apotheosis," presents the crowning moment of Topaz's vivacious but nevertheless shallow existence: her thirty-minute audience with the queen, a reward for having established in Vancouver "a branch of a Needlework Guild . . . with Royal encouragement" (p. 133).

Topaz has remained throughout her entire life, even on the frontier of Canada, just as "comfortable" as her brother; certainly her colonialism conforms just as much to convention as does his imperialism. Although she feels tremendous exhilaration when "at last . . . the open country . . . stretched before her, exciting her with its mountains, its forests, the Pacific Ocean, the new little frontier town, and all the new people" (p. 122), she lives a life of "unlimited leisure" in a closed circle of genteel women who pass their time deciding on new carpets for their church, lunching at the Hudson's Bay Lunch Room, and "sending knitted garments to the Queen of England." Despite her loud protests to the contrary, Topaz is a conventional British citizen and woman: she is loyal to her queen, to her culture, and to her socially defined femininity. Instead of being an adventurous colonial breaking new ground, as she protests, she maintains an imperial outpost for queen and country in Canada.

Ethel Wilson's novel centers on the eccentric behavior of this exuberant colonial, a woman who lives to be one hundred, and who even to the end never stops talking with excitement about a wide variety of topics. But her portrait is really a satire, albeit a gentle one, with political undertones. Despite all her humorous vitality and eccentricities, Topaz is revealed as a shallow, undeveloped human being; any depth of emotion remains hidden from her. Certainly the reader enjoys her flaunting of social codes for women, as, for instance, she "would invade the privacy of the gentleman's smoking-room" (p. 109). But even though she defends her actions by asserting that, once "you've come to Canada, you know, you . . . have to be less conventional," her unconventionality remains superficial. The narrator compares Topaz to a "water-glider" skimming "unencumbered" and unaware of the "dreadful deeps below" (p. 104). For her entire one hundred years, Topaz is cared for by other people, from her parents and her siblings to her nieces; never having to concern herself with serious decisions, she remains dependent, colonized.

Near the end of her life, she compares her virginal state to the situation of her married grandniece, Rose: " 'It isn't everyone who can love for seven years . . . Unrequited,' said Aunty complacently. . . . 'You and your happy marriages! Any simpleton can do that' " (p. 253). But Wilson shows Topaz's failure in Rose's reflection that her aunt's "vitality had been preserved and untroubled by [a] lack of awareness of the human relations which compose the complicated fabric of living" (p. 255). If Wilson, in *The Innocent Traveller*, pokes gentle fun at nineteenth-century ideals of female behavior and identity, she also demonstrates how trapped Topaz is by British conventions, how incapable she is of development in the open country of British Columbia. In one brilliant chapter, Topaz comes into contact with the "terrible enclosing night" of the rain forests (p. 193); she flees the natural surroundings in fear, speechless for the only time in her life. Topaz remains forever a colonial, sexually ("satin white until the day of her death" [p. 193]), socially ("a civilized although not a conventional being" [p. 59]), and politically ("the Royal Family moved through her life with banners streaming" [p. 89]).

As early as 1930, Ethel Wilson began fictionalizing the biographical and autobiographical material which is the basis of *The Innocent Traveller*.[2] This book, recording the rise of both the city of Vancouver and the new nation, gently satirizes the Victorian sensibility so prevalent in Wilson's own family during the nineteenth century and the early part of the twentieth.[3] The very names of this city and province emphasize their British inheritance. Her ironic tone is closest to Duncan's turn-of-the-century novel about nineteenth-century imperialism. Although the irony of *The Innocent Traveller* is primarily directed at Topaz, the book reveals as well Wilson's admiration for the vitality of such women who, like Catharine Parr Traill and Susanna Moodie, can adapt to unforeseen circumstances. But social conventions for these British women, like the imported British forms of government designed "to serve and protect," could also limit full development and stifle the creation of new social and political modes. Along with Frances Brooke and Anna Jameson, Wilson contrasts superficial British convention, embodied in this novel by Topaz's "surface" experiences, with the rugged wilderness setting to suggest the inadequacy of British traditions in the New World. Published in 1949, Wilson's fictional examination of the meaning of "colonial" complements the official investigations into the nature of Canada, most notably the 1949 Royal Commission on National Development in the Arts, Letters, and Sciences. *The Innocent Traveller* reflects the passing of an era and heralds Canada's constitutional emancipation from colonial status onto the world stage as an independent Dominion.

Ethel Wilson's career also parallels stages in Canada's political and cultural development. Born in South Africa of British parentage in 1887, orphaned at ten, she was sent to live with maternal aunts in Vancouver, although she returned to England for her formative education. As Irene Howard indicates, Ethel Bryant was raised in a strict, religious household fervently British in political and cultural orientation.[4] In 1921 she married Dr. Wallace Wilson and spent the next twenty years supporting his career; as she describes herself in a biographical essay, "Cat among the Falcons," she "did not contemplate a future in this occupation [of writer]—life as it was seemed already full."[5] Wilson thus began writing late in life, in 1930, at the same time that Canada gained national autonomy with the Statute of Westminster, 1931. Yet the fact that her first story appeared in 1937 in a British publication, the *New Statesman*, because she knew of no Canadian publishers, indicates the persistence, despite constitutional independence, of Canada's cultural colonialism. Then, just as Canada's growth toward political independence was delayed during World War II, so too was Wilson's writing career interrupted by war work. Afterwards, Wilson turned to intensive writing and her canon of five novels appeared between 1947 and 1956, a time corresponding to a heightened nationalism in Canada. Her collection of short stories was published in 1961, as Canada entered an unprecedented period of literary and cultural nationalism.

While *The Innocent Traveller*, evoking the early years of Canada's development, paid particular attention to the British and Victorian ethos out of and by which the country was formulated, Wilson's first published novel was *Hetty Dorval* (1947), which focuses quite specifically on the 1930s, from the time of the Statute of Westminster to the outbreak of World War II. The Statute of Westminster in 1931 was the culmination of the long struggle, begun by Sir Wilfrid Laurier and continued by Sir Robert Laird Borden, for independent national status. Yet many constitutional issues needed resolution, most notably the division of jurisdiction between the federal government and the provinces. The depression had sharpened the inequities among the various regions of the country and also forced the nations of the world into more isolationalist, protectionist stances. Mackenzie King returned to power in 1935 and only had begun to address the complexities of Canada's exercise of her new status on the international front when Canada entered the war against Hitler's Germany. The years from 1930 to 1950 forced Canada to face the difficulties of establishing independent international relations at a time of war and at a time when she had not yet solved major conflicts within her own community.

As Canada sought her way in an increasingly complex international scene, Wilson's narrator-protagonist from Lytton, British Columbia, Frankie Burnaby, is forced to think and act on her own in Europe. A bildungsroman, *Hetty Dorval* spans Frankie's seven years' growth from a naïve country girl of twelve to a young woman residing in Europe to broaden her education. Frankie's initiation into the complex world of adulthood circles around the title character, a "woman of no reputation,"[6] who lives for a short time in Lytton when Frankie is twelve. Frankie meets Hetty by coincidence at each successive stage of her development: in Vancouver at fourteen, on a boat to England at sixteen, and finally in London at nineteen. As a twelve-year-old, Frankie falls under Hetty's "spell of beauty and singing and the excitement of a charm that was new" (p. 21); her visits to Hetty's bungalow meet with the disapproval of her parents who send her away to school, first to Vancouver and then to London. In London, Frankie lives with the Tretheways; for Richard Tretheway she feels the first pangs of love, and for Molly, his younger sister, motherly solicitude. When these two meet Hetty, Frankie, "watching them succumbing to the flowing slow-spoken charm of Hetty Dorval," resolves to protect them from her "ensnaring business" (p. 65). Frankie's attempt to confront and to straighten out Hetty is interrupted by another complication: that Hetty's lifelong housekeeper, Mrs. Broom, is Hetty's mother. At the novel's end, Hetty goes on her way to yet another opportunistic marriage, while Frankie finally accepts the complexities within herself and in human relationships. Frankie cannot keep Richard, Molly or herself innocent; her simplistic sense of moral superiority is foiled by the complexities of European "relations." While Hetty is capable of protecting herself in a new alliance, the more passive Frankie, like Canada after the war, can only recognize and accept the complexities of relationships to others.

The novel is not overtly political, but as W. H. New notes in his concluding remarks to the 1981 Ethel Wilson Symposium, "there is more politics in Ethel Wilson's work than we have commonly recognized."[7] The novel ends with reference to the German occupation of Vienna on March 14, 1938; since Frankie is twelve at the novel's beginning, the time span of the book is 1931–38, from the Statute of Westminster to the first of Hitler's acts of aggression which precipitated World War II. Written and published after the war, the novel makes three specific references to the imminent conflict. Two connect Hetty to the atmosphere of impending doom in Europe. The first is Frankie's comment, just before her chance meeting with Hetty in London: "there was great uneasiness everywhere in the public and private mind, and the word 'War' underlay everybody's thoughts" (p. 62). Then, hurriedly returning from Paris to warn Richard of the dangers of romantic entanglement with Hetty, Frankie refers to the "impending feeling" of war in London. She has a "pre-vision of craters, rubble and death" (p. 75). Such ominous forebodings remind the reader that the narrator, the adult Frankie, speaks with a postwar consciousness. Certainly, the most extended reference to the war is the novel's final paragraph. Hetty travels with her latest male conquest, Jules Stern, to Vienna; the closing sentences connect her with the siege of that city: "Six weeks later the German Army occupied Vienna. There arose a wall of silence around the city, through which only faint confused sounds were sometimes heard" (p. 92). The ambiguity of the ending is typical of the book as a whole—does one associate Hetty with the besieged or the besieger? Beverly Mitchell argues that "the reader must infer ... Frankie's terrible awareness of the fate of a woman named 'Hester' in company with the Jewish-sounding 'Jules Stern' in a country occupied by Nazis."[8] Desmond Pacey, on the other hand, sees the novel as "a microcosm of the whole human world prior to the Great War"; the connections between Hetty and war suggest to Pacey that "the irresponsible individualism of Hetty Dorval, multiplied a million times, precipitated that conflict."[9] Further examination of the sexual politics in the novel, however, reveals that Wilson uses the event of war as a metaphor which validates both these apparently contradictory readings.

The sexual politics of *Hetty Dorval* is discovered in its landscape. Frankie's description, early in the novel, of her home, the point at which "the clear turbulent Thompson River joins the vaster opaque Fraser" (p. 6), is often quoted, as by Pacey, as an example of Wilson's "rich sense of place" (pp. 50–51);[10] it is perhaps more noteworthy for its metaphorical diction. The adult Frankie's likening of the joining of the rivers to "a marriage" (p. 7) reflects her attitude to the conventional relationship between the sexes: "as often in marriage, one *overcomes* the other, and one is *lost* in the other"; "the expanse of emerald and sapphire dancing water joins and *is quite lost* in the sullen Fraser. . . . The Fraser *receives* all the startling colour of the Thompson River and *overcomes* it, and flows on unchanged to look upon but greater in size and quality than before" (p. 7, emphasis mine). The subtlety here reverses patriarchal society's assumption that the male identity overcomes the female's in marriage; the female "receives" and thereby subsumes the

male. This reading is supported by Wilson's naming of the Lytton minister
the Reverend Mr. Thompson; coming "to pay a call" to Hetty Dorval, he is
quite vanquished by her "weapon of lightness" (p. 20). This view of relationships, wherein the male is consumed by the female, is represented most
clearly in the career of Hetty Dorval, as she glides unchanged from one
liaison to another. Although she is known in Lytton as Mrs. Dorval, her
"husband" is not with her; later, Frankie's mother reports that Hetty had
left an affair with a married man for "a rich oil man . . . who set her up . . .
in British Columbia where the riding was good and then for some reason
she up and left him" (p. 72). Hetty next marries an aged Englishman, General
Connot, for "security" (p. 52). After his death she sets her designs on young
Richard Tretheway, but at the novel's end she goes off instead with Jules
Stern to Vienna. Hetty "receives" men into her life, and each time goes on
"unchanged."

Such a reading of the novel apparently posits Hetty as a "bad woman"
despite Wilson's assertion to Mitchell that "I never wrote about 'bad' women"
(p. 74). Wilson's comment could be considered the denial of Victorian pru-
dery were it not for the fact that Hetty's sexual relations are not the only
stressful models Frankie has to learn from. It is in the portrait of the apparently healthy, even ideal, marriage of Frank and Ellen Burnaby that
Wilson subtly introduces the ironic complexity of her novel. Frankie's parents "had a hard and hard-working life" operating a ranch and they "set and
maintained the family standards in an exacting loneliness" (p. 8). Ellen Burnaby's unique qualification as a ranch wife, that she "had been at the Sorbonne," is commented on by Mrs. Dunne, the landlady of Frankie's boarding
house in town: "I always think it is so wonderful of a woman like your mother,
who's been at the Sorbonne . . . " (p. 8). She allows her incomplete sentence
to give the impression that Ellen is admirable for sacrificing herself, her
intelligence and her education, to her husband and the ranch. But surface
appearances, as in *The Innocent Traveller*, can be misleading.

Indeed, Ellen is no more sacrificial and passive than Hetty is "bad." Ellen
is the controlling force in the marriage; for example, Frank is emotionally
volatile during the confrontation with Frankie over her secret visits to Hetty,
while Ellen is the calming voice of reason. Frank "exploded" and spoke
"sharply" and "jumped up and began to stride up and down the room";
Ellen, on the other hand, "interposed . . . speaking to Father . . . 'Darling,
let's hear what Frankie has to say' " (p. 32). Because he seldom appears in
the novel, Frank is kept insignificant, distanced from the reader. In his last
scene, he is openly manipulated by his wife; visiting the bungalow where
Hetty Dorval had lived, Ellen "fell in love with the bungalow . . . whirled
round and her eyes sparkled. . . . 'Give it to me, Frank! I want it! I adore
it! Let's have it!' " (p. 46). Frankie observes the politics of the scene: "Father
played right into her hands." She notes her mother's manipulations: "I knew
exactly what she was doing" (p. 47). When Frank dies a short time later,

Ellen displays no emotion. She writes Frankie in London that she "was well, that she knew what she had to do, and that I was on no account to change the plans that they had made for me. She might even join me in a little while" (p. 61). Sister Marie-Cecile, a former teacher of Frankie's in Lytton, also writes to describe the death scene. Ellen tells the dying Frank, "Nothing can ever part you and me, Frank. We shall always be together wherever we are, my dear love" (p. 61). Sister Marie-Cecile concludes that Frankie's parents "have between them the perfection of human love" (p. 61). Surely Wilson intends some irony here, for not only is the man dead, but also it is a nun who pronounces this statement about a subject she cannot know about from personal experience. Moreover, Frankie's vision of the scene pictures her "mother leaning over my father in the immortal attitude of love" (p. 62). The Pieta iconography suggested here places the woman in a permanently dominant position. In the marriages of Hetty and Ellen, then, love and destruction are closely interwoven. Marriage as a symbol of human interaction becomes a dangerous game, wherein one identity—in this novel, the male—inevitably loses.

The novelists examined in chapter 2 all reflect the challenges to the conventional relationship between men and women typical of the first quarter of this century; the advent of independent women began a change in the balance of power between "man and wife." Both Sara Jeannette Duncan and Nellie McClung reveal the difficulties of men and women who treat each other as equal partners when they approach marriage—that traditional, patriarchal institution. Martha Ostenso's Judith is the first female character in this study to break away from the restrictions imposed by her male-dominated society; she finds power in a sexual relationship outside marriage, but then Ostenso can take her no further than domestic residence with her mate and child in Winnipeg. Hetty Dorval, on the other hand, is the first novel in this series to contain a "woman of no reputation," let alone to focus upon such a woman as the title character. Moreover, not only Hetty's transient relationships with men but also the more traditional marriage of Ellen reveals the ascendancy of women's power over men.

The challenge to patriarchal conventions in the novels discussed in previous chapters has, in Hetty Dorval, become a more general assault on men. Social events in the years between World Wars I and II explain the shift in sexual politics mirrored in Wilson's novels. From World War I women gained the vote, employment outside the home and the freedom of the 1920s "flapper" period. The depression years sent men from home in search of work, leaving women to usurp the prestige of their place as heads of the family. By the end of the 1930s, Betty Friedan points out, women's magazines portrayed an image of New Woman, "less fluffily feminine, so independent and determined to find a new life of her own."[11] Friedan's comment that "there was an aura about [the New Woman] of becoming, of moving into a future that was going to be different from the past," is applicable in retrospect not only to the changing relationships of men and women, but also to the changes in Canada's former alliances. With the Statute of Westminster Canada started to go her own way but in the troubles of the 1930s, she was as yet untried, "of no reputation," only just sensing her power. The independent and isolationist Prime Minister King, like Hetty, did not want life complicated by the affairs of others; both King and Hetty were nevertheless caught up irrevocably by another World War.[12] The new imperative for Canada, for Canadian women, as for Hetty, is to assess their new powers and the complications of an independent place in international affairs.

The epigraph from Donne's "Meditation XVII" sets the central thematic development, the desire for isolation, against the necessity of community. The generally accepted interpretation of the novel is that Frankie is forced to choose between the isolationism of Hetty Dorval and the social responsibility impressed on her by her parents, most notably her mother.[13] Frankie's thoughts upon her arrival with her mother in England support this reading: "Any positive efforts that one could discern on the part of Hetty were directed towards isolating herself from responsibilities to other people. She endeavoured to island herself in her own particular world of comfort and irresponsibility. ('I will *not* have my life complicated.') But 'No man is an Iland, intire of itself' said Mother's poet three hundred years ago" (p. 57). Frankie's confrontation of Hetty in the penultimate chapter, sparked as it is by her protective love for Richard and Molly Tretheway, is seen as her acceptance of responsibility for others and her rejection of selfish opportunism such as Hetty's. In this sense, Desmond Pacey is correct to read the novel "as another version of the classic confrontation of innocence and experience . . . in which Innocence meets Evil in the disguise of Beauty, is temporarily enchanted thereby, is made wise by Parental Wisdom, and succeeds finally in cheating Evil out of another victim" (p. 54). But such an allegorical interpretation ignores, as Pacey intimates but does not pursue, the complexities which contain Wilson's explorations of the political dimensions of her story.

Frankie is forced to grapple with the complexities of relationships which develop beyond isolationism and with her own femininity as the result of her involvement with the Tretheways and Hetty. If one keeps in mind the destructive violence inherent in Donne's "Meditation XVII," a destruction which breaks up unity, then Frankie's friendship with the Tretheways of Cliff House must be read as an allusion to "a promontorie . . . as well as . . . a manor of thy friends." Donne's "Meditation" is echoed in Frankie's diction as she describes "the harmony and confidence of our lives together, whether we were apart, or whether we were all together in Cliff House by the sea" (p. 60). Hetty is the force which threatens to tear apart "the integrity of Cliff House . . . and leave wreckage behind" (p. 75). If Hetty represents the "irresponsible individualism" which precipitated the world conflict, if she is, in other words, connected with Germany's siege of Vienna at the novel's end, then Frankie's defense of her British cousins takes on the aura of international political struggle.

Just as Canada's participation in the World War was complex, as she strove to serve the British Commonwealth while maintaining national integrity and unity, so Frankie's motivations for defending the Tretheways are mixed: "I told myself, 'Oh no, it was not Richard whom I was warning off Hetty, but Richard for Molly.' . . . I shut firmly away any personal concern about Richard." She then adds the qualification, "Perhaps" (p. 68). When Hetty accuses her of being "in love with Richard . . . [and] very jealous," Frankie counters: "I truly believe you're as selfish as a human being can be, and my friends at Cliff House are too good to be made unhappy by you" (p. 79). But Wilson again undercuts Frankie's altruistic self-image by having Frankie conclude with the childish taunt: "So there!" Frankie's foray into the complex world of adult relationships has cost her emotional pain, for "take it whichever way you like, Rick was going to be very unhappy—and so was I, as far as I could see" (p. 85). Also, and more significantly, she has had to compromise her own innocence and integrity by becoming like Hetty in order to save her friends from this "menace." She becomes aware that "inexperienced as I was . . . I had more force than I had given myself credit for" (p. 74). She decides to use Hetty's own weapon against her: "The strength of Hetty's silence would be this—that her friend . . . or lover or antagonist would waste himself in emotion and talk, and Hetty would remain serene and unwasted." She succeeds at Hetty's own game, for during the confrontation Frankie observes that "there was not the making of a quarrel . . . in the room and . . . neither Hetty nor I appeared angry. We both waited in silence for the other" (p. 79). It is at this point that "the hidden mine of Mrs. Broom" explodes, ominously connecting Frankie to the warlike violence possible in her future; even "comfortable safe ones" like Frankie can encounter sordidness and shame "in a dirty foreign place" (p. 83). Frankie has learned much about her own manipulative capacities, her own destructiveness, and the complications involved in human love.

Both *Hetty Dorval* and *The Innocent Traveller* demonstrate that beneath the comfortable veneer of community may exist latent selfishness, even evil. A supportive community allows the insular, self-concerned innocence of Topaz to thrive. Donne's "Community," from which Wilson derives the third epigraph for *Hetty Dorval*, actually implies that "good is [not] as visible as green," that it is impossible to segregate the "good or bad" in women. And no such dichotomy is found in Wilson's portraits of women. The characterization of Ellen Burnaby, for example, is connected with that of Hetty Dorval: when Ellen expresses the desire to buy Hetty's bungalow because "Nothing and no one could complicate life here," Frankie recalls Hetty's similar assertion, "I will *not* complicate my life!" (p. 47). At the end of the novel Frankie too echoes the desire for isolation from other people's invasions as she tells Hetty, "I've got my own life to live and I don't want ever to see

you again"; Hetty responds, "I understand *exactly*. . . . It is preposterous the
way other people . . . complicate one's life. It is my own phobia, Frankie,
and I understand you . . . so well" (p. 91). Neither isolation nor community
can, it seems, be clearly distinguished as either good or bad. Complexity in
relationships is as inevitable as complexity in individual characters.

Set in the 1930s, but published in 1947, *Hetty Dorval* suggests the rapid
maturation Canada underwent as she was forced out of her isolationist stance
onto the international stage. The Spanish Civil War and the rise to power
of Nazi Germany signalled the increasing complexity of the involvement of
the "world" in "war" and indeed all international affairs. A measure of Canada's position is reflected by the attitude of then Prime Minister Mackenzie
King who, according to Donald Creighton's *The Forked Road* (1976), "dis-
liked the intrusion of external affairs" (p. 68). Nevertheless, Canada was
inevitably involved in, and made aware of, the darker destructive forces in
the world and in herself. Her first battle of the war, Hong Kong, "a dirty
foreign place" (*Hetty Dorval*, p. 83), brought shattering defeat and the sus-
picion of misuse by the British. Then in 1945 the Gouzenko case shocked
Canadian naïveté into acceptance of the fact that an ally was operating a
most sophisticated spy network within her borders. Finally, Canada's wartime commitment, while upholding the dignity and heritage of the British
Commonwealth, proved as well her capacity for destruction. Even the development of nuclear energy in Canada during the war carried with it sinister
implications, as nuclear power was perverted to construction of the bomb
and the nuclear age dramatically altered international relations. In order to
defeat the enemy it seemed necessary to adopt "foreign" means of violence,
to enter the complicity of evil.

Alexandra Collins has argued tenuously that Wilson's thematic links to
four American women writers—Edith Wharton, Ellen Glasgow, Willa
Cather and Ostenso—demonstrate "her sense of Canada as a new country."[14]
But more basic than thematic similarities to American writers is the structural
parallel: in *Hetty Dorval* Wilson uses, as did Duncan before her, the "international situation" of the Jamesian novel. *The Portrait of a Lady* (1881)
particularly comes to mind because of the similarities between the relationships of Frankie and Hetty and of Isabel Archer and Madame Merle: an
older friend turns out to be a "menace." *Hetty Dorval*, like *The Portrait of
a Lady*, places an innocent girl from the new world in an old-world setting;
Frankie Burnaby of Lytton, British Columbia, confronts her values and
heritage in England. Moreover, as does Duncan's *The Imperialist* (1904),
Hetty Dorval brings a character—in this case, a woman of the world—to the
colonial backwater of Canada, thereby revealing the provincialism and par-
ochialism of that frontier community. For example, when the Reverend Mr.
Thompson, in whom Frankie as a child sees a "burning sort of goodness and
directness" (p. 20), comes to "pay a call" on Hetty Dorval, the reader can
easily perceive beneath his "directness" a very narrow-minded "sort of good-

ness," as he fishes for information about Hetty's "husband" and "home" (p. 18). Beverly Mitchell argues persuasively that the novel reveals not the "menace" of Hetty Dorval, but the destructiveness of gossip and hearsay; Hetty Dorval is condemned more by rumors of her reputation than by acts she has committed (pp. 80–83). In England, attempting, out of an inherited sense of responsibility, to rid the community of the reputed "menace" of Hetty, Frankie begins to examine the complexities of her motivations. This examination provides the vehicle of the thematic complexities of the novel for—to recall Mitchell's observation—when Frankie watches Hetty depart for Vienna, she sees the evil in what she has done. Such a reading brings this discussion of the novel full circle, for Hetty Dorval can be associated not just with the besieger, but also with the besieged. Through the structure of the international novel and the consistent point of view, Wilson adopts an American formula to explore the Canadian mentality as it is juxtaposed to the European, in general, and the English, in particular.

Just as Frankie Burnaby became aware of the darker complexities of her identity and her relationships while confronting the "menace" abroad, so Canada during and immediately after World War II became conscious of her separate identity as a nation and at the same time of the complexities in international relations. Canada's military contribution during the war was outstanding, as it had been during the Great War; after the fall of France, Canada was the largest nation aiding Britain against the German attack. The Commonwealth of Nations stood alone against Germany. Sacrifices such as those at Dieppe measured the courage and force of Canadians, but during the final stages of the war when the United States and Britain were managing the war effort, Canada began to sense that she was merely a pawn in a game run by others. When Franklin D. Roosevelt and Winston Churchill met on the *Prince of Wales* off Newfoundland in 1941, Canada was not even invited to participate; Creighton concludes in *Dominion of the North* (1957) that such exclusion shattered Canada's cherished role as "mediator . . . of Anglo-American co-operation" (p. 525). Shaken by such treatment by her two closest allies and the revelations of Gouzenko about a third, Canada took her place in the international forum, joining the United Nations and NATO, mistrustful even of her allies. She strove to be a voice of moderation and conciliation in an international scene rapidly deteriorating into the tensions of cold war. Perhaps there is no better symbol of Canada's precarious position than the completion of Confederation in 1949 when Newfoundland became the tenth province of the Dominion; Canada was now at long last a nation *ad mare usque ad mare*, but Newfoundland brought uncomfortable ties with the United States, which had a ninety-nine-year lease of armed forces bases on the island. Even Canada's closest neighbor could be a "menace."

Perhaps as always in her history, it was out of a sense of self-preservation against the powerful influence of the United States that Canada at this time became concerned with her national identity. In 1946 the Canadian Citizenship Bill established the priority of Canadian citizenship over British subjecthood. The Royal Commission on National Development in the Arts, Letters, and Sciences, established in 1949 "to give encouragement to institutions which express national feeling," made recommendations in its report of 1951 not only for the development of the Canadian Broadcasting Corporation and the National Film Board, but also for the creation of a Canada Council, which would give encouragement to the arts and letters. Canada after the war set out as never before to clarify her national identity for herself and for the international community.

A measure of Canada's newfound confidence in her nationhood is reflected in Wilson's *Swamp Angel* (1954), a novel which Hallvard Dahlie rightly argues demonstrates the maturity of "an unconscious Canadianism" in fiction rather than the insecurity of "a self-conscious one."[15] Dahlie points out that the novel is artistically effective because a journey to central British Columbia governs both its plot and its characterization. Maggie Lloyd Vardoe leaves her second husband, Edward, and travels to the interior where she takes up an occupation familiar to her from her maritime childhood, the operation of a fishing lodge. The political implications of *Swamp Angel* can be surmised even from this brief description, for Maggie's character is built on a love *ad mare usque ad mare*: she loves the landscapes of both New Brunswick and British Columbia. Moreover, the lodge reveals an international composite, from the Scandinavian owners to the Chinese boy whose help Maggie enlists.

Swamp Angel continues Wilson's central theme: the interrelation of the individual and community. Maggie's employers are the maimed Haldar Gunnarsen and his bitter wife, Vera, who becomes increasingly jealous of Maggie's competence. Maggie's search for individual peace must encompass the difficulties of her relationship with the Gunnarsens; she decides not to leave for a more lucrative, self-satisfying job in the United States, but to stay and meet the responsibilities and personal rewards of "these people . . . now her family."[16] The subplot also concerns two other women on individual quests for independence, Mrs. Nell Severance and her daughter, Hilda. Mrs. Severance, an imposing woman of eighty, once a circus juggler, is able finally to sever her memory of her past and to accept her approaching death. Throughout the novel she constantly juggles a "Swamp Angel," a small gun used in her act; when she sends the gun away to Maggie, her act of "severance" suggests freedom from the past. For Hilda the "Swamp Angel" had symbolized her parents' neglect during her childhood, and its disappearance precipitates her freedom to love, marry, and bear a child. The novel ends with Nell's death and the nurturing, by Hilda and Maggie, of their respective families.

With *Swamp Angel*, Wilson is the first novelist considered in this series who consciously examines a marriage breakdown. The impetus of its plot is delineated in the first chapter, as Maggie prepares for and completes her departure from Vardoe. Anna Jameson's *Winter Studies and Summer Rambles* (1838) had as its underlying tension the difficulties of her marriage, but the marriage did not end until after the journals' time span. *Hetty Dorval*, the first novel to examine a "bad" woman, shows Hetty walking in and out of "marriages" as suits her whim, but hers cannot be called typical bourgeois marriages. As New rightly points out, Hetty, "with her silence and withdrawal, simply uses people for her own security and moves on, always the same."[17] These various marital relationships have provided the prime venue for all these novelists to explore the politics of a changing nation. Brooke examines colonial beginnings by focusing on courtship; the journalistic, autobiographical works of Jameson, Traill and Moodie suggest a colony in revolt when they, as wives, grow stronger than their husbands. Duncan, McClung and Ostenso explore the changes in imperial relations when spouse and nation gain political equality. *Swamp Angel*, as Donna E. Smyth correctly summarizes in her study "Strong Women in the Web: Women's Work and Community in Ethel Wilson's Fiction," captures the people of the 1940s, the kind of women whom Betty Friedan would analyze in *The Feminine Mystique* (1963).[18] Beginning as it does with a woman who consciously plans the end of her marriage, this novel emerges from a Canada breaking the last vestiges of colonialism, declaring Canadian citizenship, searching for a distinctive flag. In keeping with New's challenge to critics to consider the "politics" of all of Wilson's works, we must explore the political dimensions of Maggie's declared desire for independence: "I know the kind of place I want to find and I know what I want to do. I want to have a certain kind of business. I know what I want. I've worked it all out and I know I can do it" (p. 27).

The political level of Maggie's story is implied primarily in her two marriages. Maggie felt her individuality stifled by "her outraged endurance of the nights' hateful assaults" by Vardoe (p. 23). Having left him, she rediscovers the identity she had lost after the deaths of her previous husband, Tom Lloyd, their child and her father: "she had once lived through three deaths, and—it really seemed—her own" (p. 16). With these three losses, Ethel Wilson makes clear, Maggie had lost touch with her feminine essence, that of nurturing: she had "no one to care for." "By an act of . . . fatal stupidity" she had tried to assuage her loss by marriage to Vardoe. The political implications suggested by Maggie's position between husbands is reminiscent of Emily Montague's hiatus between fathers; as Emily was a mirror of Canada in transition from French to British imperial rule, so Maggie's marriages suggest Canada's evolution from British colonial status to a more demeaning position as an American economic satellite. The generic implications of Maggie's husbands' names point to the national dimensions: Tom Lloyd's name recalls the great British Prime Minister Lloyd George, under whose leadership during the Great War Canada made strides toward national autonomy; E. Thompson Vardoe, the car salesman, is brash and enterprising, the quintessentially American-style businessman. Married to Vardoe, Maggie was "standing still" (p. 19); Vardoe sees her only in the role of subservient wife (p. 31). She rediscovers her identity as "Tom Lloyd's own widow again" (p. 36). Considering the British origin of Wilson's family, as it is reflected in *The Innocent Traveller*, *Swamp Angel* seems to advocate a reassertion of British heritage as an antidote to the increasing threat of American economics and culture in Canadian life.

Like *Hetty Dorval*, *Swamp Angel* explores, in the context of female characters, the isolation/community theme. But whereas *Hetty Dorval* studies the destructive side of feminine personality and portrays the ambiguities of communal values, *Swamp Angel* seems to embrace wholeheartedly the necessity of preserving community. Maggie's "union with Three Loon Lake" is compared to "a happy marriage" (p. 84). She takes command of the "ordering, providing, planning, cooking" at the lodge, and succeeds in doing so "cheaply and well, and with good humour" (p. 84). She provides warmth and attention both to an American tourist, Mr. Carmichael, after he is trapped on the lake by a storm, and to Vera, distraught after her attempt to drown herself. As Maggie moves from isolation to community, she finds her strength and identity renewed: "These people were now her family" (p. 140).

Wilson seems to imply that this identity is to remain distinct from the American when Maggie rejects the lucrative offer to manage Mr. Carmichael's resort in the United States and affirms her Canadian allegiances to and love for the interior landscape of British Columbia, the woods of New Brunswick, and her British heritage. However, even though Maggie commits herself at the novel's end to the people of Loon Lake Lodge, there is no guarantee of success; Vera may not recover emotionally or rejoin her husband at the lodge. Maggie senses that "if I cannot cope with Vera and her folly . . . I've failed" (p. 140); the preservation of individuals within communities is confirmed as a value and a challenging goal to work toward.

Just as *Hetty Dorval* juxtaposes three women to reveal the selfishness lurking beneath altruistic feelings, so too *Swamp Angel* contrasts different images of women to portray the difficulties and yet the hope in human relationships. Maggie's commitment to her new community is contrasted to and commented on by the formidable Nell Severance. It is Nell who gives voice to the Donne "Meditation" which stands as epigraph to *Hetty Dorval*: "We are all in it together. 'No Man is an Iland, I am involved in Mankinde,' and we have no immunity and we may as well realize it" (p. 150). When critics such as Smyth assert that Nell is a "visionary . . . saint" (p. 92) who understands the mysterious web of human interaction, they seem to overlook the irony of Nell's characterization. Despite her quotation of Donne, she counsels Maggie to leave the Gunnarsens and accept Carmichael's offer of work in the States: "Leave these tiresome people. . . . Are they really your affair?" (p. 152). Desmond Pacey's critical instincts were correct when he focused on the significance of Nell's surname, Severance; but he sees in the name only her willingness to give up the past to enable others, particularly her daughter Hilda, to move forward (p. 153). In fact, she gives up the past, symbolized by the swamp angel, with great unwillingness and self-pity, and only after public humiliation threatens the security of the little gun. The deeper meaning of "severance" derives instead from Donne's "Meditation": "a Clod . . . washed away by the Sea . . . as well as if a Promontorie were." "To sever" is to disjoin, to part, and, as the noun "severance" implies in terms of land surveyance, to break off a part from a whole. The woman who quotes Donne's theme of human community is also the woman who counsels the very destructive severance of Donne's image and who desires "immunity," not community.

While Maggie considers Nell her "greatest friend and the friend of [her] spirit" (p. 154), when Nell and Maggie are together in the penultimate chapter—the only time the reader sees them together—an essential difference becomes clear. Maggie's response that she is well aware of the difficulties of involvement and her assertion that "escape to a desert island . . . is a trouble factory. . . . I'm not escaping . . . now" (p. 149) indicate that she has matured, that she is no longer the frightened woman who ran away from her husband. The vast difference between Maggie and Nell, moreover, is delineated by their respective views of nature. Whereas Nell believes that "everything of any importance happens indoors" (p. 149), such a statement seems pointedly indifferent to the nature imagery of Donne's "Meditation." Maggie retorts, "oh, it does not," for her "involvement" with nature—in activities such as fishing, boating and swimming which occur on the meeting place of land and water, the constituents of Donne's image—has been instrumental in the renewal of her spirit and in the creation of her community.

Maggie's commitment to her new family is also directly contrasted to Nell's family history. Nell claims to have had a wonderful love with her common-law husband, Philip, her partner in the circus. However, their life together and the pursuit of their shared careers "severed" them from their child; Hilda moved from one boarding school to another as her parents travelled the world: "She was only a child, and how could they take a child away from school to Troy, to Ravenna . . . they kept strange company; they lived like vagabonds . . . it would be unhealthy, quite unsuitable for a child" (pp. 50–51). In Nell's reminiscence Philip is clearly the dominant force, controlling their careers— "it was important, Philip had said, that they should go to Ravenna"—and answering "vaguely" Nell's maternal suggestion that Hilda should travel with them. Thus, for the sake of romance and career, Nell sacrificed her maternal role: "the mother excused herself to herself but did not convince herself" (p. 51). Yet as she grows older, she demonstrates a singular ignorance of the pain she has caused Hilda. Having sent the Angel away, she asks Hilda, "You didn't like the Angel, did you?" (p. 119). The question reminds Hilda of "the absences, the felt pity, the second place, her father whom she would have liked to love," but she only admits that "it was some kind of symbol" (p. 119). Nell asks, "Of what, darling? . . . thinking there were things I should have known, things I should have seen." Only in a parenthetical entry in a letter to Maggie does Nell admit her "fault" in neglecting Hilda's childhood (p. 127).

Wilson's portrait of Nell Severance is most ambiguous; although Nell values and at times displays "perception and awareness of other people" (p. 127), Nell is also a self-indulgent, proud old woman who can claim, "I don't really care for humanity . . . it gets between me and my desires" (p. 78). She seeks "immunity" from humanity, "mankinde," as she insists upon satisfying her individual "desires" to the exclusion of Hilda who belongs to her immediate community, the family. Maggie does not commit the same mistake, even though she too severs a relationship to pursue an independent career. She applauds Nell's sacrifice of the Angel as "our ability to throw away the substance, to lose all yet keep the essence" (p. 129). Unlike Nell's destructive isolationism, however, Maggie's severance from her empty marriage with Vardoe is a necessary and positive amputation which allows her to rediscover her strengths, "to keep the essence."

Maggie, while she is characterized primarily through contrast with other women, is also defined in terms of traditionally masculine strengths. Men respond to her as an equal, respecting, for example, her proficiency in the art of fishing, particularly in the creation of flies. Mr. Spencer, who buys her products, "looked for flaws in the perfection of the body, the hackle, the wings" (p. 14). When he saw that "there were no flaws, he now regarded the young woman with some respect." Having escaped Vardoe, Maggie refreshes her spirit by camping for three days beside the Similkameen River where "in the pleasure of casting over this lively stream she forgot—as always when she was fishing—her own existence" (p. 38). "Brought up from childhood by a man, with men" in the woods of New Brunswick, Maggie has the necessary courage and independence to have "serenely and alone . . . acted with her own resources" (p. 32).

Independent in what is primarily a man's world, comfortable with men in their traditional enclaves of sport and nature, Maggie is presented as admirable in comparison with the traditional, stereotypical women in the novel. On the bus driving up the Fraser Canyon, Maggie's love of the natural world is highlighted by the selfish concerns of a gossipy housewife. Wilson uses run-on sentences to convey the noisy chatter of this busybody whose thoughts are as unsophisticated as her grammar: "Well . . . that's one thing I can't take—fishing. If you want to have your home look nice you can't have men clumping in and out with dirty boots on One time my husband brought fish home and I said Well if you want me to cook those fish you can clean them yourself and he did and by the time he finished there was fish all over the house there was scales in the new broadloom and I do declare there was scales in the drapes How he did it I don't know" (p. 54). Maggie is distinguished from the women of Three Loon Lake when, after the first season, the idle gossips speculate on the tension between Maggie and Vera. The malicious chatter, in a chorus of female voices, identifies the instigator as Vera:

> "I heard that woman Henry Corder sent you was a wonder."
> "Yes, she was fine."
> "Did you like her?"
> "I liked her all right."
> "What didn't you like about her?"
> "Oh, I liked her . . . sure, I liked her."
>
> • • • • • • • • • •
>
> "Where'd she come from?"
> "I don't know. She never said."
> "Never *said*! Got a husband?"
> "I don't know."
> "You don't *know*. Didn't she tell you?"
> "No . . ." abruptly.
> "You'd think after a whole summer . . ."
> "I know," with a half smile, "but she didn't."
>
> • • • • • • • • • •
>
> In the evening Alma Bower said to her mother Mrs Pratt, "I don't think Vera Gunnarsen's so crazy about that Mrs Lloyd." . . . And Mrs Pratt said to her friend Sally Bate, "Did you hear about that woman's been working for Gunnarsens? Kind of a myst'ry woman Vera says. Vera says. . . . " (p. 115)

Wilson juxtaposes Maggie's quiet ways to the "gabby talkers," the women concerned with fussy social conventions determining the proper hat and hairdo for weddings (p. 122).

When Henry Corder is confronted with the indirect questions about Maggie, he explodes in a tirade against "wimmin": "Can you beat it the way wimmin talk. Make up a thing out of whole cloth. . . . She's not one of those mod'n wimmin. . . . She's just not one of these gabby talkers" (p. 116). The reader is led to share the admiration of the male characters for Maggie's self-control as she struggles with her painful emotions and difficult experiences. Typed by the women as "one of these man's women" (p. 116), Maggie is valued for the qualities which distinguish her from her contemporaries, the kind of women—whom Betty Friedan was to describe in *The Feminine Mystique*—whose world is limited by the role of housewife, whose intellect and emotion are fed on stories about getting and keeping a husband, whose energy finally degenerates into idle gossip and petty annoyance. In contrast to "mod'n wimmin," Maggie is independent, efficient, controlled—in "essence," masculine.

With her masculine talents and control and her feminine awareness of and response to others' needs, Maggie is forced to grow through the process of coming to terms with an irrational feminine force. Vera, whose antipathy to her lot in life pushes her to jealousy of the competent Maggie, is one of the "mod'n wimmin," weak, lacking in control. Though Smyth argues that Wilson shows sympathetic understanding of Vera in the comment that other women would understand the fatigue caused by Vera's workload (p. 92), the authorial comments actually make clear that Wilson despises women like Vera. Vera "was not intelligent . . . [and] had not the support of simple philosophy" (p. 87). Although Vera's husband is bullheaded and cantankerous, Wilson observes that "living with [Vera] could hardly be called a pleasure" (p. 72). Vera's primary problem, that she cannot reason her way out of her emotional dilemma, contrasts Maggie's knowledge that she will "have to make [her] way on [her] own power" (p. 99).

Despite Wilson's obvious admiration for Maggie and her dislike of Vera, however, the difficulties Maggie experiences in applying her masculine "power" in her relationship with Vera demonstrate the limits of her "fine talk and . . . all her fine thinking" (p. 142). Maggie has to discover a deeper power within herself "to cope with one unhappy being" (p. 142). After unsuccessfully attempting to drown herself, Vera stumbles to Maggie's cabin; the ensuing scene recalls Maggie's restoration of the exhausted Mr. Carmichael, but the diction and imagery suggest a deeper psychological dimension. The atmosphere of their meeting echoes the microcosm of Donne's "Meditation": "A room lit by a candle and in a silent and solitary place is a world within itself . . . it has a singularity" (p. 146). The encounter focuses on the effect on Maggie; when she realizes "with horror" what Vera has tried to do, Maggie "came to herself." "Without speaking," Maggie "drew Vera into the cabin." Wilson emphasizes the absence of words during Maggie's ministrations to Vera; "still not speaking," Maggie dries Vera and prepares a fire. In this crisis Maggie is forced to abandon words: "it seemed to her the least important thing that she should speak and make words." When Maggie, "her heart failing her," tries to talk away Vera's fear of madness, her words are useless. The only effective response Maggie makes to Vera's anguished cry—"I hate you I love you I hate you Maggie I love you . . . don't ever leave me!"—is to cradle Vera in her arms and speak to her as a mother would to a disturbed child: "Maggie, bending, drew Vera up and held her strongly and softly in her arms until the trembling and crying went quiet. . . . She could not think what to say . . . 'There then,' she said . . . patting Vera gently as she held her in her arms, 'there then . . . there then' " (p. 147).

Such a passage recalls the icon of the Pieta used in *Hetty Dorval*, but here the image of two embracing women also suggests Maggie's recovery of her lost child. Maggie's embrace of Vera is also one of truth, as Vera's Latinate name implies. Maggie goes beyond the rational power of "simple philosophy" and words—because she does not know "what words you use to exorcise the Evil One"—to embrace another individual with what she quite incorrectly terms "helpless compassion." She becomes a truer individual by acknowledging the irrational element which Ostenso's Caleb Gare could not control and therefore not accept, and she learns the tremendous healing powers of her feminine compassion. Wilson does not allow the situation to conclude on a note of naïve optimism, however; Maggie knows that "it's not going to be easy" to remain with the Gunnarsens, but "perhaps there's a way" (p. 154). In the deliberation over the future of the lodge, she advises that Vera should not be brought to the lake "till she says she wants to go," that they all do "a little more petting, a little helping." When Henry Corder exclaims defensively, "I couldn't pet anybody—never done such a thing in all my life," Maggie promises, "I'll teach you, Henry" (p. 153). She has just learned herself.

Like Frances Brooke's *Emily Montague* two hundred years earlier, Wilson's novel dramatizes the need to go beyond the controls and limitations of a masculine "philosophy" of human relations. A dominating man such as Edward Vardoe, who sees his wife only in terms of conventional roles, must be vanquished, abandoned. This action enables Maggie to draw strength from the masculine side of her nature, suffocated during their marriage. Once released from the prison of conventional femininity, she is able to stand on her own, to carve out aggressively the lifestyle she wants, to live independently. This portrait is distinctive to the first half of the twentieth century in its ambiguous treatment of sexual roles. Like Pearl in *Purple Springs*, Maggie Lloyd is an uneasy composite of masculine and feminine traits; both women are somewhat too good to be true. Maggie achieves independence, through masculine powers, in what is primarily a man's world, yet she acquires the powers of feminine nurturing and manages the domestic arrangements of the lodge with a "good housewifery" which would be the envy of Catharine Parr Traill. Wilson and McClung assert, more than they render, the feminine quality of their apparently "masculine" protagonists. McClung tried to avoid the implications of her characterization simply by giving Pearl a sentimental romantic marriage at the novel's end. Wilson, on the other hand, seems to realize the problems raised by her creation; her authorial intrusions indicate a conscious manipulation of conventional sexual types. Disliking, as does McClung, the gossips such as Vera and the irrational forces which control women, Wilson nevertheless structures the plot of *Swamp Angel* around Maggie's discovery of the nurturing feminine "essence" to complement her masculine strengths. Although the androgynous ideal is awkwardly realized, it seems to be the goal of the narrator as well as of the plot.

Wilson's development, seen in her characterization of Topaz, Hetty and Maggie, has its corollary in the generic growth of her work. *The Innocent Traveller* finds its models in the British writers Wilson acknowledged to

Pacey as her primary literary influences: Henry Fielding, Daniel Defoe, E. M. Forster, Anthony Trollope and Arnold Bennett (p. 16). *Hetty Dorval* followed the American "international" novel in its theme and structure. *Swamp Angel*, however, is a composite, a combination of British and American influences. Whereas *Hetty Dorval* maintains a first-person point of view, *Swamp Angel* returns to a third-person narration with an omniscient author who, as does the narrator in *The Innocent Traveller*, often intrudes into the story. Yet, when Wilson describes Maggie fishing in the Similkameen, her style also suggests the influence of Ernest Hemingway, particularly his fishing sequences in *The Sun Also Rises* (1926). Moreover, entire chapters are rendered in dialogue only, a dramatic form which Hemingway had experimented with in such short stories as "Hills Like White Elephants." The mode of all these literary influences, it must be noted, is decidedly masculine. In a letter to Pacey stating her literary preferences, Wilson indicates dissatisfaction with the craft of both Jane Austen and Virginia Woolf (p. 21). Consequently, her preference for and admiration of a masculine style of writing repeat the tension of Maggie's struggle between the poles of her masculine and feminine psyche. The plot and character development of *Swamp Angel* dramatize the necessity of feminine strengths, while the style remains primarily in the masculine tradition. The book moves toward an eclectic style as its protagonist grows toward androgyny.

This novel's theme and technique also comment on Canadian consciousness at the midpoint of "her" century. "Human relations," muses Maggie, "how they defeat us" (p. 142), yet she remains committed to her wider family, despite the slim hope of success. She has found the independence she wanted, and is learning more and more about her long dormant and even previously hidden strengths. Canada, likewise, at midcentury had solidified her autonomy as a nation with her membership in the United Nations, a wider "family" than the British Commonwealth of Nations. Yet the growing cold war between the superpowers and the war in Korea manifested the grave difficulties of attaining peace in the international community. While remaining committed to her growing role as mediator in international affairs, Canada also set out as never before to explore her cultural and national identity. Creighton opines in *Dominion of the North*, "the appointment, in April, 1949, of a Royal Commission on National Development in the Arts, Letters and Sciences, implied that the preservation of Canada's intellectual and spiritual independence was now recognized as an urgent matter of both public and private concern" (p. 579). As already noted, in the early years of the 1950s, Canada began to establish its own institutions for the development of the arts: the Stratford Shakespeare Festival in 1953, the Canadian Broadcasting Corporation in 1952, the Royal Winnipeg Ballet in 1953 and the National Ballet of Canada in 1951. Yet the irony in the development of the dance companies and the Stratford Festival is that the artistic directors, the chief architects, were imported from Britain. The British control of Canadian culture, coupled with the increasing dominance of the United States in the Canadian economy, are prominent reminders that Canada has always been and still is a composite of British and American influences; in the 1950s, Canada strove, like Maggie, toward independence, but could not yet formulate the qualities of her uniqueness.

Like Frankie Burnaby, Canada was thrust prematurely into a complex adult world. Like Maggie Lloyd Vardoe, Canada found herself on a difficult path toward independence, caught between the influences of the two great nations which have been so prominent throughout her history, and caught as well in an increasingly tense international community. But Maggie and Frankie have one thing in common with their creator, a love of the British Columbia landscape. The roots of their identities are in that landscape, and Wilson's fame is ultimately that of a British Columbia writer. Wilson is, in this sense, a regional and pioneer writer, and her novels, particularly *Swamp Angel*, are unabashedly steeped in the British Columbian landscape. This setting is in its appellation a composite of British and American influences; the British and American heritages, Old World and New World, meet in this westernmost province of Canada. Just as Hugh Finlay in *The Imperialist* speculated on the possibility of formulating a new identity for himself and his newly adopted country in the wilderness of British Columbia (p. 184), so Wilson, through her fiction and her characters, explored this land and pointed the way for Canadians to discover the uniqueness of their experience.

NOTES

1. Ethel Wilson, *The Innocent Traveller* (Toronto, 1949), p. 229.

2. Peter Hinchcliffe, "Ethel Wilson," in *Profiles in Canadian Literature 3*, ed. Jeffrey M. Heath (Toronto, 1982), p. 110.

3. George Woodcock, "Innocence and Solitude: The Fictions of Ethel Wilson," in *The Canadian Novel: Modern Times*, ed. John Moss, (Toronto, 1982), p. 179.

4. Irene Howard, "Shockable and Unshockable Methodists in Ethel Wilson's *The Innocent Traveller*," *Essays in Canadian Writing* 23 (Spring 1982): 107–34.

5. Ethel Wilson, "Cat among the Falcons," in *The Masks of Fiction*, ed. A. J. M. Smith (Toronto, 1961), p. 30.

6. Ethel Wilson, *Hetty Dorval* (1947; Toronto, 1967), p. 33.

7. W. H. New, "Critical Notes on Ethel Wilson: For a Concluding Panel," *The Ethel Wilson Symposium*, ed. Lorraine McMullen (Ottawa, 1982), p. 143.

8. Beverly Mitchell, "The Right Word in the Right Place: Literary Techniques in the Fiction of Ethel Wilson," in *The Ethel Wilson Symposium*, ed. McMullen, p. 85.

9. Desmond Pacey, *Ethel Wilson* (New York, 1968), p. 56. R. D. McDonald also notes that "Hetty and destruction are continually associated" ("Serious Whimsey," *Canadian Literature* 63 [Winter 1975]: 47).

10. Cf. as well H. W. Sonthoff's cryptic comment that "descriptions of the Fraser and the Thompson River . . . seem . . . outside the main line of the story" ("The Novels of Ethel Wilson," *Canadian Literature* 26 [Fall 1965]: 34).

11. Betty Friedan, *The Feminine Mystique* (New York, 1963), p. 33.

12. Donald Creighton makes this point about King's leadership, briefly near the end of his *Dominion of the North* (Toronto, 1957), p. 500, and in more detail in his *The Forked Road: Canada 1939–1957* (Toronto, 1976), pp. 68–69.

13. See Pacey's elaboration of this interpretation in his *Ethel Wilson*, p. 55. Hinchcliffe gives a more general summary of critical approaches to Hetty Dorval in his article in *Profiles 3*, ed. Heath, p. 107.

14. Alexandra Collins, "Who Shall Inherit the Earth? Ethel Wilson's Kinship with Wharton, Glasgow, Cather, and Ostenso," in *The Ethel Wilson Symposium*, ed. McMullen, pp. 61–72.

15. Hallvard Dahlie, "Self-conscious Canadians," *Canadian Literature* 62 (Fall 1974): 10.

16. Ethel Wilson, *Swamp Angel* (1954; Toronto, 1962), p. 140.

17. W. H. New, "The 'Genius' of Place and Time: The Fiction of Ethel Wilson," *Journal of Canadian Studies* 3 (February 1968): 40.

18. Donna E. Smyth, "Strong Women in the Web: Women's Work and Community in Ethel Wilson's Fiction," in *The Ethel Wilson Symposium*, ed. McMullen, pp. 87–95.

4

"A Canadian Theme... Just As Much a Personal Theme": Margaret Laurence, Canada and the 1960s

Hagar Shipley, protagonist of Margaret Laurence's *The Stone Angel* (1964), looks back over her ninety-odd years and recalls "as a child" spending "hours in our huge warm... kitchen" watching the housekeeper "slap and pat pastry." As the pampered daughter of Manawaka's first merchant, Hagar "used to think how sad to spend one's life in caring for the houses of others."[1] She herself "learned to cook after [she] was married" because she had "had no premonition" that she would spend her womanhood "caring for the houses of others," first as hostess in her father's house, next as housewife in her husband's, and finally as paid housekeeper for a Vancouver merchant. Her present home is the reward of her years of servitude: "it is mine. I bought it with the money I worked for." And it is all that she has: "If I am not somehow contained... in this house... then I do not know where I am to be found at all" (p. 36). The story of Hagar, then, is that of a modern bondservant, housebound all her life, despite her early expectation of high estate.

Laurence presents the women of Manawaka in novels which, unlike those of some earlier women writers, are not overtly political. Unlike Anna Jameson, Sara Jeannette Duncan and Nellie McClung, Laurence does not feel the need to argue national politics. Laurence, like Catharine Parr Traill and Susanna Moodie, and especially Ethel Wilson, places the women's experiences at the forefront of the works. Yet while the political is as implicit in her works as in the previous writers', Laurence signals a new stage of independence for Canada and for women when she confidently uses different women's perspectives to portray their individual experiences. In the context of the enthusiasm generated in the artistic community of the 1960s by the formation of the Canada Council, *The Stone Angel*, Laurence's 1964 novel, was a major step in the exploration and expression of uniquely Canadian experience.

If the central consciousness of each of Laurence's Canadian novels is female, she nevertheless struggles to find her own voice; the controlling motif in the Manawaka novels is the individual's fight for independence. And the source of this theme and plot is political; Laurence discovered it in the struggle of colonized Africans for freedom from the colonialist British. In 1943, Margaret Wemyss married Jack Laurence, a British civil engineer, and travelled with him on his postings to Somaliland in 1950 and the Gold Coast in 1952, where they remained until 1957. Aware from an early age that she wanted to be a writer, Margaret Laurence began in this decade to transcribe African stories. She published a collection of these, A Tree for Poverty (1954), as well as her own short stories about African life. Finally, she produced her first novel, This Side Jordan (1960), about the struggle for independence in Ghana. In her later novels, the country's political struggle became the analogue of the individual woman's quest for self-determination.

Her only "directly autobiographical"[2] book is a travelogue of her experiences in Africa, The Prophet's Camel Bell (1963). Hers was a dual perspective: as the wife of a white technocrat she was part of the imperialist power structure; as a writer trying to produce a collection of Somali poetry and tales, she had to overcome the language barrier and the Africans' distrust of her as a white, Western female. Not surprisingly, The Prophet's Camel Bell presents a portrait of imperialists and colonized. She begins with the admission that she had come to Africa with a confirmed prejudice "that the overwhelming majority of Englishmen in colonies could properly be classified as imperialists, and [her] feeling about imperialism was very simple—[she] was against it."[3] Laurence believed that she was not of their ilk and that the Africans would clearly see the difference. At the end of her odyssey, however, by recognizing the colonialist in herself, she understands: "This was something of an irony for me, to have started out in righteous disapproval of the empire-builders, and to have been forced at last to recognize that I, too, had been of that company" (p. 228).

If she discovers the colonialist in herself, she finds as well, in the African colonial history, a parallel to her experience as a Canadian. In conversation with Donald Cameron, she further explains the similar "pattern" of her African and Canadian writing: "I was dealing with something which was just as much a Canadian theme and just as much a personal theme: the whole process of every human individual coming to terms with your own past . . . and getting to the point where you can see yourself as a human individual no longer blaming the past . . . but finding a way to live with your own past. . . . This kind of inner freedom has been a continuing theme."[4] If Laurence was a colonialist, her sympathy is with the colonized whose struggle for emotional freedom forms the structural principle of her subsequent fiction.

And, as she explains in "Sources," an essay she wrote for *Mosaic's* issue on "Manitoba in Literature: An Issue on Literary Environment," having witnessed the African writers' "exploration of the past," when she came to write about her "own people, [her] own place of belonging," she found "the pattern" was the same.[5] Her experience of African colonialism, then, clarified her understanding of Canada and, by extension, of herself.

Thus, as she explains in "Sources," when she began in the early 1960s to write about Canada, she expressed her "continuing theme" by "approaching [her] background and [her] past through [her] grandparents' generation, the generation of pioneers of Scots-Presbyterian origin" (p. 81). As a result, *The Stone Angel* explores the pioneer, the colonial, past of both Laurence and Canada; not surprisingly for a person who could identify with both colonized and colonizer in African politics, Laurence approaches her protagonist, Hagar Shipley, with feelings she describes in another reflective essay, "Ten Years' Sentences," as "ambiguous . . . because I resent her authoritarian outlook, and yet I love her, too, for her battling."[6]

Laurence's own struggle, which she wages in her creation of heroines in conflict, is to come to terms with her maternal grandfather, the dominant, colonialist figure in her childhood. She tells Cameron that he appears as Grandfather Connor in the collection of short stories, *A Bird in the House* (1971), and she explains the conjunction of actual ancestor, fictional character and herself: "My grandfather . . . was a terrible old man . . . who had an enormous sense of his own independence. . . . I really hated him as a kid . . . but when I got to the end of those stories I realized that . . . I was an awful lot like him in this way . . . because that very tenacity which he had, I also had. . . . I do not want to be an authoritarian figure as he was, but I recognize that, like Hagar, there is a good deal of the matriarch in me. . . . I don't think I ever would have known those things about myself if I hadn't written *The Stone Angel* and *A Bird in the House*" (p. 99). The mature narrator's conclusion to this book echoes Laurence's dual response to African politics: "I had feared and fought the old man, yet he proclaimed himself in my veins."[7]

Laurence's personal exorcism seems to have struck a chord in the Canadian populace for, as she explains to Clara Thomas and Irving Layton, "Canadians saw [Hagar] as their grandmother."[8] The "matriarch," who is at the same time a victim, is a figure with whom Canadians, colonized as they still were in 1964, could readily identify. Certainly one does not need Laurence's extratextual comments to realize the political implications of Hagar's personal experience. The dates corresponding to major events in Hagar's life suggest that Laurence is aware of the historical dimension of her novel. In the time present, Hagar is ninety years of age, and through a series of flashbacks, she relives her past. Laurence deliberately divides these flashbacks into three stages: the years before, during and after her marriage. Hagar's first son is seventeen when World War I breaks out; thus he is born in 1897. Since there is a ten years' difference between her sons, John is born in 1907.

Hagar, born in 1870 and married in 1894, leaves her husband when John is twelve, in 1919. John dies in the middle years of the Depression, and Hagar ends her recollections with a brief reference to the many sons lost in World War II. Each period covers a quarter-century: Hagar marries when she is twenty-four; she lives with Bram Shipley for twenty-four years; and the third period of her reminiscences covers the twenty-five years between the two World Wars.

These three periods of Hagar's past correspond with three stages in Canada's development as a nation. British troops, after quelling the Red River uprising, finally left in 1871 and the building of an independent nation under Sir John A. Macdonald proceeded; in 1870 and 1871, respectively, Manitoba and British Columbia joined Confederation. This period ended with the ascension of the Liberals under Sir Wilfrid Laurier in 1896. The Liberals completed the task of Macdonald's national policy, aided by a rise in prosperity and national confidence, but undermined by imperial questions which culminated in the 1917 election wherein the French and English were split as never before; fighting as a member of the British Empire had dismembered Canadian unity. And the period between the wars was that of the Great Depression. These three periods, therefore, contained the economic conditions of depression, followed by prosperity and depression, as well as the political conditions of union and separation.

The memories of Hagar, whose life spans the history of Canada before the renewed nationalism of the early 1960s, end in the mid–1930s on the Depression prairies with the death of her favorite son, John, when she herself was "transformed to stone" (p. 243). Hagar, in the time present, is a ninety-year-old "matriarch," as harsh and life-denying as she has ever been. Her past, which she recalls in flashbacks, demonstrates the tremendous cost of survival in the world of the Canadian frontier. W. L. Morton, a historian who Clara Thomas speculates has influenced Laurence's thinking,[9] argues quite convincingly in his 1961 essays on *The Canadian Identity*, that "Canadian life . . . is marked by a northern quality, the strong seasonal rhythms . . . the wilderness venture . . . the return from the lonely savagery of the wilderness to the peace of the home . . . the puritanical restraint which masks the psychological tensions set up by the contrast of wilderness roughness and home discipline."[10] Hagar's time present, in conjunction with her memories, explores the strengths and the weaknesses inherited from this communal past. As Laurence concludes in "Sources," Hagar "is very much a person who belongs in the same kind of prairie Scots-Presbyterian background as I do, and it was, of course, people like Hagar who created that background, with all its flaws and its strengths . . . and this is the place we are standing on, for better and for worse" (p. 84).

As the publication date of Morton's book and the great popularity of *The Stone Angel* indicate, Canadians in the early 1960s were greatly interested in their past and its influence on their present, in this "place we are standing on." Indicative of this preoccupation was the 1958 election of John George Diefenbaker with the largest majority ever accorded a leader in Canadian history. Not only did Diefenbaker present Canadians with a vision of developing a great nation of the North; he also evoked Canada's pioneer past— sixty-two when he became prime minister, he was proud of his family's settlement in Saskatchewan, and profoundly impressed by the prairie dwellers' determination. His frontier experience, like Hagar's, evoked immediate interest.

The first period of Hagar's reminiscences of her Canadian past, the years of her childhood and adolescence which culminate in her marriage, focuses both on her fear of the female image required of her by the pioneer community much like that of Diefenbaker's past and on her subsequent assumption of the masculine toughness required by her society. In the "uncouth land" of Manitoba, the "feeble ghost" of Hagar's mother, who died giving her life, becomes in Hagar's mind a symbol of feminine weakness (p. 3). When Hagar is asked by her brother to assume her mother's role in order to comfort their dying brother Dan, Hagar "stiffened" in resistance, the "frailty" of the "meek woman" being too threatening a role for Hagar (p. 25). This early denial of a compassionate pose costs Hagar much torment, for she desired "above all else to do the thing he asked, [but was] unable to bend enough" (p. 25); it is to "stoney" Hagar as much as to her mother's tombstone that the title of the novel refers.

Likewise, the concept of "angel" helps to explain why Hagar at least attempts to act benevolently. The expectation that woman be "The Angel in the House"—to use the title of Coventry Patmore's popular poem of the Victorian era—was a subtle way of glorifying the subservient position of woman as wife and mother.[11] The spiritual and moral pedestals upon which women were placed in the nineteenth century were devices by which the society, organized for the benefit of males, kept women in their colonized place. Laurence specifies this colonial implication when Hagar remarks that her "mother's angel" was "bought in pride" by her father, Jason Currie, in order to "proclaim his dynasty" (p. 3). Men, in dominating women, dehumanized them; "angels" were, inevitably, "stone."

Laurence thus quite deliberately sets the twenty-five years of Hagar's formative years in the era of dynasty-making under the aggressive, almost ruthless, economic policies of Sir John A. Macdonald. In his tough drive to unite the provinces from sea to sea by rail, Macdonald strove to establish the "Kingdom of Canada," a nation founded on the same principles and institutions as Britain but independent of her. The foundations of this new nation, in Macdonald's "National Policy," determined that the country would be forged, almost arbitrarily, by the power of economics. Although Macdonald's promise to British Columbia to build a railway within ten years of its joining Confederation was not fulfilled within the designated period, the railway was nevertheless completed and the nation's territory was satisfactorily extended. Into this society Hagar is born and from it she learns the inevitability of masculine domination.

Jason Currie, like Macdonald, strives for progress, expansion and a personal fortune on the basis of man's labor; while he outwardly prizes a respectable gentility in women, he inwardly despises their frailty and meek subservience to social conventions. Such ambivalence, discussed by Anna Jameson in 1837, is reflected in an inscription on one of the Manawaka tombstones—"Rest in peace./ From toil, surcease. / Regina Weese. / 1866"— and Hagar's memory of Regina Weese as a "flimsy gutless creature, bland as egg custard" (p. 4). The fact that Regina's name means "queen" emphasizes the irony of her subservient position, an irony like that in the phrase "angel in the house." A further political irony of the name Regina rests in its reminder that Victoria Regina ruled during those early years of Confederation and, as Ged Martin recently pointed out in "Queen Victoria and Canada," was actively involved in the decisions which forged the nation.[12]

The negative effects of colonization are revealed in Hagar's repression of her masculine and feminine qualities. As the country is brought under the "peace, order and good government" of Ottawa, Hagar too conforms outwardly to the "neat and orderly" image expected of women (p. 5), but in the process, she rejects the loving nurture of her innate femininity. Although she "didn't want to resemble him in the least," she nevertheless "take[s] after" her father, "sturdy like him . . . [with] his hawkish nose and stare that could meet anyone's without blinking an eyelash" (p. 8). Jason Currie praises her for her "backbone" and remarks surreptitiously to his housekeeper, "smart as a whip, she is . . . if only she'd been—" (p. 14). Hagar overhears and understands his unspoken thoughts that her admirable qualities are those masculine traits which are sadly lacking in Currie's own sons who "took after our mother, graceful unspirited boys" (p. 7).

Repression of the feminine, of all "natural" emotions of love and nurture, in individuals as in society as a whole, leads inevitably to perversion of both feminine and masculine impulses. Indeed, the unnatural development of Hagar's masculine qualities and her concomitant aversion to her femininity can be explored further from such a specifically psychological perspective as that of Karen Horney's 1926 paper entitled "Inhibited Femininity," republished in 1967, at a time of growing interest, in Feminine Psychology. Horney explores the origins of the "masculinity complex of woman," that "complex of feelings and fantasies that have for their content the woman's feeling of being discriminated against, her envy of the male, her wish to be a man and to discard the female role."[13] Horney discovers several factors in the childhood of the female which contribute to this complex, the two most significant being those predominant in Hagar's society: the valuation of the male and the perceived "notion that the woman's position is precarious and one of danger." The little girl turns "away altogether from the female role and take[s] refuge in a fictitious masculinity for the sake of security" (p. 79).

If Hagar makes herself a good "son," she also conforms to the patriarchal requirements of a daughter; despite her instinctive need to leave her father's house when she is twenty-one, Hagar "stayed and kept [her] father's accounts, played hostess for him, chatted diplomatically to guests, did all he expected (p. 45). Hagar's observance of the female role "expected" of her is a "diplomatic" necessity; victimized by her father because of her inferior sex and age, she responds by imitating and appeasing him, by "tak[ing] after" him as a son while "play[ing] hostess for him" as a daughter.

The political analogue of this psycho-sexual confusion is the Canadian "love" of things British, a point which Laurence makes when she has Currie send Hagar "East" to learn "how to dress and behave like a lady" (p. 43). Laurence reveals here an interior form of colonialism in Canada, for the westerner sees "down East" as a settled and prosperous, a culturally superior, region. But the vague reference of "East" points as well to the imperial seat of culture and politics for nineteenth-century Canada, Great Britain, and reminds the reader that in the three decades following Confederation, Macdonald's Conservative party was attempting to forge a nation on the British model, partly in defensive response to American republicanism and its loud, frequent calls for the liberation of the colonized peoples to the north.

Thus, too, the economic language describing Hagar upon her return from the eastern finishing school establishes the economic basis of Currie's personal, like Macdonald's national, dreams. While Hagar stands before her father, she feels "a thing and his"; Currie pronounces the end product "worth every penny. . . . You're a credit to me" (p. 43). In the five years following Confederation, the Macdonald government acted swiftly to ensure the future of the nation, buying up the Hudson's Bay lands, making British Columbia a province long before it had sufficient population to warrant such status and promising economic links with the East by means of the railroad. W. L. Morton emphasizes, in his historical study of the formation of Canada, *The Kingdom of Canada* (1963), Macdonald's great spending and skillful political maneuvering which succeeded in buying the nation into being.[14]

The cost of Macdonald's relentlessness, however, is not measured so much by the political repercussions of the Pacific Scandal, but by the 1885 use of the railway, built with the intention of uniting the country, to transport Canadian militiamen to Saskatchewan to crush the Riel rebellion. Colonization is domination by force; white, male technology and economic and military might overpowered Canada's natives and "virgin" nature. Such racial discrimination is reflected in the novel when Currie refuses to allow "any son of his" to go "gallivanting around the country with a half-breed" (p. 20). As Hagar is "antimacassared" to become a "thing and his," so the wilderness and the native people of Canada are massacred to become a "Victorian," British-styled "Kingdom of Canada."

Hagar, not surprisingly, perpetuates her father's colonizing compulsion in her marriage to Brampton Shipley. Shipley, looking like "a bearded Indian" (p. 45) and associating "with half-breed girls" (p. 47), threatens her refined and repressed instincts. She sets about to remake Shipley not just in her own image, but also in her father's. As the finishing school in the East had fitted her into the "costume" her father desired, so she imagines Shipley "rigged out in a suit of gray soft as a dove's breast-feathers" (p. 45) and her father's approval "when he saw how Brampton Shipley prospered, gentled, learned cravats and grammar" (p. 50). As Macdonald strove to forge a British nation in Canada, it is Hagar's intention to turn her husband into a refined, "Eastern," facsimile of her father.

The twenty-four years of Hagar's marriage, which ends just after World War I, show her, while leaving home to establish her own family, continuing, in fact, to be her father's daughter. This period in her history corresponds to that of Canada, "of age" as an independent country, still dominated by British political issues. Laurier continued Macdonald's policy of building a nation equal in status to Great Britain; however, the issue of imperialism ultimately divided Laurier's party and the country. The governing principle of Laurier's leadership was the maintenance of national unity in the face of divisive threats, especially that of the conflict between English and French. Nevertheless, the Boer War, the rising threat of Germany, and finally World War I forced Canada to commit herself to participation in what the French-Canadians saw as British concerns. Canada's decision to side with the Empire in World War I brought about the defeat of the Laurier Liberals and the racial split which Laurier fought so hard to avoid. The same irony recurs in *The Stone Angel* when John, son of British Hagar and "Indian" Bram, turns against his mother's domineering love and her expectation that he display the "get-up-and-go" of his grandfather, and retreats to his father's "coarse way" with women (p. 174).

Siding with the British in foreign conflicts, then, led to disunity in the Dominion; Hagar's overinvolvement with her father and his code of behavior contributes, even before the destruction of her relationship with her beloved John, to the breakdown of her marriage. Taught by Currie's society to value male strength, Hagar's sexual response to Bram is that of frigidity, as "stoney" as her "angelic" acceptance of patriarchal domination: "I never let him know. . . . and I made certain that the trembling was all inner. . . . I prided myself upon keeping my pride intact, like some maidenhead" (p. 81). Denying her sensuality, she can at most conform outwardly to the role expected of her. Imagining herself upon marriage as "chatelaine" of the Shipley place (p. 51), she finds herself the day after her wedding "work[ing] and scrubb[ing] the house . . . as though . . . driven by a whip" (p. 52). She "worked like a dray horse thinking: *At least nobody will ever be able to say I didn't keep a clean house*" (p. 112). And, at harvest time, she "served the food . . . never letting on how I felt about it, Hagar Currie serving a bunch of breeds and ne'er-do-wells and Galacians" (p. 114). Ever her father's daughter, Hagar evinces a colonizer's disgust for people she sees to be of inferior race and, even more, for herself when she, of the "inferior" sex, is forced to serve them.

Hagar, this demoted "chatelaine," is ninety before she is able to see beneath her sense of social respectability to the psychological problems— her devaluation of her erotic nature and dissatisfaction with her subservient female role—which originated from this very respectability which required her to accept her society's male superiority and domination. Only at the point of death is she able to recognize, in her memories, the missed opportunities and frustrated potential in her relationship with Bram; she realizes that Shipley was "the only person close to me who ever thought of me by name" rather than by her social roles of "daughter . . . sister . . . mother" (p. 80). Again, the source of her inhibited femininity, as she intimates, lies in social opinion: "People thought of things differently in those days. . . . I never spoke of it to anyone" (p. 81). The symbol of her social pretensions intrudes into the bedroom of the Shipley place; her "black leather traveling trunk . . . [with her] former name on it in neat white paint, *Miss H. Currie*" (p. 80) proclaims her continued "maidenhood," her acquiescence to her father's concept of socially creditable but unfulfilled femininity.

Hagar's continued references to eastern influences are but one of the vehicles by which Laurence suggests the wider political dimensions of her protagonist's personal experience. National disunity and the loss of a generation of men were the legacy of Canada's involvement in "foreign" wars; Laurence repeats this national dilemma in the breakup of Hagar's marriage and the loss of her sons. The final section of her reminiscence spans the twenty-five years between World War I and World War II. We can conveniently label this period of Hagar's story "matriarchal," for once free of Shipley's disturbing but potentially liberating love, she recreates, in her relationships with her sons, her father's destructive "patriarchal" role. As the direct result of her authoritarian nature, Hagar loses both her sons. While the eldest, Marvin, enlists underage in World War I, never to return to his mother's home, the novel reaches its apotheosis in the relationship between Hagar and her favorite son, John, whose death is but the last estrangement in a history of "lost men" (p. 6).

The psycho-social origin of this destruction of a Canadian man of John's time derives, again, from the patriarchal legacy. He is the natural product of colonizer and colonized; in John as in Canadian society of the time, the two camps could no more coexist as equals than could male and female. Hagar's possessive love for John precludes her recognition of his separate identity, much less of her husband's share in their children's heritage. When the infant John is brought to her, she notices he has "black hair . . . black as my own . . . forgetting for the moment that Bram was black-haired too" (p. 122). Hagar repeatedly connects the objects of her love, stressing to John that it is "a great pity your grandfather never saw you, for you're a boy after his own heart" (p. 123). Hagar is "stone" blind to the rich potential of the present when John expresses interest in "where Bram had been born" (p. 125) and Bram answers, "In a barn. I thought you'd have told been [sic] that by now. Me and Jesus. Eh, Hagar?" Hagar, refusing to see any humor or meaning in Shipley's origins, ignores both John's need to understand his relationship with his father and the saving power in Shipley's spirit.

Hagar forces her psychologically damaging colonialist attitudes on John throughout his childhood, telling him not only of his dead grandfather, but also of his Scottish ancestry, giving him the "Currie plaid-pin" which she had received from her father, and exposing him to European art in a determined, though undoubtedly unconscious, act of cultural imperialism. She never acknowledges her colonized child's need for self-determination, just as she rejected the vital spirit and natural independence of Shipley, whom she treated as her social and racial inferior. She attempts to shape John, as she had Bram, into her own image, as she herself had been made the stone angel of her father's image.

Hagar displays the same type of colonialist mentality which came under attack in the writings of Frances Brooke and Anna Jameson, as she devalues the details of her prairie life on the basis of the standards inculcated by her father and the Eastern finishing school. Brooke and Jameson both cautioned against such behavior, suggesting that "eastern" conventions should not govern human relationships in the New World; settlement in Canada held the opportunity for creating a new social order molded, as Traill argued, to the "circumstances" of life in the backwoods. Hagar's inability to adapt forces her to flee her marriage and Manitoba; she takes John and moves to the more "British," urban life of Vancouver where she can live as a genteel spinster.

The central political event in 1919, the year of their move, was the Winnipeg General Strike, the culmination of the growing labor revolt, against social and regional inequities, which made labor a political force. But, as Morton explains in *The Kingdom of Canada*, during the 1920s and 1930s, the conservative public and government, fearing repetition of the Revolution in Russia, made internal security, including spying on revolutionaries, a responsibility of the Royal Canadian Mounted Police, and passed Section 98 into the Criminal Code to allow the government to act against any " 'unlawful associations' without the usual restraints imposed by Canadian law" (p. 431).

In this light, Hagar's spying on John's "association" with half-breeds and his rebellion against her "restraints" take on political overtones. In his affair with Arlene Simmons, "doing it . . . on [Hagar's] Toronto couch in broad daylight" (p. 208), John rejects her sexual constraints, her Eastern standards of behavior and, in that the Simmons family is socially inferior to the Curries, her British pride of class. Hagar plots to separate the young couple, finding in the Depression scarcity of jobs ready cause for her interference; she asserts, "the money's the main concern," and demonstrates this conviction with the horrifying picture of John's future "living on relief, perhaps with children" (p. 211). Hagar, as "depressed" as her time in history, rejects his self-determination and his assumption of the adult responsibilities of parentage. That the young lovers' deaths result directly from Hagar's destructive unconscious is symbolized in her sleepless vigil and her fantasy that "some hobo who had ridden the rods this far and wanted food and lodging, a despairing man, perhaps . . . might be tempted to ransack the house" (pp. 238–39). Her personal guilt manifests its political dimension in the fact that the threatening figure in her fantasy was a central image of the "despairing" Depression years, a "hobo," one whom the colonizing class feared would "ransack" and overthrow the patriarchal "house."

Hagar's retrospective narration ends at this point with her brief conjecture that John would probably have died anyway in World War II, which points to Canada's next loss of a generation of men. The years between his death and the time present are not, for her, worthy of consideration because, "that night he died, [her] son died," Hagar was "transformed to stone" (pp. 242–43). Canada, too, was an angel turned to stone in that, during the 1950s, Louis St. Laurent failed to meet the challenges of a new age; he delayed implementation of the Massey Commission's recommendation on the formation of a Canada Council and he did not pursue the adoption of a distinctively Canadian flag. St. Laurent and C. D. Howe concentrated instead on developing the economy of the country—"the money's the main concern"—but in so doing, they ignored the threat to independence by giving increasing control of the Canadian economy to Americans. Canadians seemed unconcerned for, as Betty Friedan has observed about the conditions in American society which contributed to the creation of "the feminine mystique," the returning war veterans and the war-weary population desired the peace and security of a prosperous lifestyle which forced women to return to the home, to the victimized acceptance of the belief that femininity was fulfilled through their social roles as wives and mothers.[15] In the 1950s, Canada and Canadian women seemed petrified in their passive acceptance of the legacy of colonialized grandmothers such as Hagar Shipley.

One can speculate on the national implications of Hagar's colonized identity in 1960 as opposed to Stacey MacAindra's liberation in Laurence's 1969 novel, *The Fire-Dwellers*. From her beginning, Canada has been formed and governed by older men, father figures, from Sir John A. Macdonald to Laurier and "King," "uncle" Louis in the 1950s and finally Diefenbaker and Lester Pearson. During the 1960s, on the other hand, Canadians, in the process of throwing off such "governors," fervently embraced the youngest man ever elected prime minister, Pierre Trudeau.

The early 1960s were characterized by political and cultural soul-searching.

Public confidence in Diefenbaker waned, partly because of his scandalous mismanagement. At a deeper level, as Robert Bothwell, Ian Drummond and John English point out, "Canadians were embarrassed by their conservative reputations."[16] In the United States, the youthful, flamboyant leadership of John F. Kennedy, the youngest man ever elected president, seemed to be a harbinger of an American renaissance. In comparison, Diefenbaker seemed "locked in the prison of his own past and his narrow beliefs" (p. 263). The ambivalence felt by Canadians toward Diefenbaker and by extension their pioneer heritage was reflected in the series of minority governments elected under Lester Pearson from 1963 to 1968; Canadians could not wholly expurgate Diefenbaker and the past, nor could they unhesitatingly endorse Pearson's leadership. As Claude Bissell has noted in the first essay of *The Literary History of Canada* (1976), "at the opening of the 1960s, Canadians were aware that a new political age had begun, although its contours were still vague."[17] The publication of *The Stone Angel*, about a woman "locked in the prison of [her] own past," was extremely timely.

By 1969 when Laurence published *The Fire-Dwellers*, the Canadian political situation had drastically altered. A sense of nationalism climaxed in the Centennial celebrations, the 1967 Montreal World Exposition and the 1968 election of a majority government under Trudeau. Trudeau, with his cosmopolitan flaunting of conventional mores, stirred Canadians with his vision of creating in Canada a Just Society which would be a model for the rest of the world. As George Woodcock notes in his *Canada and the Canadians* (1973), Trudeau "provided, as Diefenbaker did in the previous decade, a vehicle for the idea of themselves as a nation that was stirring among Canadians of all origins. He continued the work done by Expo in the previous year, the work of self-revelation by which Canadians were beginning to see themselves, no longer . . . under some overwhelming shadow of France or Britain or America, but rather as a people capable of originality, adventurousness, radical-minded, open to the future."[18] For Canadians at the end of the decade, in Woodcock's phrase, "the image . . . was one of liberation."

Accompanying the volatile politics and growing nationalism of the 1960s was increasing agitation, by the Women's Liberation Movement, for women's rights in society. Highly influential texts were published: the English translation of Simone de Beauvoir's *The Second Sex* in 1961; Betty Friedan's *The Feminine Mystique* in 1963 and Kate Millet's *Sexual Politics* in 1969. Judith Hole and Ellen Levine, in their *Rebirth of Feminism* (1971), record how the women's movement began in the early 1960s as a response to these books and the American civil rights movement; in 1968, women from both countries convened in Chicago for the "first national [sic] women's liberation conference."[19] The consciousness-raising of women reached Canada at about the same time as the more indigenous social phenomenon, Trudeaumania. Both movements signalled revolutionary changes in Canadian society.

Reflecting—but also questioning—this cultural scene is Laurence's characterization in *The Fire-Dwellers* of Stacey MacAindra, a woman who strives for freedom from her domestic trap but ultimately elects to stay within the traditional roles of wife and mother. In the late 1960s, Canada and many of her female citizens strained, not entirely successfully, to break out of past molds; the political implication of *The Fire-Dwellers* is that Canada and Canadian women must come to terms with, and not simply reject, their pasts. Says Laurence to Bernice Lever: "a great many of the protagonists in my books . . . find it's not a total freedom that they achieve, that there is no such thing. What they achieve is . . . a great deal more understanding of themselves."[20]

The Fire-Dwellers is even less overtly political than *The Stone Angel*. Indeed, as it tells of the domestic life of Stacey MacAindra, a thirty-nine-year-old housewife living in Vancouver with her husband of sixteen years, Mac, and their four children, Katie, Ian, Duncan, and Jen, *The Fire-Dwellers* seems, on first reading, to resemble such lightweight women's novels as Constance Beresford-Howe's *The Marriage Bed* (1982). There are no grand adventures beyond everyday events, no clearly defined political or social themes. Nevertheless, oblique references are made to the world outside the fiction. Mac takes a job selling a vitamin product and, while he works long hours trying to succeed with the new company, Stacey worries that he is wasting his life selling such a questionable American commodity. Stacey spends most of her time trying to cope with her restless children and tired husband; her own battle is ostensibly with alcohol, but actually it is against the boredom of her traditional life as housewife.

Certainly this first-person narration uses some of the language of the Women's Liberation Movement. Stacey is addicted to the popular magazines' self-help articles which she asserts are "articles . . . written by male anarchists";[21] Friedan reports her discovery that the 1950s "image of woman as housewife-mother has been largely created by writers and editors who are men" (p. 47). Stacey rebels against this identity, against being known "only as Mac's wife or the kids' mother" (p. 95). Despite her love for the children, she also feels incompetent as a mother. Unlike Hagar who prided herself on her orderly housekeeping, Stacey gets "bloody sick of trying to cope. I don't want to be a good wife and mother" (p. 174). When her lover, Luke, jokes that she looks like "a woman who . . . makes good pastry," Stacey quips back that "it sounds like an insult" (p. 179). Voicing the cry of many housewives, Stacey exclaims, "I don't have any time for myself" (p. 172). She is a woman of her time, seeking liberation.

But Stacey's limited success derives not from political changes effected by the Women's Liberation Movement, but from her own inner resources; unlike Hagar, she is in touch with her emotions, her unconscious, and her feminine qualities of relatedness. She has, concludes Laurence in "Sources," "some human warmth and ability to reach out and touch others . . . to change and to move into new areas of life" (p. 83). Thus, the novel goes beyond the conventional rhetoric and political solutions of the Women's Liberation Movement to probe the psyche of this particular woman and her self-liberation.

Critical reaction to *The Fire-Dwellers* indicates that many readers cannot see this. In her bibliographical essay on Laurence, Helen M. Buss observes that "this novel is the most neglected of Laurence's Canadian works in terms of individual critical consideration."[22] The reviewers seemed to be afraid or unable to take a firm stand on this "woman's novel," implying that Laurence is naive in finding meaning in a housewife's mundane life. Laurence, in turn, took issue with such criticisms in conversation with Graeme Gibson: "*The Fire-Dwellers* received some real put-downs from a number of male reviewers. They didn't even say it was a bad novel; it was just that if anybody like Stacey existed, they just would rather not know" (p. 200). The *Times Literary Supplement* dismissed this "extremely depressing funny novel"; the un-named reviewer felt that Stacey would benefit from "a short course" at the "institute in California which trains unhappy couples to quarrel properly."[23] This evasive sarcasm indicates the reviewer's defensive rejection of a novel which is difficult and unsettling to read.

F. W. Watt's 1969 review in the *Canadian Forum*, however, is more subtle in its blame by praise: "This book contains flaws enough to sink half a dozen books by lesser novelists."[24] The problem is that Stacey is "merely a middle-class mother of four." Watt then praises Laurence's talent because readers "learn to care about her and come to believe that what she thinks and feels and tries to do matters." Laurence, he claims, gives fresh "vision and insight even with the stale material" she has chosen. Watt simply dislikes Stacey's "perpetual chatter of complaint and self-mortification"; he finds the "rich, poignant emotional existence of the spinster-teacher in *A Jest of God*" far more artistically successful. His preference for the latter novel supports Laurence's contention, expressed in her interview with Lever, that male reviewers "found Stacey threatening . . . [whereas] Hagar . . . was an old woman, she was too far removed from them, and Rachel . . . was a spinster, you know, pathetic, they didn't have to worry about her. But Stacey was a wife and mother, and if their own wives and mothers had thoughts like hers they just didn't want to know about them" (p. 37).

As both woman and writer, Phyllis Gotlieb expresses "relief" and "heartfelt thanks" that Laurence has produced such a "whole woman" in Stacey. Yet Gotlieb would seem to agree with Watt that the "territory" of the novel is too limited, that Laurence's "material is easily available and explored and mapped without much artistic risk; it is limited and cannot be expanded."[25] This review, like the others, is riddled with such ambivalent, even contra-dictory, phrases.

Buss is therefore right to question why "Stacey, representative as she is of the millions like her in the Canadian population, receives little comment from those sociologically-oriented critics who see Laurence as defining the

Canadian identity" (p. 9). The source of such indifference apparently lies in the widespread feeling that the housewife, the mother, cannot be suitable material for artistic vision, for comparison to weighty issues such as national identity. Laurence seems to have anticipated such reaction when she has Stacey declare, "if I could only talk about it. But who wants to know, and anyway, could I say?" (p. 17). This defensiveness stems, one must assume, from the inculcated assumption that women, housewives, are of "low . . . human worth." This is the same internalized value which Shulamith Firestone, in Hole and Levine, cites as the reason most women never try to change their social position (p. 228).

Buss's challenge can be answered if one adopts, for instance, the critical approach which Ken Hughes takes to *A Jest of God* (1966); Stacey, like her sister Rachel, then becomes an embodiment of "a post-colonial Canada moving uncertainly yet with hope onto the stage of the world."[26] *The Fire-Dwellers* extends this national analogy into a study of the liberation of the North American housewife; Laurence explores in fiction what *The Feminine Mystique* studied in specifically political and sociological terms. In her article "Ivory Tower or Grassroots?: The Novelist As Socio-political Being," Laurence explicitly connects her "feelings of anti-imperialism, anti-colonialism, anti-authoritarianism" and her "growing awareness of the dilemma and powerlessness of women, the tendency of women to accept male definition of ourselves, to be self-deprecating and uncertain, and to rage inwardly."[27] Distraught at the possibility that one of her sons narrowly missed being hit by a car, Stacey resists the impulse to shower him with affection. "Restraint," she cautions, "some wise *guy* is always telling you how you're sapping the national strength" (p. 14; emphasis mine). This socially accepted aphorism, suggesting that it is in the male interest to suppress the woman's natural impulse, repeats the political position of *The Stone Angel*.

As Laurence tells Lever, her work is not simply allegorized theory: "I'm very pro women's movement but at the same time I would never write a book simply to advance a cause" (p. 9). While Stacey remains an autonomous character of fiction, like Laurence's other protagonists, she nevertheless demonstrates a cornerstone of women's liberation theory and practice, which, according to Hole and Levine, is the "process of relating the personal to the political," that is, realizing that the individual woman's situation has "a social cause and probably a political solution" (p. 125).

In fact, Stacey continually "relates" her individual problems to larger "social causes" and "political solutions." The title of one of those articles, which she so compulsively reads, written by men for women's magazines: "Nine Ways the Modern Mum May Be Ruining Her Daughter" (p. 14), pinpoints the primary focus of *The Fire-Dwellers*' psychological exploration: mother-daughter relationships in both the past and the present. Stacey, as she worries about her interaction with her daughter, remembers her relationship with her own mother. Elizabeth Waterston points out in her *Survey*

(1973) that in the women's literature of the late 1960s, the "device of setting different generations of women in contrast to each other ... focuses the problem of women's roles, women's status, and women's potential."[28] Indeed, Stacey's position is at the center of three such generations: "I stand in relation to my life both as child and as parent ... whichever way I look, God, it looks pretty confusing to me" (p. 47). She has no clear knowledge of herself as a woman, perhaps because the roles of mother and daughter continue to prove so ambiguous.

The only defined female role model in Stacey's life is negative. Mrs. Cameron, as presented in the flashbacks of the novel and her more fully developed portrait in A Jest of God, is a woman very similar to Hagar in her respectability, her class-consciousness and her lack of honesty and affection. As Denyse Forman and Uma Parameswaran correctly note, in Manawaka "the watchword is conformity. ... This code of behavior entails a repression of the life force. Feelings are replaced by pseudo-intellect and shallow rationalizations. Mrs. Cameron is a staunch conformist."[29] As a teenager, Stacey fought the demands that she be ladylike by fleeing to dances "every Saturday night, jitterbugging. Knowing by instinct how to move, loving the boy's closeness, whoever he was, loving the male smell of him" (p. 12). Between Stacey and her mother lies the conflict of decorum and the "life force" of passion.

The ominous presence which shapes both their lives is Mr. Cameron, the "town undertaker ... capable only of dressing the dead in between bouts with his own special embalming fluid" (p. 8). Mrs. Cameron, whose upstairs gentility depends upon his buried death-in-life, proves the destructiveness of the interiorization, the acceptance of masculine values in her dependence on "codeine and phenobarb" (p. 302) and her never-ending, whining criticisms of her daughters. Her resemblance to Hagar gives credence to Laurence's description in "Ten Years' Sentences" of Stacey as Hagar's "spiritual grand-daughter" (p. 15). These Manawaka women demonstrate the negative result of traditional socialization; Stacey predicts, "if I live to be ninety, I'll be positively venomous" (p. 81).

Stacey realizes that she is repeating the image of motherhood propagated by her mother. Over the course of the novel she is struck several times with a sense of déjà vu, as she argues with her daughter as her mother had argued with her about habits of dressing, drinking and dating. In the midst of one such argument Stacey questions why she keeps on trying to set "a good example. Example of what? All the things I hate. Hate, but perpetuate" (p. 5). She feels "it's my duty to appear to be doing my duty, that's all," and dismisses her maternal role as "a farce" (p. 46).

The difficulties of communicating with her own children force her to understand that while her mother might have seemed to have "the consolation of believing herself to be unquestionably right about everything," "maybe she didn't either" (p. 302). The acceptance of her ties with her mother is neither easy nor total; she has no answer to the "current pop psychology article... entitled 'Mummy Is the Root of All Evil?' " (p. 304). Whereas Hagar could only flee the image of womanhood presented by her society and protect herself behind a veneer of masculine resolution, Stacey is able to perceive the psychological complexities which create women like Hagar and her mother, and ultimately herself. With this knowledge Stacey discovers the power to free the angel from her house, to communicate her human emotions to her own daughter, and to let her daughter fully enter womanhood: "she's on her own" (p. 302).

Just as Stacey battled with role models from the past, Canadians in the 1960s reacted against restrictions inherited from their ancestors and, by the end of that decade, were forced to accept the complexities of changing their collective image. Despite the growth of national pride, Canada still suffered a tremendous inferiority complex and was only beginning to wrestle with its origins. When George Woodcock founded a journal devoted to criticism of Canadian literature in 1959, there were many academics who openly wondered where he would find enough material to last more than four issues.[30] Reviewing "the Canadian personality" in 1961, Bruce Hutchison wrote: "We are the last people to realize, and the first to deny, the material achievements of the Canadian nation.... The Canadian audience at a political meeting (a significant little test, if the glumest), [is] the most stolid and dead-panned ever known... and our politicians truly reflect us in their stodgy competence."[31] Canadians, to some extent, still perceived themselves as frozen by the past. But that self-image was changing even as Hutchison wrote those words. In fact, his essay is primarily an expression of rising national pride. By the time Laurence published *The Fire-Dwellers*, nationalism had flowered in Expo '67 and the Trudeaumania which swept the country in the following years marked Canada's efforts to change her rather stodgy image to that of a swinging jet-setter. The euphoria of Expo year and Trudeaumania telegraphed to Canadians that their nation, after one hundred years, had finally come into her own.

Artists in all fields attempted to reflect this newfound Canadian nationalism and identity. Laurence herself comments to Gibson on the fact that when she began to publish "we still had... a kind of colonial mentality, a great many people felt that a book written by a Canadian couldn't possibly be good" (p. 200). In the two decades since the war, however, a sizable body of literary work had appeared and what could be called a Canadian literary tradition had been established.[32] The popularity of Canadian artists increased; courses in Canadian literature and history were demanded in universities, colleges and high schools. Not only was *Canadian Literature* still publishing ten years after its founding, but others with the same objectives, such as the *Journal of Canadian Fiction*, were established.

In contrast to such nationalistic positivism, *The Fire-Dwellers* seemed, despite the success of its protagonist in breaking the mold of the patriarchal

social past, to strike a discordant note of insecurity and anxiety. The ambivalence of the reviews suggests, along with a defensiveness about sexual
roles, the possibility that the novel was not at all timely. But as Clara Thomas
recognizes, "with Stacey comes the shock of recognition, and though we
have much preferred to suggest panaceas, from pills to extension courses,
to the hosts of such women, Stacey's voice . . . says, 'ATTENTION MUST
BE PAID.' "[33] In light of what we know now about those nationalistic years,
Laurence actually tapped the national psyche more accurately than Canadians wished to admit at the time. Looking back on the cultural nationalism
of the 1960s, George Woodcock has concluded that it was "a decade of almost
uncharacteristic euphoria"; "economic setbacks, changes in global conditions, threats to our precarious unity, have changed that mood to a more
anxious one."[34]

As well, Laurence was one of the few public commentators of the 1960s
who connected national and feminine issues; she concludes the description
to Gibson of the "colonial mentality" of Canadian publishing: "Women for
a long time in some ways have not only been regarded by men as second-
class citizens—they have even regarded themselves in this way" (p. 200).
Stacey's negative feelings are often projected onto God, the Father whom
she sees oppressing her, forcing her into the divinely ordained role for woman
and rebuking her for failing to conform to its standard. She lashes out at
this patriarchal image: "You try bringing up four kids. . . . Next time you
send somebody down here, get It born as a her with seven young or a him
with a large family and a rotten boss, eh? Then we'll see how the inspirational
bit goes" (p. 168). Stacey, like Hagar, is subject to the patriarchal values of
a God and a father who constantly remind her of her own inferiority. The
psychological conditioning of Canadian women by their patriarchal society
has changed very little from Hagar's time to Stacey's. In her portrait of
Stacey, then, one finds Laurence's analysis of this anxiety which is at once
national and social.

And Laurence, consistent with her habit of connecting women's psychological and social situations with the "state" of Canada as a colonized country,
does argue, in The Fire-Dwellers, the destructiveness of patriarchal values
to both women and Canada. She sets the novel in the city of Vancouver—
named after Captain George Vancouver—in the province of British Columbia—a compilation of British imperialism and American republicanism. Stacey's comment on her personal situation is appropriate to this society:
"Whichever way you look, it seems pretty confusing to me" (p. 47). The
setting is an ironic reminder of Duncan's The Imperialist (1904), in which
Hugh Finlay thought it possible to forge a new identity, individually and
nationally, on the west coast—Stacey, the 1969 variant of woman and country, is a mass of confusion and self-doubt. The beloved landscape of Wilson's
heroines brings no easy solutions to identity quests. Instead of news of

optimistic social programs, and more frequent than fantasies of Edenic scenery north of Vancouver, Stacey hears radio and television reports of war in Southeast Asia and of violence in American cities. Apocryphal wars and rumors of war are nightmare visions which stop only when she musters the courage to face her problems and her past. Laurence challenges the anxieties and naïve self-images of both Canada and her Canadian heroines.

In the late 1960s, however, most Canadians persisted in their dreams of innocence. Along with the strong nationalism, a very conscious anti-American feeling displayed itself; Canadians defined themselves by what they perceived they were not. Mordecai Richler, for example, who in the early 1960s ridiculed Canada for its provincialism, compared Canada to the Americans and concluded that "we are nicer."[35] The nationalism of 1967–68 climaxed at the same time that the United States, escalating the war in Southeast Asia, was strongly criticized by the international community. A little Canadian flag decal on the backpack of a Canadian in Europe brought immediate positive reaction. Furthermore, American cities just across the border from cities in southern Ontario were in flames, as rioters looted many neighborhoods torn by racial strife. Comparatively, Canada seemed to have achieved "peace, order and good government." *The Fire-Dwellers*, however, suggests that beneath Canadians' smug feelings of superiority lies a fear of just such violence.

The political narcissism of Expo year allowed Canadians to ignore the signs of the times, the national troubles growing between the French and English. When Quebec Labour Minister Pierre Laporte was assassinated by the Front de libération du Quebec (FLQ) in October 1970, Canadians awoke to the painful truth that political assassination could happen here. The October Crisis brought home to Canadians the fact that they were not immune from violence, that military rule was not impossible; in retrospect, the threat to Stacey of violence which the Canadian media portrayed as indigenous to some war-torn country in Asia or a strife-ridden city in the United States makes *The Fire-Dwellers* prophetic. Canada no longer seemed a safe place.

Clara Thomas correctly notes, in "The Novels of Margaret Laurence," that Stacey's "internal and external situation[s]" are complexly orchestrated: "Stacey's consciousness is invaded at all times . . . by the horrendous presence of our world's immediate communications system" (p. 59). And the problem of communication between individuals is certainly a major theme as well. Stacey rarely expresses her feelings and thoughts to anyone, least of all her husband. Mac is a threatening enigma, as was her father: "Perhaps it isn't that the masks have been put on, one for each year like the circles that tell the age of a tree. Perhaps they've been gradually peeled off, and what's there underneath is the face that's always been there for me, the unspeaking eyes, the mouth for whom words were too difficult" (p. 170). This image from her unconscious epitomizes her fears of nullity and death, the difficulties of communication between the sexes, the doubts of her own worth as a woman, all of which have their corollary in the images of destruction broadcast to her from a world dominated by Americans.

That Stacey feels threatened both by her father and husband and by Americans suggests a political dimension to her marriage which becomes further evident when one considers Mac's occupation. Salesmanship links him to the drummers of the American frontier, the business entrepreneurs of the American republic. He spends his spare time in his study, alone, isolated from his wife and children. His ambition leads him to compete against his new manager; his fear of failure forces him to use his wife and children to impress his boss with his commitment to the product. Through Mac's characterization Laurence dramatizes the growing influence on Canadians of the American control of the Canadian economy and way of life. Man's domination of woman becomes, in this novel, American domination of Canada.

Mac is typically American, not only in his domination, but also in his isolationism. Stacey complains to her lover: "he doesn't talk any more hardly at all can you imagine what it's like to live in the same house with somebody who doesn't talk or who can't or else won't and I don't know which reason it could be" (p. 197). When Mac accuses her of adultery with his wartime buddy, Buckle Fennick, Stacey attempts to communicate her innocence, but is met with the impersonal male rejection she has always feared, ever since she saw her own father lock himself away from his wife. In a voice which is "almost not his voice at all," Mac tells her, "Leave me alone, can't you? Can't you just *leave me alone*?" (p. 166). He hates her dependence on him and attempts, like the United States throughout its history, to cut himself off from moral and emotional involvement with his satellites.

Tempted to flee this difficult marriage, Stacey longs for an affair with a man so that she "would have done something that belonged only to me, was mine only" (p. 211). As Stacey sits ruminating by the sea, from a nearby "dwelling half-concealed in undergrowth" (p. 170) comes its "occupant" (p. 175), Luke Venturi, wearing "a brown-and-off-white Indian sweater in thick wool with Haida or something motifs of outspread eagle wings and bear masks" (p. 176). He is an escapist alternative to Mac, associated with Indians rather than Americans, less powerful in that he is younger, unthreatening. Luke fits into Stacey's fantasies of escaping to the Cariboo country, for he relates his experiences in the Cariboo and then invites Stacey "to come along and see" it with him. Stacey longs to escape because there are "too many people here, too many crises" (p. 211). The point here is that Canada, like Stacey, may be escapist in turning from her difficult but essential relationship with the United States and in trying to evade her own domination of the Indians by romanticizing them, by "going Indian."

Whereas Hagar in the 1920s retreats from marriage to her "Indian" into British conventions, Stacey, in the late 1960s, chooses to continue the difficult marriage with her "American" husband. While Luke Venturi offered temporary, immature escape, "adventure," he also, as his Christian name after the physician of the Gospels implies, performs a healing role in her emotional life. He encourages her to stop "trying to be a good example" (p. 180), to break out of the mold of "the angel in the house." Laurence makes the connection with *The Stone Angel* explicit when Luke tells a sobbing Stacey, "You're not alone," and she insists "that's where you're wrong" (p. 179)—these same words were exchanged by Hagar and the Rev. Mr. Troy (p. 121). But where Hagar remains ultimately alone, islanded by her lifelong pride, Stacey, through her experience with Luke, learns that, as he insists, "that's where [she is] wrong" (p. 179). In a comment that could be equally addressed to Canadians with their persistent sense of inferiority, Luke admonishes her, "you keep on communicating your own awfulness to yourself, and nothing changes" (p. 192). With his help, Stacey, unlike Hagar, is able to "change" from repression and escapism, to struggle more bravely with the dominant male side in her life, as Canadians must coexist with Americans.

Laurence signals this positive change in Stacey in the final chapters which take place a few months after the affair with Luke. She no longer needs to get drunk. And she and Mac have stopped the sham of sending the children to Sunday school to placate Mac's clergyman-father; the powers of the patriarchal past, which had bedevilled Stacey and Canadian society for so long, have faded. He is only a retired preacher suffering from glaucoma and dizzy spells, uncertain of the success of his past work as a spiritual leader. Stacey can now call Mac's father "dad" for the first time: "Strange—it's only a name now . . . only a way of identifying Matthew" (p. 281). But she is also, in naming Matthew "Dad" and in inviting him to come and live with them, accepting the inevitable omnipresence of her "American" husband's connections.

Stacey's realization, "Temporarily, they are all more or less okay" (p. 308), is the novel's highly tentative resolution; Stacey's future remains as uncertain as that of Canada as, in the late 1960s, she accepted, despite many idealistic left-wing protests, the American presence in every corner of her house. One might conjecture that the unpopularity of this novel resulted in part from the refusal of Canadian literati, with their consistently anti-American radicalism, to accept a protagonist who, in their eyes, capitulates to this less-than-attractive but financially responsible and historically established husband instead of fleeing with her hippie lover to the idealized North. Stacey does not cling to the imperial past, as did the earlier Hagar and her Canada, but she chooses, from her limited options, the most pragmatic. As Laurence tells Gibson, "her real self-discovery was that she was a survivor. She was not going to crack up" (p. 202).

If one looks at Stacey's decision to remain with Mac, not with disappointed idealism, but with a realization of the complexities of North American life, her position can be seen as difficult, but mature. So, too, "Canadian destiny," according to Morton in *Canadian Identity*, "is an evolution in progress" (p. 83). The media reports of world violence remind us that Stacey, like Canada, "is free, within the limits of world power politics, to continue to work our [her] own destiny." But in electing to remain with her family, when she could just as easily have run away, Stacey epitomizes what Morton defines as the essence of the Canadian psyche: "monarchical allegiance. . . . the final governing force in Canada is tradition and convention. . . . Canadian nationhood has . . . put the proposition that association and equality are not incompatible terms, that nations may in free association, by careful definition and great patience, make mutual accommodations of sovereignty without loss of independence" (pp. 85–86).

Laurence's two novels, presenting as they do portraits of a pioneer and of that pioneer's "grandchild," span the first century of Canada's history as a nation. These novels subtly suggest the tremendous changes in Canada's culture and sense of nationalism which occurred during the decade of the 1960s. In both novels—to recall Laurence's comments on the influence of her experience in Africa on her Canadian writing—what is chronicled through a focus on the interior "states" of the protagonists is the emergence of both Canada and Canadian women from their colonial positions. Viewed in this light, Hagar and Stacey show more differences than similarities. Hagar remains totally colonized all her life whereas Stacey overcomes that "psychic" conditioning and achieves some measure of liberation.

In keeping with its future-directed message, *The Fire-Dwellers* is experimental, a postmodern novel, whereas *The Stone Angel* remains as highly structured and traditional in form as its heroine's psyche. The value of change and growth is the hope Laurence posits for women, for Canada and for the novel. This prescription for women, and by extension for the nation in the 1970s, can be discerned in Laurence's growth toward a more feminine form in her writing; the "personal" and the "political" unite as her style moves away from the colonial confines of the masculine novel. In *The Stone Angel*, as Laurence tells Cameron, she attempts to capture the "idiom" of Hagar's generation (p. 113), but the novel's form, the use of first-person narration and the chronological sequence of the flashbacks exhibit the order and control of a masculine mind, as befits a work wherein the main character is, throughout her life, dominated by her father.

The Fire-Dwellers, on the other hand, experiments with a variety of techniques to convey Stacey's emotional reality. Laurence uses interior monologue rather than first-person narration; she eschews chronological structuring of past events in favor of short memory flashes brought on by stimuli in Stacey's present. The result is a montage which more closely approximates the way humans perceive and experience daily life. The novel is loose and open-ended; the fragments and voices in the world around Stacey are there for her to assimilate, and she does manage some acceptance of the chaos, but without total understanding or the illusion of order. Feminine writing, according to Anais Nin, attempts to escape the masculine writer's tendency to use "explicit and direct statement" in order that the writer might "match the way we truly see and feel, in images resembling the sequence of film." The feminine writer tries to break down the concept of distance between author and character in order to see a character "from within."[36] Laurence explains to Cameron that she attempts to portray each heroine in a style reflective of that character; her creative approach is comparable to that of a "method actor, [I] get right inside the role . . . to try and feel my way into their skull in such a way that I respond in the writing the way they would respond" (p. 102). Not only does *The Fire-Dwellers* portray a woman who partially frees herself from her personal colonized situation, at a time when Canada too was pulling away from her colonial past, but also Laurence's technique moves decisively from a masculine to a feminine mode of expression.

Life in Africa taught Laurence about her own colonialism and provided her with the distance to help her understand her Canadian background. When she began to "set down her time and her place," she maintained distance from it by living, during the 1960s, as a divorced mother of two in England. "Living in England," she explains to Margaret Atwood, "convinced me that my real place was in Canada. I was writing from my Canadian background, this is my spiritual home."[37] Subsequently, toward the end of the sixties she returned to Canada more often, first as a writer-in-residence. Then, during the summers she purchased a cottage near Lakefield where she took up permanent residence in 1974. Although she claims that "there is certainly no sense of nationalism in a political sense in my work," Laurence's personal odyssey has given Canadians "a very strong sense of who they are, where they came from and where they may be going." While she makes no overt political statements in her novels, these works are political in that, in Laurence's words, they give "voice to our history, to our legends, to our cultural being."[38] The colonial period, for Margaret Laurence and for Canada, is finished, but not forgotten.

NOTES

1. Margaret Laurence, *The Stone Angel* (1964; Toronto, 1968), p. 34.

2. Laurence is insistent in interviews that her novels are not "directly autobiographical," but she does concede that *A Bird in the House* (1971) is the exception. She tells Graeme Gibson in *Eleven Canadian Novelists* (Toronto, 1972), p. 197, that the short stories are "drawn from my childhood."

3. Margaret Laurence, *The Prophet's Camel Bell* (Toronto, 1963), p. 16.

4. Donald Cameron, *Conversations with Canadian Novelists* (Toronto, 1973), p. 98.

5. Margaret Laurence, "Sources," *Mosaic* 3 (Spring 1970): 81.

6. Margaret Laurence, "Ten Years' Sentences," *Canadian Literature* 41 (Summer 1969): 15.

7. Margaret Laurence, *A Bird in the House* (1971; Toronto, 1974), p. 207.

8. Clara Thomas, "A Conversation about Literature: An Interview with Margaret Laurence and Irving Layton," *Journal of Canadian Fiction* 1 (Winter 1972): 66.

9. Clara Thomas, "Myth and Manitoba in *The Diviners*," in *The Canadian Novel: Here and Now*, ed. John Moss (Toronto, 1978), pp. 116–17.

10. W. L. Morton, *The Canadian Identity* (Toronto, 1961), p. 93.

11. Marlene Springer, *What Manner of Woman* (New York, 1973), p. 130.

12. Ged Martin, "Queen Victoria and Canada," *American Review of Canadian Studies* 13 (Spring 1983): 215–33.

13. Karen Horney, "Inhibited Femininity," in *Feminine Psychology* (New York, 1967), p. 74.

14. W. L. Morton, *The Kingdom of Canada* (Toronto, 1963), p. 345.

15. Betty Friedan, *The Feminine Mystique* (New York, 1963), pp. 174–77.

16. Robert Bothwell, Ian Drummond and John English, *Canada since 1945: Power, Politics, and Provincialism* (Toronto, 1981), p. 261.

17. Claude Bissell, "Politics and Literature in the 1960s," in *The Literary History of Canada*, gen. ed. Carl F. Klinck, 3 vols. (Toronto, 1976), 3:3.

18. George Woodcock, *Canada and the Canadians* (London, 1973), p. 235.

19. Judith Hole and Ellen Levine, *Rebirth of Feminism* (New York, 1971), pp. 115–16.

20. Bernice Lever, "An Interview with Margaret Laurence," *Waves* 3 (Winter 1975): 12.

21. Margaret Laurence, *The Fire-Dwellers* (Toronto, 1969), p. 56.

22. Helen M. Buss, "Margaret Laurence—a Bibliographical Essay," *American Review of Canadian Studies* 11, no. 5 (Autumn 1981): 8.

23. "Other New Novels," *Times Literary Supplement*, May 22, 1969, in *Margaret Laurence: The Writer and Her Critics*, ed. W. H. New (Toronto, 1977), p. 197.

24. F. W. Watt, "Review of *The Fire-Dwellers*," in *Margaret Laurence: The Writer and Her Critics*, ed. New, pp. 198–99.

25. Phyllis Gotlieb, "On Margaret Laurence," *Tamarack Review* 52 (1969): 76–78.

26. Ken Hughes, "Politics and *A Jest of God*," *Journal of Canadian Studies* 13 (Fall 1978): 43.

27. Margaret Laurence, "Ivory Tower or Grassroots?: The Novelist As Socio-political Being," in *A Political Art*, ed. W. H. New (Vancouver, 1978), p. 24.

28. Elizabeth Waterston, *Survey: A Short History of Canadian Literature* (Toronto, 1973), pp. 72–73.

29. Denyse Forman and Uma Parameswaran, "Echoes and Refrains in the Canadian Novels of Margaret Laurence," in *Margaret Laurence: The Writer and Her Critics*, ed. New, p. 91.

30. W. H. New, "Rhythms of Discovery," *Canadian Literature* 100 (Spring 1984): 8.

31. Bruce Hutchison, "The Canadian Personality," in *Man and His World*, ed. Malcolm Ross and John Stevens (Toronto, 1961), p. 189.

32. Sandra Djwa, "Canadian Poets and the Great Tradition," *Canadian Literature* 65 (Summer 1975): 42–52.

33. Clara Thomas, "The Novels of Margaret Laurence," in *Margaret Laurence: The Writer and Her Critics*, ed. New, p. 60.

34. George Woodcock, *The Canadians* (Don Mills, 1979), p. 301.

35. As quoted in Bothwell, Drummond and English, *Canada since 1945*, in the context of a lengthy discussion on the growth of anti-Americanism between 1964 and 1967, p. 278.

36. Anais Nin, *The Novel of the Future* (New York, 1968), pp. 27, 59.

37. Margaret Atwood, "Face to Face," *Maclean's* (May 1974): 46.

38. Bernice Lever, "Literature and Canadian Culture: An Interview with Margaret Laurence," in *Margaret Laurence: The Writer and Her Critics*, ed. New, pp. 26, 27.

5

"To Refuse to Be a Victim": Anti-Americanism in the Early Novels of Margaret Atwood

Walking down the aisle of a supermarket, Marian McAlpin, a market research analyst in Margaret Atwood's *The Edible Woman* (1969), resents the techniques used to "lower your sales resistance to the point at which all things are desirable."[1] The music "from the concealed loudspeakers" and the "deceptively-priced or subliminally-packaged" merchandise trick her into "doing precisely what some planner in a broadloomed office had hoped and predicted she would do." Successful merchandising depends on "which detergent had the best power-symbol" and "which tomato juice can had the sexiest-looking tomato on it." Despite Marian's attempts "to defend herself with lists," she finds "her hands twitching with the impulse to reach out and grab anything with a bright label." "Just because she knew what they were up to didn't mean she was immune"; *The Edible Woman* dramatizes the extent to which even human relationships are not "immune" from the profit motive of a consumer-oriented society.

A society which so devotes itself to materialism is the setting of much of Margaret Atwood's poetry and fiction. In a 1972 interview with Graeme Gibson, Atwood draws a parallel between the psyches of her heroines and Canada:

What I'm really into . . . is the great Canadian victim complex. If you define yourself as innocent then nothing is ever your fault—it is always somebody else doing it to you, and until you stop defining yourself as a victim that will always be true. It will always be somebody else's fault, and you will always be the object of that rather than somebody who has any choice or takes responsibility for their life. And that is not only the Canadian stance towards the world, but the usual female one. Look what a mess I am and it's all their fault. And Canadians do that too. Look at poor innocent us, we are morally better than they. We do not burn people in Vietnam, and those bastards are coming in and taking away our country. Well, the real truth of the matter is that Canadians are selling it.[2]

As poet, novelist, literary critic and social activist, Atwood has been instrumental in shaping Canada's understanding of herself as a nation. Although she disclaims the labels "nationalist" and "feminist," her statements about the American control of the publishing industry in the early 1970s, for example, raised national consciousness enough to effect change: "Canadian writers of my generation started to read Canadian literature in self-defence; we got tired of people telling us there wasn't any."[3]

Her volume of poetry, *Power Politics* (1971), highlights the central subjects and metaphors in her work: the sexual tactics employed by men and women and the Canadian political experience. The emphasis Atwood places on these two political arenas validates Susan Mann Trofimenkoff's call for a closer study of the relationship between feminism and Canadian nationalism. Trofimenkoff argues that contemporary writing of women's history implies that "the major driving force of history is not the struggle between classes or the oppression of one class by another but rather the relationship between the sexes."[4] The study of women by intellectual historians interested in nationalism, she suggests, will discover "a combination of economic, demographic and political factors." Certainly, Atwood's works, describing Canadian and feminine oppression from the perspective of female personae in poetry and female narrators in novels, present, as George Woodcock suggests, "the proposition that . . . all Canadian attitudes are . . . related to the central fact of victimization."[5]

Although Atwood admits to Linda Sandler, "I probably am a feminist," she cautions against reading her characters as "role models. I don't try to resolve the problems of living, deal out the answers, and I'm not dealing with my female characters as members of a separate species."[6] Her first two novels, *The Edible Woman* (1969) and *Surfacing* (1972), nevertheless share a concern with female roles; in each book conventional behavior is required of the protagonist. Each heroine then suffers an identity crisis as she wrestles with her growing awareness of her dual, if not multiple, personalities which "surface" after she has rejected the imposed image. Each at first defensively reacts by seeing herself as a victim of male domination, but then comes to recognize that this colonial attitude is a way of hiding the truth of her own culpability: that she had willingly inculcated the sexual role models prescribed for her by a patriarchal society, that she had become a "sellout."

These heroines, who so readily suggest feminist and nationalist struggles, are also apparently autobiographical. They closely correspond in age to Atwood, with their flashbacks, like Atwood's past, consisting of a childhood in postwar Canada. Like Marian in *The Edible Woman*, Atwood once worked for a market research firm; like the narrator of *Surfacing*, Atwood's parents "carried Peggy into the Quebec north woods when she was six months old. The family spent half of each year in the woods—mostly in northern Quebec."[7] Atwood's essay in *Maclean's*, "Travels Back: Refusing to acknowledge where you come from is an act of amputation," further amplifies the connections between her childhood and adolescence and those of the heroine of *Surfacing*: "twice a year, north when the ice went out, south when the snow came, the time between [was] spent in tents; or in the cabin built by my father on a granite point a mile by water from a Quebec village so remote that the road went in only two years before I was born. . . . I didn't spend a full year in school until I was 11."[8] These first two novels present portraits both of Atwood's own experience and of her countrywomen's contemporary history.

The Edible Woman, narrated by Marian McAlpin, a recent university graduate who is working for a market research firm, Seymour Surveys, demonstrates the difficulties, for women of the 1960s, of living within conventional norms. The novel's three sections conform to the patterns of conventional courtship fiction: in Part One, Marian becomes engaged to Peter Wollander, an articling law student; in Part Two, preparations are underway for the planned spring wedding; in Part Three, Marian breaks off the engagement and plans to search for a new job. The deviation from the traditional happy ending in marriage, undercutting both sentimental love stories and traditional relationships between men and women, typifies the connection of aesthetic and social innovation, which extends the national-sexual parallels in Atwood's work.

Set in the mid–1960s, *The Edible Woman* suggests that the production and promotion of goods for mass consumption have pervaded relationships between men and women by restricting the roles available for women in the consumer society of postwar Canada. "I can't tell [the office] yet," muses Marian about her engagement, "I'll have to keep my job there for a while longer" (p. 102). That Marian becomes engaged on a Labor Day Weekend ironically indicates the mutually exclusive choices open to women in 1965: career or the "labor" of childbirth within a respectable marriage. "I was expected to have one or the other," Atwood explains in "The Curse of Eve— Or, What I Learned in School," her speech for the 1976 Gerstein Lectures at York University, "and this is one of the ways in which I hope times have changed."[9] There was no such hope in the society of *The Edible Woman*.

Sex-directed education was an effective form of male domination in Marian's youth. When she and her roommate are asked why they have such "crummy" jobs, they can only defend themselves with the rhetorical question, "What else do you do with a B.A. these days?" (p. 55). The postwar male arguments against the increasing numbers of women enrolling in postsecondary institutions were that higher education was wasted on the woman who would become just a wife and mother and that the woman who pursued a career was taking a job from a male who needed it to support his family.

But Betty Friedan discovered that intelligent women, bored by their re-
petitive work as housewives and mothers, only feel fulfilled as women, wives
and mothers when they use their intelligence in activities outside the home.[10]

Unfortunately for these women, Friedan notes, in the period between
1945 and 1960 sex-directed education "added its weight to the process by
which American women . . . were shaped increasingly to their biological function" (p. 148). In the Gerstein Lectures, Atwood tells of her similar, Canadian experience of the university professor who tried to dissuade her from
graduate work by asking whether she "wouldn't . . . rather get married"
(p. 13). So, too, Marian's education "through highschool and college" was
tempered by her assumption, inherited from her parents, "that I was going
to marry someone eventually and have children, everyone does" (p. 102).
Marian's parents "worried she would turn into a high-school teacher or a
maiden aunt or a dope addict or a female executive, or [far worse than this]
. . . would undergo some shocking physical transformation, like developing
muscles and a deep voice" (p. 174). Her engagement calms their "fears about
the effects of her university education" (p. 103). The need for female education was one of the central themes of Anna Jameson's writing, and the
heroines in both Sara Jeannette Duncan's *The Imperialist* (1904) and Nellie
McClung's *Purple Springs* (1921) raise themselves beyond the realm of conventional roles by their advanced education. Marian's education has no such
liberating influence.

When her roommate states her intention of becoming a single parent,
Marian wonders "about the job at the art gallery" Ainslie had talked of
seeking; "what has having a baby got to do with getting a job at the art
gallery?" responds Ainslie. "You're always thinking in terms of either/or"
(p. 41). One can hardly blame Marian; her society has taught her to think
that way. And, in light of the job opportunities open to her at Seymour
Surveys, her desire for marriage is also understandable. For while her "kind
of job is only to be expected" of female college graduates, the masculine
name of her firm underscores the fact that "the executives and the psy-
chologists . . . are all men" (p. 20). While hoping that she is "being groomed
for something higher up," Marian can at best look forward to "turn[ing] into
Mrs. Bogue or her assistant," overseeing other women. When required to
join the pension plan, Marian imagines that "somewhere in front of me a
self was waiting, pre-formed" (p. 21); the fact that this future is notably one
of spinsterhood reinforces her "either/or" attitude to career and marriage.

In reaction to the limitations of this pink-collar ghetto, Marian comes to
view Peter as a "rescuer from chaos, a provider of stability" (p. 89). But her
next thought points to the threat to her identity posed by their engagement:
"Somewhere in the vaults of Seymour Surveys an invisible hand was wiping
away my signature." Marriage eradicates the career steps she has made;
when Mrs. Bogue announces Marian's engagement at the office party, "she
had . . . made it clear . . . that she would be expecting her to leave her job

whether she wanted to or not" (p. 168). Mrs. Bogue, representing "management" as she does, "preferred her girls to be either unmarried or seasoned veterans with their liability to unpredictable pregnancies well in the past." Marian accepts her society's rules for its "girls" by growing detached from her work; she is all too soon ready to quit. When Peter asks her when she wants to get married, Marian responds in "a soft, flannelly voice [she] barely recognized, saying, 'I'd rather . . . leave the big decisions up to you" (p. 90). In "Alice in Consumer-Land," John Lauber astutely observes: "That flannelly voice is the voice of society, of its traditional expectations about woman's role, incorporated within her own personality and responding automatically, before her conscious mind can act."[11] Paralyzed between the roles of career woman and wife, Marian has no identity, no power of self-direction.

What happens to Marian as she slips, barely conscious of her ambivalent desires, into the "sargasso-sea of femininity" (p. 167), happened, according to Friedan, to thousands of her contemporaries: "they learned that truly feminine women do not want careers, higher education, political rights— the independence and the opportunities that the old-fashioned feminists fought for" (p. 11). Women were removed from the world around them, rarely involved in social issues. Atwood uses third-person narration in the second part of the novel; Marian has "lost her voice," become distanced from the reader as from herself. Her passive removal from involvement in the world mirrors that of Canadian society during the 1950s. According to Donald Creighton's 1976 examination of Canada after the war, "Uncle" St. Laurent played the role of "an affectionate *pater familias*, tenderly watching over the welfare and interests of his large Canadian family," instituting social welfare programs with a show of paternal largesse; meanwhile, "direct American investment in Canada . . . more than tripled during the twelve years from 1945 to 1957."[12] Only a few people such as Walter Gordon questioned the price of the standard of living enjoyed by Canadians; voices like Canadian economist B. S. Keirstead's were more common, patronizingly asserting that it was "somewhat naive to suppose that in some fashion this [American] investment constituted a menace to Canadian independence."[13] Hugh G. J. Aitken in 1961 might optimistically propose that "the vitality and creativity of . . . cultural life" would "maintain a sense of identity in the face of economic integration with the United States,"[14] but by the mid–1960s Atwood and many more Canadians realized that American investment meant American influence of Canadian social and cultural identity. *The Edible Woman* exposes the concomitant process of domination, the growing threat to woman's identity by a male-controlled and increasingly consumer-oriented society.

Indeed, the central motif of the novel is the "sexual sell" of market research. The questions Marian asks various men about their reactions to a commercial jingo for Moose beer are intended to measure the appeal of the masculine stereotypes in the song's images. Most of the products tested at Seymour are meant for the woman and the home—as Friedan argues, "the really important role that women serve as housewives is to buy more things for the home. . . . the real business of America is business. But the perpetuation of housewifery, the growth of the feminine mystique, makes sense (and dollars) when one realizes that women are the chief customers of American business" (p. 197). Pondering a girdle advertisement, Marian perceives that the "sort of person who would have enough response . . . to go and buy the object" is actually trying to purchase a "self-image . . . getting their own youth and slenderness back in the package" (p. 93). Mrs. Bogue is so "sold" by her job that she instructs her assistant to tell the employees that they are working to "better the Lot of Womankind" (p. 109). Even Ainslie, the most independent woman in the novel, says "every woman should have at least one baby . . . like a voice on the radio saying every woman should have a hair-dryer" (p. 41); the "sexual sell" extends to the manipulation of woman's biological destiny.

The woman as consumer is also consumed, as a packaged product, like a cake prepared and edible for male consumption. In her attentions to clothing, Marian consciously conforms to the accepted social image. At Peter's suggestion, she plans to "have something done with her hair" and buy a dress "not quite so mousy as any she already owned" (p. 208). The hairdresser "treated your head like a cake: something to be carefully iced and ornamented" (p. 208). Marian "thought it would be a good idea if they would give anaesthetics to the patients . . . she didn't enjoy feeling like a slab of flesh, an object. . . . Her whole body felt curiously paralysed" (p. 209). Marian "feels like a callgirl," and is encouraged to conform by an advertisement in a magazine she reads while under the dryer: "Girls! Be successful! If you want to really Go Places, Develop Your Bust" (p. 210). She succumbs to the socially imposed facade both because she feels a loss of control, "she was intimidated by [the male hairdresser's] official surroundings," and because she undergoes the operation "of her own free will." When she buys a red dress, the saleslady assures her, "It's you, dear" (p. 208), and goes on to pressure her to purchase a girdle, not because she needs one, but because "the saleslady who . . . was thoroughly corseted herself said she ought to. . . . 'that is a close-fitting dress and you wouldn't want it to be obvious that you haven't got one on, would you?' " (p. 221). Marian understands that "it had seemed like a moral issue"; a woman who does not wear a girdle is seen as "loose." Her hair and clothes, by contrast, are acceptably alluring; Peter approves of the final product: "Darling, you look absolutely marvellous. . . . And I love you especially in that red dress" (pp. 228, 231). "Yum, yum," says Peter to his edible woman (p. 227).

In her relationship with Peter, Marian begins to recognize herself as a product and him as a threat. With his collection of guns and cameras, he fits the socially approved male image of hunter projected by the Moose beer commercial. Once engaged, he assumes an attitude of ownership: "now that she had been ringed he took pride in displaying her" (p. 176). Marian imagines that with his "brand of logic" Peter would "go out and buy . . . one of those marriage-manuals": "if you got something new you went out and bought a book that told you how to work it" (p. 150). Certainly logic pervades his occupation, law, which is itself a form of domination by means of legalizing patriarchal power. Peter is, according to Ainslie, "nicely packaged" and Marian sees him as "ordinariness raised to perfection" (p. 61), the finished product of a masculine society, a success whose triumph necessitates the domination of others. At the engagement party Marian imagines Peter's future in terms of a typical American leisure scene: "forty-five and balding . . . standing in bright sunlight beside a barbecue with a long fork in his hand. . . . She looked carefully for herself in the garden, but she wasn't there and the discovery chilled her" (p. 243). Peter's typical male interests in hunting and photography coalesce at this point; he "raised the camera and aimed it at her . . . to get a couple of shots."

Marian's fear of being photographed is well explained by John Moss: "a camera can steal the soul. The basis for such a belief is not superstition but the intuitively sophisticated equation of appearance with reality. . . . Identity is clearly a complex living thing. A static literal image . . . on film destroys intrinsic vitality and dimension, the qualities ultimately defining the soul, which is thereby lost."[15] Knowing that in the red dress she is "a perfect target," Marian runs from the party before Peter can capture her; in doing so, she runs for her very life, rejecting the two-dimensional image of woman which she had allowed Peter, and by extension society, to impose on her.

Marian's rebellion began, albeit unconsciously, the night of their engagement. Her sudden flight after drinks at the Park Plaza, her hiding under Len's bed, the unexpected embrace of the stranger, Duncan, whom she meets in a laundromat, and her inertia as she sits on her bed at the end of Part One, indicate that although she has outwardly assumed the pattern of passive femininity expected by Peter, inwardly she has begun to withdraw from this version of womanhood. The focus of Atwood's satire emerges in Part Two as Marian becomes increasingly unable to consume food; the split between her mind and body becomes a metaphor of her rejection, not only of consumerism, but also of herself as a commodity packaged as fiancée, bride, wife and mother. Her half-formed perception leads her to identify, at the start of Part Two, with the "victim" in the market research survey (p. 107). When Marian's fellow-workers, reacting to a failed survey on menstruation, show concern only for the product test and the client, Atwood has Marian absent-mindedly draw "a row of moons across her page; crescent moons, full moons, then crescent moons pointing the other way, then nothing: a black moon" (p. 110). This action, while also a parody of anthropological studies of woman, indicates that at some level of her being Marian is grappling with a deeper dimension of femininity.

In her exploration of *Woman's Mysteries* (1976), M. Esther Harding maintains that "to understand woman . . . it is necessary to take into account her moonlike character and to gain some insight into the law of change which governs her."[16] Viewing her co-workers and the "vast anonymous ocean of housewives," Marian understands the perversion of "the law of change" by consumerism: "their fluidity sustained somewhere within by bones, without by a carapace of clothing and makeup . . . and the continual flux between the outside and the inside, taking things in, giving them out, chewing, words, potato-chips, burps, grease, hair, babies, milk, excrement, cookies, vomit, coffee, tomato-juice, blood" (p. 167). Because she realizes that "at some time she would be—or no, already she was like that too; she was one of them, her body the same, identical," she becomes anorexic, more and more detached in her reaction against the socially approved image. She offers Peter the substitute woman of cake, in itself a parody of the woman as object popularized at stag parties by the woman emerging from a cake. Her comment, "You've been trying to destroy me, haven't you. . . . You've been trying to assimilate me" (p. 271), uses the political language of a minority group speaking to a conventional, powerful majority, of a colony to an imperial power, of a woman to a man.

Formally, as Atwood tells Gibson, the novel is an "anti-comedy" which rejects the happy ending of "your standard eighteenth-century comedy" (p. 21). This formal deviation from the British model has its correlative not only in Marian's rebellion against Peter, but also in the mind-state of the nation in the early 1960s. Canada continued the process of turning away from the British while enjoying the prosperity of the American way of life. Robert Bothwell, Ian Drummond and John English note, for instance, that in July of 1960, "Beverly Baxter wrote his last London Letter for *Maclean's*," and soon after *Maclean's* came out with a "special issue: 'America 1960—a 100-page report on the people all the shouting is about.' "[17] The United States had John F. Kennedy; Canada had John George Diefenbaker. Canadians were increasingly "embarrassed about their conservative reputations," and Diefenbaker stood for the British heritage; Lester Pearson, on the other hand, was on good terms with the Americans. Bothwell, Drummond and English maintain that Pearson, trained in the international field of diplomacy, distrusted the "irrational in politics and also the values of the past" (p. 270) and that as he moved the country toward a sense of itself as a nation distinct from Britain, Pearson was also convinced of the necessity of being on "the American team" (p. 279).

Others such as Hugh MacLennan saw the danger of the gradual American domination of Canada. George Grant's *Lament for a Nation* (1965) interpreted the defeat of Diefenbaker as the end to any hope that "an alternative to the American republic [might be] built on the northern half of this continent."[18] And by 1967, polls indicated a shift in public opinion from 1965; more Canadians thought that Canada should take steps to ensure its national independence from foreign economic control. *The Edible Woman* is, in a sense, Atwood's early lament, for although the novel is set in a Toronto

easily recognized by anyone who has lived there, the city is never named
and therefore represents, as Atwood says, "any Northeast, commercial, tech-
nological city."[19] The thrust of the novel's satire is that Canadian society's
materialistic values are indistinguishable from those of the United States.

Certainly, as Atwood suggests to Gibson, the traditional "comedy solution
[of marriage] would be a tragic solution for Marian" (p. 25). In the very short
third section of the novel Marian struggles by herself, but now "thinking
. . . in the first person singular again" (p. 278); she is cleaning her neglected
apartment, seeking a new job, even eating. Sherrill Grace, in her thematic
study of Atwood, *Violent Duality* (1980), emphasizes the negative connotations of the circular structure of the book and concludes that "Marian
returns to the point from which she began."[20] But Grace overlooks the strong
positive elements in the conclusion: that it is spring, a traditional time of
rebirth, and that the baking of the cake is, as Atwood herself tells Gibson,
"an action. Up until that point she has been evading, avoiding" (p. 25).
Lauber extends Atwood's reading: "through baking a cake, a traditionally
feminine action . . . Marian . . . symbolically . . . represents . . . her unwillingness to be eaten" (p. 28). Atwood describes the novel to Gibson as "pessimistic" but she also acknowledges that although "the ideal would be
somebody who would neither be a killer or a victim, who could achieve
some kind of harmony with the world, which is a productive or creative
harmony. . . . [and although not] actualized [in *The Edible Woman*] . . . it's
seen as a possibility finally, whereas initially it is not" (p. 27).

The tentative nature of the novel's ending and of Marian's future is foreshadowed in her ambiguous relationship with Duncan, the graduate student
in English, whom she often meets in a laundromat. The setting of their
rendezvous suggests the lifestyle emerging in the 1960s; both men and
women go out to do the laundry once done by women in the home. But the
possibility that he is meant by Atwood to represent an admirably liberated
male is negated by his compulsiveness in ironing; it is a form of "relieving
tensions": "you straighten things out and get them flat" (p. 142).

On the question of androgyny, Atwood explains to Margaret Kaminski
about "counterparts and complements. Your counterpart is someone who is
the mirror reflection of yourself, and your complement is someone who
supplies those elements that are lacking in you" (p. 12). Duncan plays the
role of "counterpart" most effectively; when Marian dons his dressing-gown,
Duncan observes, "you look sort of like me in that" (p. 144). She enjoys his
wit and imagination, qualities she shares. But Atwood clarifies Duncan's
purpose as a mirror-image when his roommate expounds on *Alice's Adventures in Wonderland* (1865) as a "sexual-identity-crisis book." This exposition
suggests the structure of *The Edible Woman*: "one sexual role after another
is presented to [the heroine] but she seems unable to accept any of them"
(p. 194). At one point Alice "goes to talk with the Mock-Turtle" who, like
Duncan, is "enclosed in his shell and his self-pity, a definitely pre-adolescent

character"; in the bedroom scene between Duncan and Marian, he slips under the bedclothes "like a turtle into his shell" (p. 253). Duncan is insecure and passive; as an animus projection he demonstrates Marian's weak self-esteem and undeveloped sense of identity. They both are, in essence, children, he regressively protected by his roommates, and she shaped first by her parents' plans for her future and then by Peter's.

In his inability to "move out" from his surrogate parents—"they spend so much time fussing about my identity that I really shouldn't have to bother with it myself at all" (p. 201)—Duncan mirrors not only Marian's loss of identity as she faces marriage but also that of the thousands of North American women who accepted "the feminine mystique" in order to protect themselves; they willingly donned the roles of homemaker and motherhood to avoid participation in the world. Such an "evasion of growth," concludes Friedan, "consists in a systematic denial and repression of one's own personality, and an attempt to substitute some other . . . standard of absolute goodness by which one tries to live, suppressing all those genuine impulses that are incompatible with the exaggerated and unrealistic standard, or simply taking the personality that is the popular cliché of the time" (pp. 279–80).

There is suggested at the end of the novel a perhaps more subtle purpose to Duncan's role. Marian muses that in the case of Peter her woman of cake "as a symbol [of their relationship] had definitely failed"; Peter "hadn't devoured it after all" (p. 271). But Duncan consumes the remains of the cake, "mostly the head," while playing "head-games" with Marian, confusing her with various interpretations of her relationships with men, suggesting at one point that "the real truth is that it wasn't Peter at all. It was me. I was trying to destroy you" (p. 281). Marian has "a sinking feeling" (p. 280) that she has been wrong in her analysis of her relationships with Peter and Duncan, but as she "sat watching the cake disappear," she experiences "a peculiar sense of satisfaction to see him eat as if the work [of baking the cake] hadn't been wasted after all" (p. 281). Duncan is revealed for the "cannibal" he is, and as such, is actually a symbol of the kind of man with whom Marian was programmed to become involved.

Duncan is a child-man who "bring[s] out the Florence Nightingale" in "every woman" (p. 100); immediately after their spontaneous embrace at the laundromat, Marian "stared for a long time at an advertisement with a picture of a nurse in a white cap and dress. She had a wholesome, competent face" (p. 101). Then, after their night together, when Duncan says that "she wasn't the first," Marian realizes that "the starched nurse-like image of herself she had tried to preserve as a last resort crumpled like wet newsprint" (p. 264). Duncan's action of eating the cake confirms for Marian that men do play on the nurturing, biological function of women to manipulate them into subservient roles by appealing to "the better half" to live their lives for the welfare of husbands and children. Duncan warns her to "be careful . . .

you might do something destructive: hunger is more basic than love. Florence Nightingale was a cannibal, you know" (p. 100). In light of Marian's anorexia, the "hunger" to which he alludes is the desire for self-fulfillment, for self-realization.

Friedan points out the "progressive dehumanization" of American children robbed of their identities by mothers who, frustrated with the limitations of their own lives, end up living through their husbands and children, becoming so involved that the children lose all self-motivation and self-confidence (p. 278). Atwood, in *Survival* (1972), analyzes the presentation, in Canadian literature, of women who "have internalized the values of their cultures" in terms of the Rapunzel fairy-tale. In Canadian novels the Rescuer "is not much help" and his "facelessness and lack of substance as a character is usually a clue to his status as a fantasy-escape figure." Canadian heroines are "stuck in the tower, and . . . [must] learn how to cope with it.[21] At the end of *The Edible Woman*, Marian sees that Duncan is an inadequate "rescuer" and chooses the risks of independence. The conclusion is thus positive in that she is taking control of her life, as Friedan states women must do: they "must refuse to be nameless, depersonalized, manipulated, and live their own lives again according to a self-chosen purpose. They must begin to grow" (p. 298).

Yet the ending of the novel is problematic because the question remains: what can she do? Canada, too, began at the end of the decade to take some steps toward control of her own house. And what could Canada do? There have been two forms of economic nationalism in Canadian history. Sir John A. Macdonald's "national policy" which forged the nation, and C. D. Howe's economic policies used American entrepreneurship and finance to develop the nation, at great cost to Canadian independence; they ignored the national implications of their economic policies. But men such as Walter Gordon proposed a form of economic nationalism whereby national independence would be protected by tariffs on trade and regulation of foreign investment. The economic nationalism mirrored in *The Edible Woman* is that of Macdonald and Howe as Atwood demonstrates the danger of American consumerism to Canadian society.

Certainly a consumer society propagates patriarchal values; in a world controlled by multinational corporations, women and Canada remain colonies. Atwood portrays the male characters' fears of the "radical views" of "liberating" unconscious drives toward self-realization: "Politically Peter is conservative" (p. 67). And the "home" situation of Duncan offers Atwood's most humorous satire of the "colonial mentality" of Canadians. Duncan's roommates, Trevor and Fischer, from Westmount in Montreal and Vancouver respectively, have been in the "braingrinder" of literary studies so long that they "don't sound as though [they are] from anywhere" (p. 98). All of their literary studies are of British literature, particularly Victorian novels, and their apartment contains touches of Victoriana: "There's so little elegance left," muses Trevor, "especially in this country. . . . we all ought to do our bit to preserve some of it" (p. 193). These men preserve imperial standards just as Peter propagates American materialism. Atwood embodies the hope of change solely in the female character's revolt against man and his world.

The change in Canada's position as a nation in relation to the United States is best symbolized by movement from cooperation between Lester Pearson and John F. Kennedy in 1963 to hostility between Pearson and Lyndon Baines Johnson in 1965. In these two years American escalation of the war in Vietnam caused Canada to reassess her closeness to this aggressive neighbor. With the assassinations of the Kennedys and Martin Luther King, and the explosion, in American cities south of the Canadian border, of racial strife and student revolt, Canadians began to think of themselves as a "nicer" people. Bothwell, Drummond and English note that by 1967 "the Canadian sense of inferiority was replaced by a strong gust of moral righteousness which exalted many of those values which had embarrassed Canadians in 1960: their placidity, caution, and even innocence" (pp. 341–42).

Atwood's *Surfacing*, published in 1972, examines with painful precision the complex development of the "nice" image of Canada in the late 1960s. On the "surface," the first two-thirds of the novel seem apolitical. A young woman in the company of her new lover, Joe, and a married couple, David and Anna, return to her parents' island home in the northern Quebec wilderness to search for her father who is reported missing. The camaraderie of the four young adults soon breaks down into various maneuvers of sexual politics. And the narrator's "cool" exterior is shattered when she finds what appears to be her father's drowned body in the lake; the experience releases a flood of memories previously sealed from her—and the reader's—consciousness. The marriage and divorce which she had cited as the reasons for her rift from her parents turn out to be her whitewashed version of an illicit affair with a married man, her college art teacher, and the resulting abortion which he had arranged. Her admission of the true story, of her complicity in allowing the abortion, brings her a deep sense of her own evil. Her previous insistence on her innocence as a "nice" victim of both male aggression and the American killer instinct is revealed as a shield behind which she hid her own guilt.

Although Atwood makes few direct temporal or geographical references, she specifies a politically significant historical period. David studied theology in New York "during the 60s."[22] This phrase places the time present of the novel after that decade, in the early 1970s. The narrator says that she has been away from her parents' home since the time of her "marriage" and that David and Anna "got married about the same time I did" (p. 40). Since David and Anna have been married "nine years," the narrator's abortion took place during 1962–63, the time period so crucial to Canada's sense of identity as distinguished from the American. Unlike *The Edible Woman*, which concentrates on feminist issues and only indirectly makes political analogies, *Surfacing* focuses directly on specific national and political issues—American domination of the Canadian economy and destruction of her natural, northern resources, the independence of Quebec, the threat of nuclear weapons—by uncovering the period of the 1960s from the narrator's past when these issues were so politically relevant.

Atwood also presents these concerns through specific, satiric commentary within the "fiction." In the first chapter, as the foursome enters the landscape of "needle trees and . . . gray granite and . . . tourist cabins" (p. 9), signs appear "saying GATEWAY TO THE NORTH"; "the future is in the North, that was a political slogan once," reflects the narrator, remembering Diefenbaker's vision of northern development which caught the imagination of the Canadian people in the 1958 election. Her next thought—and juxtaposition within the narrator's stream of consciousness is one of Atwood's vehicles of political commentary—expresses fear of the American "rockets" in Canadian territory; beneath "an innocent hill" lies "the pit the Americans hollowed out" (p. 9). The American pressure that Canadian armed forces acquire nuclear weapons was as controversial in the early 1960s as the cruise missile testing over western Canada in the 1980s. The Cuban missile crisis in 1962 and the later Bomarc missile debate—whether or not Canadian planes would be equipped with nuclear warheads—shook the confidence of the Canadian people in the Diefenbaker government, and the nuclear arms question continued to plague the Pearson administration. Significantly, an anti-nuclear weapons movement, organized in 1960, was called "The Voice of Women." But for this female narrator, as for Canada in the early 1960s, American destructive capability is, as yet, an overwhelming threat.

In the first chapter, Atwood refers twice to the debate over the sovereignty of Quebec. As the narrator crosses the border into Quebec with her friends, she thinks, "now we're on my home ground, foreign territory" (p. 11). She is many times politically dispossessed: as an Anglophone in Quebec; as a Quebecker in Canada; and as a Canadian in North America. The chapter ends with a mélange of slogans painted on roadside cliff faces, one of which alludes not only to separatist aspirations but also to General de Gaulle's famous 1967 balcony cry, "QUEBEC LIBRE" (p. 15). Catherine McLay comments that the "French-English relationships" are the "first evidence" in the novel of the theme of separation.[23] It is an issue which Atwood extends both beyond provincial-federal to international conflicts and beyond political to individual isolation and self-determination.

Atwood develops the theme of independence primarily in terms of Canadian dislike of American domination. The narrator's antipathy for Americans and their way of life intensifies through the novel just as nationalistic feelings grew in Canada during the mid–1960s. At the start, such criticisms are muted, almost incidental, as the narrator makes passing comments on the landscape around her. She refers three times to the white birches in this part of the country not yet afflicted by "the disease . . . from the south" (p. 7). Anti-American comments become more strident and frequent as the novel progresses. "Surveyors" felling trees are transformed in her imagi- nation to "advance men, agents" who are "plotting the new shoreline" (p. 113). The rise of the lake level, she surmises, will depend on "who got elected, not here but somewhere else" (p. 132). And her nationalistic feelings become more explicit: "My country, sold or drowned, a reservoir: the people were sold along with the land and the animals, a bargain, sale, *solde*. Les soldes they called them, sellouts." These references, an expansion of the hunter-hunted motif of *The Edible Woman*, emphasize Americans' exploitive attitude.

The narrator's experience of Americans is typical of Canadians of her generation. In her childhood, Americans were seen as "harmless and funny and inept and faintly lovable, like President Eisenhower." This World War II general was popular among both Americans and Canadians who saw in his stability as family man and golfer the strength necessary to contain the Russians. The familial image of Eisenhower, however, kept both publics ignorant of his administration's covert operations, for example, in the 1954 overthrow of the communist government in Guatemala. After the Vietnam War, such questionable foreign policy was general knowledge, and the nar- rator of *Surfacing* now sees American smiles as "teeth bared . . . friendly as a shark" (p. 66). She perceives the "dynamite" exploitation beneath the sporting interest in nature (p. 66) of the fishermen and Bill Malstrom, of the Detroit Branch of the Wildlife Protection Association of America. When Malstrom appears "prepared to make . . . an offer" for her father's property to establish "a retreat lodge, where the members could meditate and observe . . . the beauties of Nature, and [adding in contradiction] maybe do a little hunting and fishing" (p. 94), the narrator reacts with distrust, contemptuous as she is of his reference to Michigan, his home state, "as though it was something to be proud of." As Margaret Laurence records in *The Fire- Dwellers* (1969), the urban turmoil in Detroit, Michigan, in particular the racial riots in 1965, had shocked and dismayed Canadians.

David further feeds the narrator's paranoia with his hypothesis that Mal- strom is "a front man for the C.I.A.," which wants the property as a "snooping base" in preparation for the eventual war between the two countries over fresh water rights. His speculation reads like the plot summary of a novel such as *Ultimatum* (1973) by Richard Rohmer; both David and Rohmer tapped the growing fear that Canada would not be immune to interference such as experienced by Chile in the CIA-backed overthrow of its legally elected government. The narrator would not "sell-out," she assures David, but ponders that urban Canadians would be "apathetic" in such a war, "they wouldn't mind another change of flag" (p. 97). Her reference to the flag is a reminder not only of the adoption of the Canadian flag in 1965, a formal symbol of Canadian independence from Britain, but also of the Canadian need, in that same decade, to assert that independence in the face of American foreign policy.

The narrator's attitude is self-righteous; she comments only on other people's apathy, not her own. However, as Atwood has cautioned in her conversation with Gibson, we should be wary of the narrator's sense of victimization. The irony of her attitude to America—the key political statement of the novel—emerges when the two "American" fishermen reveal that they come from Sarnia and Toronto, and that these Canadians, in turn, had mistaken the narrator and her friends for Americans. This passage redefines the narrator's anti-American bias; the American way of life becomes a metaphor to describe an exploitive attitude to nature, and consequently to people: "It doesn't matter what country they're from, my head said, they're still Americans, they're what's in store for us, what we are turning into" (p. 129).

This passage, even more significantly, reveals her and, by extension, Canada's paranoic projection onto Americans of their own guilt and violence. Her anger at the "senseless killing" of the heron makes her want to "swing [her] paddle sideways, blade into [the fisherman's] head" (p. 128). And when she finally admits to the abortion, her guilt and subterfuges are unmasked: "I let them catch it [the foetus]. I could have said no but I didn't; that made me one of them too, a killer" (p. 145). Her paranoia that "the innocents get slaughtered because they exist" (p. 128) is a projection, onto another people, of characteristics which, in the course of the novel, she is forced to acknowledge as her own.

The narrator's view of men, moreover, undergoes similar transformation from defensive criticism to mature understanding. At first, she sees her "husband" and David as predators, just as bent on destroying women as the Americans are determined to exploit Canada. The "Pill," with its negative side effects, is something the "bastards . . . come up with" that "work[s]" while "killing you" (p. 80). Man's love of woman is only a war game of power politics wherein the male gains "a victory, some flag . . . [to] wave, parade" (p. 87). Anna's relationship with David clearly represents for the narrator such power politics. Their marriage depends on a "little set of rules . . . break one of them [and you] get punished" (p. 122). David, a "second-hand American" (p. 152), illustrates how the American lust for power over nature has been extended to the masculine domination of women: "the only relation they could have to a thing like that was to destroy it" (p. 116). The narrator sees Anna, moreover, as a compliant victim, "desperate, her body her only weapon . . . she was fighting him because if she ever surrendered the balance of power would be broken and he would go elsewhere. To continue the war" (pp. 153–54). In this cruel marriage the narrator sees a more extreme form of her own female passivity. Watching Anna apply the makeup David requires her to wear in order "to look like a young chick" (p. 122), the narrator explains, with obvious reference to men's magazines such as *Playboy*, the process by which Anna has inculcated society's feminine image of "a seamed and folded imitation of a magazine picture that is itself an imitation of a woman who is also an imitation, the original nowhere" (p. 165). Her own "husband" "arranged" the abortion and, recalling the commodity metaphor of *The Edible Woman*, "fixed [her] . . . as good as new" (p. 145). The constant repetition of "he said" in her version of the abortion underlines the fact that her passivity is a defensive mechanism to ward off her own guilt and sense of evil. The "husband" and David, seen by the narrator, are "American" because they are male; she has deceived herself into believing that she is the victim of a masculine ethic which she equates with American lust for power.

The narrator has locked herself into what Atwood in *Survival* labels "victim position two: To acknowledge the fact that you are a victim, but to explain this as an act of Fate, the Will of God, the dictates of Biology (in the case of women, for instance) . . . or any other large general powerful idea" (p. 37). Charles Hanly provides a means of understanding the formative factors of the narrator's neurotic nationalism and feminism in "A Psychoanalysis of Nationalist Sentiment," an article which seeks to analyze the "complex emotion of loving veneration for the nation and hostility toward some other or others."[24] He explains that "nationalistic feeling arises out of the repression of the conflicts generated by . . . development in the sexual instinct during early childhood" (p. 306). What is valuable in his study for a consideration of *Surfacing* is his contention that "nationalist sentiment require[s] a hate object": the source lies in "a pattern for dealing defensively with destructive impulses" (p. 308). The goodness of the parents is transferred to the nation while the "evil image" of the parents is projected onto some "outsider." This pattern clearly emerges in the childhood memories of Atwood's heroine. Her affair and abortion, she finally admits, came about because she "was not prepared for the average, its needless cruelties and lies" (p. 189). Her parents did not "teach us about evil, they didn't understand about it"; her mother taught them that "fighting was wrong" (p. 72). Because of their "perilous innocence," she felt she could never explain to them about her affair or the abortion (p. 144); she admits, however, that "their totalitarian innocence was my own" (p. 190). Because she "couldn't accept . . . that mutilation, ruin [she'd] made, [she] needed a different version" (p. 143), placing all blame on men and Americans.

Through the actual and symbolic return to her childhood home in search of her missing father, the narrator comes to recognize her own capacity for evil. But even more significant is her discovery, in her "roots," of how her socialization has denied her essential femininity. Her father, who had "admired . . . the eighteenth-century rationalists" (p. 38), and her mother, who kept a diary but entered "no reflections, no emotions" (p. 22), had taught her techniques of survival in the bush, but were unable to teach her to survive as a woman in civilization. She remembers herself as a child hiding "behind open doors at birthday parties" (p. 71), becoming "crafty" in order to avoid the "tricks and minor tortures" of other children (p. 72). "Being socially retarded" made her an object for "torment and reform" (p. 72) by her peers more adept in their consumer-oriented society. She "prayed to be made invisible" (p. 73) and succeeded by "imitating the paper dolls" (p. 42) of girlhood play. Like Marian in *The Edible Woman*, she uses clothing as her "camouflage." Searching through her childhood scrapbooks for "where I had come from or gone wrong," she discovers commercial advertisements of "ladies, all kinds: holding up cans of cleanser, knitting, smiling, modelling toeless high heels and nylons with dark seams and pillbox hats and veils" (p. 91). She internalized this "sexual sell": "it wasn't a lie, I did want to be those things." Photographs of her as a teenager, "in the stiff dresses, crinolines and tulle," evince that she "was civilized at last, the finished product"; but "after the formal dresses," she notes, "I disappeared" (p. 108). The abortion which "emptied, amputated" her essential nature as woman (p. 144) was the final act, in a lifelong process of psychological violence inflicted on her by a society dominated, just as were the worlds of Hagar and Stacey, by patriarchal values. Whereas Stacey's instinct to love her children overcomes the inhibition of "some wise guy telling you you were sapping the national strength," Atwood's narrator capitulates to the dominant belief of the essential worthlessness of her biological function when she dresses up as "the finished product" and then consents to the abortion for her lover's convenience.

Evelyn J. Hinz and John J. Teunissen conclude their archetypal analysis of *Surfacing* with speculation that the general "cultural upheaval, political unrest, and violence" of Western society precipitate "the manifestation . . . of the archetype of the Grieving Mother" in Atwood's vision.[25] The present study demonstrates the specific political and social issues in Canadian life out of which Atwood's novel emerges. Primarily, *Surfacing* reflects the anti-American component of Canadian nationalism in the late 1960s and early 1970s. It is worth noting that Bothwell, Drummond and English's 1981 study of the evolution of Canada in the 1960s expresses Canada's emerging consciousness of an American threat in language quite similar to Atwood's. They observe that in 1964, "doubts about Johnson's international activism rarely *surfaced* in Canada," but by 1966 there existed "a fear that the nation might fall prey to the *virus* sweeping the United States" (pp. 274, 278; emphasis mine). Atwood's prime concern, however, is that the consequent "Great Canadian victim complex" is so defensive that it inhibits the development of consciousness of both the country and its individuals. *Surfacing* reveals the complexity and complicity of such an attitude of injured innocence.

Other historical assessments likewise qualify the "nice, innocent" image Canada had of itself in the late 1960s. Peter Stursberg, in his 1980 *Lester Pearson and the American Dilemma*, questions the "high moral tone" of Pearson's speech at Temple University calling for a halt to the bombing in

Vietnam and concludes that "the speech had the effect of actually delaying Johnson's order to halt the air raids."[26] An even sterner indictment of Canada's peaceful image emerged in William Cobban's November 1971 article— a date much closer to the publication of *Surfacing*—"Dealing Out Death Discreetly: The Traffic in Canadian Arms." Cobban explodes with an arsenal of statistics any belief Canadians may have had about this country's international peace-keeping role. Cobban demonstrates that since the mid–1950s Canada has been "circumspect about how it cashed in on the international arms market."[27] In light of Cobban's article, Pearson's call for a halt to the bombing in Vietnam smacks of hypocrisy, for "half of the work Canada does for the American defence industry is in the production of aircraft and related components. . . . Peace in Vietnam would be a severe blow to our aircraft industry" (p. 24).

Moreover, while Canadians felt aghast at American racial tensions, "sometime in 1962 or 1963," point out Bothwell, Drummond and English, "the Quiet Revolution became the Quebec Problem" (p. 288), which culminated in the October Crisis of 1970 and the imposition of the War Measures Act. Canadians were forced to recognize that their nation too was torn by racial animosity which could erupt into urban violence and political murder, to fear, along with Atwood's narrator, that they "are all Americans now" (p. 169). Canadians could no longer hide behind their self-created image as an orderly, peace-loving nation. Criticism, for the narrator and for contemporary Canada, must become self-criticism.

Atwood conveys the American-Canadian comparison by the subtle manner in which she has modelled *Surfacing* on James Dickey's *Deliverance* (1970). Two critics have recently compared these novels, with differing conclusions. Evelyn J. Hinz stresses their similarities, seeing both as artistic responses to the spiritual emptiness of Western society.[28] Rosemary Sullivan argues that the primitivism in Dickey provides "emotional intensity" whereas in Atwood it engenders "moral scrutiny."[29] Dickey, she maintains, celebrates the American myth of self-preservation; that is, Gentry's experience of eros proves that he is, as Dickey says, "really a born killer" (p. 16). Gentry's proof of masculinity supports the view of Atwood's narrator of the typical American instinct to assert power over nature.

The primitivism in *Surfacing*, however, provides more than just a forum for "moral scrutiny." Hinz convincingly argues that "a consideration of the sexual and national differences" reflected in the novels must be done in light of the "cultural decadence and the loss of religious symbolism" which constitute the "major impetus behind the primitivistic impulse in Dickey and Atwood" (p. 91). To understand *Surfacing* in comparison to the American ethos as captured in *Deliverance*, one must see the rise of North American feminism in the context of the decline of traditional patriarchal religion. For example, Mary Daly in her *Beyond God the Father: Toward a Philosophy of Women's Liberation* (1973) argues that "creative eschatology must come by way of the disenfranchised sex."[30] In the past, Daly contends, history evolved when "a particular eros or sense of belonging... provide[d] the identity of a group to the exclusion of others"; the women's movement on the other hand offers "a real leap in human evolution" because "our transformation is rooted in being" (p. 35). Consequently the Christographic images in *Surfacing* emphasize not merely general religious decadence but specifically the inadequacy of patriarchal religious iconography: "bland oleotinted" pictures of Jesus (p. 145) at the narrator's Sunday school suggest He is "tired-looking" (p. 55); Christ is referred to as an "alien god" (p. 14) and God is a "dead man in the sky watching" (p. 45). One can understand the limitations of the narrator's nationalism and feminism only in light of the ultimate development of her spiritual consciousness.

Daly comments that "nationalist movements do not liberate women... because national freedom is identified with male freedom" (p. 54). When the narrator of *Surfacing* discovers that "feeling was beginning to seep back into me" (p. 146), she finally stops using nationalism and feminism as excuses for the "belief that I am powerless" (p. 191). She has, as Hinz and Teunissen argue, regained contact with her essential nature *as woman*, rediscovered the eros principle of her consciousness, long before supplanted by the masculine rule of logos (p. 229). Her childhood painting of mother and child becomes her "mother's gift," her "guide" (p. 158), to a matriarchal perception that "everything is alive, everything is waiting to become alive" (p. 159). At the novel's close, the narrator utilizes the resources of her maternal power to reject her passive innocence and to resolve that her "lost child... must be born, allowed" (p. 191). Deciding "to prefer life," she commits herself not to any nationalistic or feminist ideology but instead to a deeper, psychological form of "worship" (p. 140). The primitivism in Atwood creates religious ecstasy, an older form of worship and self-knowledge.

Atwood herself, in the interview with Sandler, rejects "party loyalties": "What's important to me is how human beings ought to live and behave. ... If people end up behaving in anti-human ways, their ideology will not redeem them" (p. 26). When at the end of the novel the narrator asserts that "the pervasive menace, the Americans... can be watched and predicted and stopped without being copied" (p. 189), she is acknowledging that in the past she "copied" the American way not only when she became a "killer," but also when she accepted her own victimized position as woman and as citizen. The statement summarizes the national, feminine and literary aspects of Atwood's novel. If Canadians are to develop their own humanity, they must cease copying the American drive for prosperity at the expense of nature, just as women must cease accepting male dominance of their psyches; but more profoundly, Canadians must "give up the old belief that [they are] powerless," must "refuse to be a victim" and accept responsibility for their development.

In the interview with Gibson, Atwood has spoken of the necessity of

23. Catherine McLay, "The Divided Self: Theme and Pattern in Margaret Atwood's *Surfacing*," in *The Canadian Novel: Here and Now*, ed. Moss, p. 39.

24. Charles Hanly, "A Psychoanalysis of Nationalist Sentiment," in *Nationalism in Canada*, ed. Peter Russell (Toronto, 1966), p. 305.

25. Evelyn J. Hinz and John J. Teunissen, "*Surfacing*: Margaret Atwood's 'Nymph Complaining,' " *Contemporary Literature* 20, no. 2 (1979): 236.

26. Peter Stursberg, *Lester Pearson and the American Dilemma* (Toronto, 1980), p. 224.

27. William Cobban, "Dealing Out Death Discreetly: The Traffic in Canadian Arms," *Saturday Night* 86 (November 1971): 23.

28. Evelyn J. Hinz, "The Masculine/Feminine Psychology of American/Canadian Primitivism: *Deliverance* and *Surfacing*," in *Other Voices/Other Views: a Collection of Essays from the Bi-centennial*, ed. Robin W. Winks (New York, 1978), pp. 75–96.

29. Rosemary Sullivan, "*Surfacing* and *Deliverance*," *Canadian Literature* 67 (Winter 1976): 12.

30. Mary Daly, *Beyond God the Father: Toward a Philosophy of Women's Liberation* (Boston, 1973), p. 34.

6

"Still Fighting the Same Bloody Battles As Always": *The Diviners* and *Lady Oracle*

In the time present of *The Diviners* (1974), Morag Gunn is amazed to find herself "an established and older writer."[1] Reflecting on the "large number of writers young enough to be her children," Morag echoes Margaret Laurence's own feelings when she muses that she "reads their work out of fascination, not duty." In an interview with Donald Cameron, Laurence discusses the "exchange" between the generations of writers; she will not "go on writing novels all my life" because "soon I will have said what I have to say for my generation, and in my idiom and about my time."[2] "Older writer is the right phrase," Morag concludes, "takes some mental adjustment, though. Meditation. Assimilation." Morag, like her creator, belongs to the generation of women writers who can, indeed, "assimilate." The novel ends, as it begins, with a time present made satisfying by the success of Morag's mature "adjustment" to herself, to her role as writer, and to her society.

The "exchange" between the two generations of women writers culminated in the publication of Margaret Laurence's *The Diviners* in 1974 and Margaret Atwood's *Lady Oracle* in 1976. Certainly the internal evidence of the former suggests Laurence's consciousness of Atwood's novels. The liberated Morag's lifestyle bears a striking resemblance to that of the narrator at the end of *Surfacing* (1972): Morag is raising an illegitimate child outside the institution of marriage; she maintains a profoundly close yet transient relationship with her lover, the father of the child. Furthermore, both protagonists have experienced a "marriage" dominated by the male who symbolically denies his offspring; *Surfacing* is the story of a woman who undergoes an abortion and abortion is a recurring topic in *The Diviners*. Finally, Atwood's critical work, *Survival*, which came out in 1972, described the imprisonment of women by the conventions of society with reference to the fable of Rapunzel and her tower; Laurence echoes this analysis in the "Memorybank Movie" specifically entitled "The Tower," wherein Morag feels stultified by her marriage and consciously recites the Prince's call to Rapunzel.

The Diviners shows not only Laurence's awareness of Surfacing and Survival but also her development beyond the premises of these works and, indeed, her own earlier novels. The Edible Woman (1969) and The Fire-Dwellers (1969) are, like Surfacing, open-ended in that the plot of each concludes with a woman wiser for her experiences and prepared to face life with a different perspective; these works analyze problems and offer only brief and tentative alternatives. But Morag has moved into an independent existence; the focus of the flashbacks is her growth toward that liberation. The Diviners, therefore, addresses and answers the question of the form liberation takes in 1970s society; Morag is the first fully liberated woman in this series of novels under study.

Laurence characterizes Morag as strong-willed, independent and artistic. The portrait painted by her Scottish lover emphasizes "her eyes, clearly and unmistakably the eyes of Morag, angry and frightened, frighteningly strong" (p. 310). This picture is created just after Morag has insisted that she is "not on call" to him, that their meetings must suit her convenience as well as his so that she can have the time she needs to write. Throughout her life, Morag insists that people not "tell me what to do . . . it's the one thing I can't stand" (p. 280). It is fitting that she receives the Currie plaid-pin in the penultimate section of the novel; since her ancestral clan had no "crest or coat-of-arms" Morag adopts those of the Currie ancestors whose battle-cry is "Gainsay Who Dare" (p. 353). She is liberated because, except during her temporary marriage, she "dares" refuse everyone who attempts to "gainsay" her independence.

This allusion to The Stone Angel (1964) demands comparison of Morag and Hagar. Both are strong-willed women but, unlike Hagar, Morag strives to maintain her essential femaleness, her sense of relatedness to those near and dear to her. There are many scenes in the time present wherein Morag's writing is interrupted by visits from her daughter and neighbors. Despite her frustration that such intrusions have become "the pattern of life," Morag affirms that "the only thing that could be said for it was that if no one ever entered that door, the situation would be infinitely worse" (p. 286). Her commitment to the paramount value of relatedness allows her to accept interruptions of her own free will; if her work suffers, her independence does not. Ella, her poet-friend from university days, says, "if you would kindly examine your own life, you would see that quite a few people have been lasting in it." Indeed Morag does work at her relationships with Pique and her neighbors while she also maintains contact with Ella, her Scottish lover and Jules, the father of her child.

The tension between independence and relatedness indicates not only that Laurence moves beyond Atwood but also that she is developing the theme of Ethel Wilson's novels. Laurence mentions in her reflective essay, "Ten Years' Sentences," that Wilson wrote her a complimentary letter after reading one of her early short stories and that they maintained a lifelong friendship.[3] This friendship certainly influenced the younger writer's work. For example, the heroine of *Swamp Angel* (1954), Maggie Vardoe, leaves her dominating husband and strives for an independent lifestyle in a wilderness setting, much as does Morag. *Swamp Angel* demonstrates that a woman can act out of her masculine strength and sense of independence while also working at necessary relationships. This novel, however, focuses only on the difficulties of Maggie's first year and her future is only vaguely, if optimistically, imagined. And Maggie's resolve to remain in relationship with her employer's family and the young Chinese boy who joins their business does not involve the close, complex commitments of lover or children. Laurence concludes with Morag's acceptance of and involvement in life's vital complexity.

Atwood concludes her 1974 profile of Laurence, "Face to Face," with a lengthy review of *The Diviners*, pointing out that "Morag's discoveries and decisions are paralleled to a certain extent by Margaret Laurence's own, although Laurence made them first."[4] Despite Laurence's protests against the autobiographical approach to her fiction, she has admitted that "in this novel I came closer to portraying myself than in any other"; the story of Morag is her "spiritual autobiography."[5] The bulk of the novel, made up of the "Memorybank Movies," records the process of Morag's colonization and her eventual liberation from that position. As noted in the earlier chapter on Laurence, the political implications of that process have not been overlooked by Laurence or her critics. Jane Leney has analyzed Laurence's African fiction and concluded that *This Side Jordan* (1960) can be viewed as an early study of colonizer and colonized of which *The Diviners* is a more mature and complex exploration.[6]

Laurence herself, in *The Prophet's Camel Bell* (1963), cites O. Mannoni's study, *Prospero and Caliban: The Psychological Study of Colonialism* (1956), which taught her to understand colonizers as people who have "fled because they cannot escape men as they are."[7] The presentation of Morag's marriage with Brooke Skelton most clearly demonstrates Mannoni's theory; however, Morag's colonized position lends to Mannoni's definition of colonizer a sexual dimension he no doubt did not intend, but which Laurence most definitely does. Brooke himself is a colonial exiled from India, the place of his birth, and he attempts to recreate another colonial situation with Morag in order to protect himself, as he says, from "the world of Others" (p. 187). The dates of their marriage and separation correspond to those of Indian independence and the Suez crisis, as Ken Hughes notes in his political reading of the novel; from this perspective, Brooke becomes an "unrepentant imperialist...

the last phase of the British Canadian connection within the framework of the imperial ideal." In Morag, whom Hughes exhorts us to see "as the embodiment of Canada," we are to witness "the de-colonization of a psyche."[8]

Morag becomes aware of her colonized position in this marriage by the growing detachment of her interior self from her exterior image. Patriarchal social domination is manifested in the clothes she wears, "clothes that Brooke will like on her," and her own colonized mentality is proven when she has her hair permed the way "Brooke likes," conceding that "it does look more feminine" (p. 180). The extent to which he restricts her world is reflected in the conventional clothes he prefers; both her "tailored suits . . . with pastel blouses, sometimes frilled" and the "little black cocktail dress" suggest that Morag has assumed what Susan Brownmiller has termed the "artificial esthetic" of femininity.[9] Brooke limits her even further when he refuses to have children and talks Morag out of the idea of part-time work, arguing, quite ironically, that at twenty-four she is "still very young for that kind of limited life" (p. 181). He asserts his domination verbally, declaring, "You're mine. My woman. I'll protect you always" and further humiliates her by continually addressing her as "child" and asking, before entering her, "Have you been a good girl, love?" (pp. 182, 200). Such diminutive terms of affection reflect his patronizing attitude to his "little woman."

Morag begins to rebel against this colonization with what seems at first to be motiveless violence, throwing, for example, "a Benares brass ashtray through the kitchen window" (p. 180), perhaps unconscious that the artifact evokes the Indian struggle for independence. She comes to the self-knowledge she needs for successful rebellion only after she returns to Manawaka to attend her foster-mother's funeral. There she is confronted by the past she had denied when she met Brooke: "that was wrong, the turning away, turning her back on . . . them" (pp. 202–3). When she meets Christie, attention is drawn to her "smart" appearance; she reacts by hating "this external self who is at such variance with whatever or whoever remains inside the glossy painted shell" (p. 203). The Christian name of Prin, whose funeral is a catalyst for Morag's self-understanding, is "Princess." And the title of this, the largest section of the novel, comes from a line of "the hymn Prin used to like the best" (p. 207), "Halls of Sion." The hymn, in referring to "those halls of Sion" which are peaceful and harmonious because "the Prince is ever in them," causes Morag to realize that she had "expected, those years ago, marrying Brooke," that he would be the rescuing Prince of the Rapunzel fairy-tale; indeed, she had seen Brooke as "a prince among men" (p. 153) and had responded with "gratitude and care" the first time he called her his woman (p. 162). Morag recognizes that her colonized position resulted from her need for the protection of a man who could gain her entrance into a higher social class than that of her family in which there was no prince, only "Prin," the fat, common, yet loving woman who brought peace to the world of Morag's childhood.

But in Canadian history as in the stories of Canadian women, one cannot read the colonizer as the only villain and rebellion as the only solution. Atwood, in *The Edible Woman*, implies the psychological and social roots of Marian's rationalization. Likewise, the narrator of *Surfacing* discovers that her hatred of males and Americans delayed her recognition of her own violence. But even when women such as Stacey in *The Fire-Dwellers* understand their own limitations, they still have to deal with oppressive external forces and they manage, too, without total rejection. Morag struggles first to assert her own identity while remaining on amicable terms with Brooke; only after he proves determined to maintain his dominance does she realize that remaining in the marriage is, for her, conscious self-destruction. Canada, as reflected in the novels of the nineteenth-century writers as well as Sara Jeannette Duncan and Nellie McClung, developed her identity within the imperial framework. Even Wilson's post–World War II novels implied the need of maintaining the British heritage as a safeguard against the encroachment of American materialism. Hughes, who recognizes that Laurence clearly establishes the national parallels of Morag's marriage, tends to simplify, to make sweeping generalizations about complex historical movements. For instance, after noting that the end of Morag's marriage "coincides exactly with Suez (1956)," he goes on to claim that after Suez "even the most diehard imperialist could have no further illusions about the eternality of the British empire," without taking his analysis any further (p. 43). But Morag's, and Canada's, divorce proceedings, while certainly more decisive than the fictional and national resolutions which had gone before, were much more complex.

Although there was a definite cultural and political shift away from things British after the war and during the 1950s and 1960s, these historic changes were not embraced by even a majority of Canadians. Desmond Morton argues that at the time of the Suez crisis "opinion polls . . . showed a small majority of support for Britain," that "these were the same Canadians who had grumbled as Louis St. Laurent created a distinct Canadian citizenship, abolished appeals to the Privy Council in London, and firmly if discreetly removed crowns, Union Jacks, and other historic symbolism from the public scene." Contrary to Hughes, Morton concludes that "the Suez affair gave British sympathizers a focus for their discontent."[10] And in 1958, Canadians voted John George Diefenbaker the largest majority in Canadian political history in response to his appeal to nationalism and his vision of developing a nation of the North, yet he was also a staunch monarchist; Canada's imperial connection remained strong well into the mid–1960s. *The Diviners* reflects this duality of nationalism and colonialism, for in 1960 Morag moves to England, partly with the intent of seeing the homeland of her Scottish ancestors, but primarily because she believes it the literary center of the world. She may have broken the outward bonds of colonization with Brooke, as Canada did with its "badges of colonialism," but she is still in search of a home she assumes will be British.

Morag's first steps on the road to an independent existence are chronicled in a separate section of the novel, entitled "Rites of Passage," and spanning the years from 1957 to 1967. During this decade Canada was moving much more rapidly along its nationalistic course, but as Morton notes, the roots of divisiveness were well planted, threatening to grow beyond control. One third of Canadians were living below the poverty line, and the majority of these were native people and Metis (p. 216). Diefenbaker lost his mandate in 1963 in part because he could not communicate with, or trust, many of the Quebec members of Parliament in his caucus; the regional split in voting in 1963—the West voting Conservative and the East, especially Quebec, voting Liberal—brought "Canadians . . . face to face with their history" (p. 233). Lester Pearson's Liberals struggled to build a new nationalism, claiming that they represented Canadian unity in diversity; in 1964 Pearson established the Royal Commission on Bi-lingualism and Bi-culturalism. But the national euphoria of Expo year was undermined by Charles de Gaulle's use, in Quebec, of the slogan of Quebec independence, after which René Lévesque formed the *Mouvement souveraineté-association*. On the national scene one finds a country trying to come into her own, to accommodate the disparate elements of her history; in the novel, a woman tries to discover *"the sound of [her] own voice"* (p. 210), to come to terms with her own personal past.

Laurence finds an analogue for Morag's search in the plight of the Indian, more particularly in the offspring of French and Indian, the Metis. Leslie Monkman, in a thematic study of the Tonnerre family in the Manawaka series, concisely points out that the Tonnerres are "established in *The Stone Angel* as 'French half-breeds' opposing the values of white civilization associated with Hagar Shipley." In contrast to Hagar, who is defined by her pride of class, Morag's "understanding of herself and her world . . . is directly linked to her relationship with Jules."[11] From childhood Morag shares an unspoken affinity with this racial outcast from Manawaka society; she finds in his oppression a mirror of her own alienation as the unkempt ward of the town scavenger. Her chance meeting with Jules "Skinner" Tonnerre in Toronto precipitates her break with Brooke, just as in *The Fire-Dwellers*, Stacey's accidental meeting with Jules' sister, Valentine, helps to put her troubles into perspective. Morag "knows . . . that she does not want to stay with Brooke" even before meeting Jules, but when Brooke arrives home and is outraged to find an Indian sitting in his kitchen, drinking his scotch with his wife, Morag "walks out" (p. 220) and begins her rebellion against Brooke's imperial standards.

This use of the Metis to parallel the position of Canadian women is another conceptual advance Laurence makes beyond Atwood who, in *Surfacing*, uses Indian spiritual iconography as only a minor motif. The Indian comes to *The Diviners*, of course, already laden with well-known political significance. Laurence reinforces the reader's historical knowledge by recalling that the Metis were once the "prairie horselords" (p. 334), by contrasting the Scots' and Metis' versions of the Battle of Batoche and by connecting her fictional characters with individuals from prairie history—Jules' grandfather fought with Louis Riel. As Clara Thomas points out, when Morag first meets Jules in the Nuisance Grounds, she recognizes that "he, too, has a tradition behind him [which] includes two hero-ancestors from long ago."[12] For both Metis and orphaned Scots-Canadian, maturity comes with the understanding and acceptance of their mutual ancestral heritages.

While many prairie writers use Metis for various purposes, Laurence does so to reinforce the theme of sexual oppression and to draw attention to the plight of contemporary Indians. In the 1970s, the Canadian Federation of Native Peoples actively pressured Ottawa to settle Indian land claims and to change the system of welfare administered by the Department of Indian Affairs. Led by Harold Cardinal, president of the Alberta Indian Brotherhood, the native people in 1969 rejected the government's proposed new policy presented to Parliament in the so-called "red-paper." Cardinal answered this paper with the publication of his polemic, *The Unjust Society* (1969), the title of which parodies Pierre Trudeau's 1968 election slogan, "the Just Society."[13] Laurence's novel seems designed, in part at least, to support such protest against colonialist, in this case, racist society. Finally, when Jules draws Morag's attention to his French ancestry, Laurence brings to the novel the nationalist aspirations of Quebec which exploded in the October Crisis of 1970. In her choice of a Metis as soul-mate for Morag, Laurence specifically places her protagonist in the context of numerous oppressed minorities and contemporary racial and cultural tensions.

Published in 1974, *The Diviners* also draws parallels between Morag's liberation and that of the Women's Liberation Movement. Morag's desperate attempts to satisfy her sexual and emotional needs while resisting the conventional woman's love-making strategies demonstrate Laurence's quarrel with such superficial advice on attracting men as Helen Gurley Brown advances in *Sex and the Single Girl* (1962). A humorous passage relates Morag's machinations to catch a man, during which "she dislikes and feels alienated from herself with a lot of makeup on" (p. 261). Her search for a sexual relationship which allows independence leads her, after divorce, to sterile, virtually anonymous one-night stands. After sex, Harold, one such man of the evening, repeats the line Luke asked Stacey in *The Fire-Dwellers*: "You wanted that for a long time, didn't you" (p. 263). Unlike Stacey, Morag does not answer; she is annoyed by "the arrogance in his voice" and hurt by "the casualness of this association" (p. 263). A sexual affair cannot help Morag as it did Stacey. In fact, after violent sex with an acquaintance of her landlady, Morag decides *"never again to have sex with a man whose child I couldn't bear to bear"* (p. 270). Morag feels that it is "damned unfair" to have to curtail her sexual fulfillment but this choice is, as Laurence emphasizes by using military and political diction, a psychological breakthrough: Morag "feels as though she has fought the Crimean War"—a notably imperialist war—"single-handed, and won" (p. 270). The "de-colonization of [her] psyche" is underscored when Brooke appears briefly with his new wife who fits the socially accepted image Morag has rejected. No sex is better than sex without love, but such freedom, which precludes relationships, is a pyrrhic victory indeed.

The solution to Morag's impasse lies in a newly defined marriage of equals. Immediately after this last scene with Brooke, Laurence reintroduces his successor: Jules visits Morag and love between them is good, "both equal to each other's body in this urgent meeting and grappling." Reversing the traditional missionary position, Morag "knows he has reached whatever core of being she has." Their love confirms her chosen path; she meets him as an equal, independent: "Listen, Jules, just don't tell me what to do, eh? It's the one thing I can't stand" (p. 280). Laurence has not chosen an easy course for her heroine, and she depicts the triumphs as well as the frustrations to be expected of a woman who elects to reject socially prescribed relationships, while yet striving to "reach out her arms and hold people" (p. 150).

Morag fulfills her feminine need for relatedness not only in loving Jules, but also in bearing their child, Pique. In contrast, Hagar Shipley went to Vancouver with her child when she left her husband, but then remained just as oppressed as before. Laurence could, of course, have made life easier for Morag simply by not introducing the child into her life. But Laurence, in creating Pique, is taking issue with the more extremist members of the Women's Liberation Movement who, she conveys to Atwood in "Face to Face," "state as a general principle that women should not have children" (p. 43). In the same interview, Laurence insists upon the necessity of maintaining communication with "our husbands, our sons, our lovers," and of satisfying the very "normal human desire" to have children. Morag's struggle for self-actualization differs from Germaine Greer's revolutionary call in 1970 for women to end the patriarchal capitalist system by refusing marriage and motherhood.[14] Laurence, through Morag, aligns herself with the older, turn-of-the-century feminists such as Nellie McClung who centered women's rights on the nurturing role of woman. Morag's decision to have a child answers an unspoken need which Brooke had refused to satisfy; while living with Jules she decides not to "do anything to try not to" become pregnant (p. 228). Jules has "known [her] forever" (p. 220), and the child is a link with the past she has so long denied.

Morag's decision to have a child of her own is not unrelated to her struggle to produce a literature of her own. Laurence explores the common assumption that the roles of mother and author are mutually exclusive by deliberately parodying earlier literary models of struggling artists. The pregnant Morag finds herself in Vancouver in a rooming-house which she calls "Bleak House"; the reference not only emphasizes that Morag's literary instruction, most notably under Brooke's tutelage, was in British literature, but also contrasts her care of Pique to Charles Dickens' notorious difficulties with his large family.[15] Moreover, the landlady gives Morag an attic room in exchange for "cleaning, cooking, doing the dishes" (p. 241) and the section is entitled "Portrait of the Artist as a Pregnant Skivvy," parodying James Joyce's definitive *non serviam* of the male artist who feels he must exile himself from family, country and religion in order to create. Morag recalls that Virginia Woolf "once said [a woman] . . . must have a room of her own," while considering, ruefully, that she herself "feels too tired and lousy most evenings to do any writing at all" (p. 242). This reference to Woolf recalls that artist's struggle for artistic recognition in a field dominated by men, and the emotional traumas brought on, in part, by her decision not to have a child.[16] Morag's self-irony, while demonstrating her strength and awareness, also serves to remind the reader that the female writer's struggle must be differentiated from that of the male—Laurence shows Morag's youthful desire to discuss with John Donne and John Milton their anti-feminist opinions as a fanciful and yet valid step in her maturation as a writer. The key difference is explained when Morag ponders the American novel by Thomas Wolfe, *You Can't Go Home Again* (1940), and wonders whether for her "it may be the reverse which is true. You have to go home again, in some way or other" (p. 248). The masculine criteria for art emphasizes the need for distance from familial experience; Morag strives to create while maintaining relations, while finding "home."

She moves to England in 1960 because she sees "London as a kind of centre of writing" (p. 271). After three years in London, she abandons that "fantasy—Morag getting to know dozens of other writers, with whom she would have everything in common. In fact, only a few of her friends are writers, and . . . publishers' parties in London are no more appealing to her and no less parochial than they were in Canada" (p. 294). She learns that when she returns to Canada, "she won't ever again feel that she must be missing out on a lot in these ways." Like Hagar, Morag had been raised on stories of her Scottish forebears, but she discovers that Sutherland is not "the land of my ancestors"; that place is "Christie's real country. Where I was born" (p. 319). The entire "Memorybank Movie" of her stay in England is prefaced by Morag's commentary that "her quest for islands had ended some time ago, and her need to make pilgrimages had led her back" to Canada (p. 293). Her personal and literary discoveries correspond to the awakened nationalism in Canada, for Morag returns "back home" to Canada in 1967, Centennial year, to acknowledge the Manawaka scavenger, Christie, as her father.

As she attempts to produce literature "different" from that of the dominant British and American models, Morag's writing, along with her relationships with men, is decolonized. When Brooke reads the manuscript of her first novel, he questions whether "the main character . . . expresses anything which we haven't known before"; Morag responds internally: "No. She doesn't. But *she* says it. That is what is different" (p. 202). Her next novel,

Prospero's Child, is a contemporary remodeling of Shakespeare's play set vaguely on "some island in some ocean very far south" (p. 270) and dealing with the political theme of colonization in terms of a marriage. In her protagonist's need to "reject nearly everything" about the husband she "worships" "in order to become her own person," Morag seems in her fiction's content and form to explore and exorcise her experience with Brooke. When she describes her novel *Jonah*, written in England, Morag not only, and for the first time, sets her fiction in Canada; she also uses Christie as the model for her title character. Her fiction returns home even before she does.

Morag's literary career mirrors both Laurence's own and the development of contemporary Canadian art. As noted in the conclusion to chapter 3, the Canadian artistic community in the 1950s, including the Stratford Shakespeare Festival and the National Ballet Company, not only performed British material but also used British expertise in the establishment and operation of these institutions. However, over the decade it provided employment and training for Canadian actors and technicians; consequently, with governmental financial patronage working through the Canada Council, Canadian theaters appeared throughout the sixties in all regions of the country, and Canadian playwrights began to write and to see their plays performed. John Ripley notes in *The Literary History of Canada* (1976) that "within a dozen years [1960–72] a coast-to-coast chain of twenty-three Anglophone and Francophone companies would offer a total of 6,489 performances in a single season (1971–2), and that 3,112 of these would feature Canadian plays."[17]

When Laurence published *The Stone Angel* in 1964, the novel was seen as a pioneering venture, but both Claude Bissell and W. H. New claim in retrospect that she was "the major novelist of the sixties," the best of many.[18] Likewise, Morag finds, in the seventies, in Canada, the literary community she had sought in London during the early sixties. A glance at the number of writers in the early seventies in Canada reveals the ethnic variety of the literary material being published in Canada. As Elizabeth Waterston rightly remarks, "Canada has continuously absorbed writers from a very wide range of countries. . . . Wherever they come from, these writers will be the literary ancestors of future generations of Canadian writers. With them, Canada moves into the new world—the global village of the 1970's."[19] One of the biggest changes in Canadian society during the 1960s and early 1970s resulted from the increased contact Canadians experienced with foreign cultures as more travelled to Europe and the Southern Hemisphere. Also, the change, in 1965, in immigration policy brought larger numbers as well as peoples of different nationalities to Canada. "Between 1965 and 1973," report Robert Bothwell, Ian Drummond and John English "average immigration was well over 150,000," in contrast to "the five years prior to the 1965 White Paper [when it] averaged less than 100,000."[20] As well, Canada "reached out her arms" in the October 1970 recognition of China. In a variety of ways, then, these years exposed Morag and Canadians to other people.

Atwood comments in "Face to Face" that *The Diviners* is "at once the most 'international' of Laurence's books and the most national. 'They are not,' says Laurence, 'mutually exclusive' " (p. 39). Certainly Morag is the only Manawaka heroine who travels extensively, both within and outside Canada, the one who interacts with people from the greatest range of cultures. But while the cultural mosaic of Canadian society became more international, the foreign policy of the first Trudeau administration attempted to move Canada to a position more isolationist than that of his predecessors. Bothwell, Drummond and English conclude that Trudeau "shunned international commitment and action more strenuously than any Canadian prime minister since Mackenzie King. . . . Like King, Trudeau believed that his greatest contribution to international affairs would be the maintenance of a united Canada" (pp. 372–73). Just as Wilson's novels dramatized the dangers of such isolationist attitudes, so too *The Diviners*, in its departure from extremist feminist thought and in its advocation of the necessity of maintaining relationships, counters such self-serving forms of independence. As befits a character whose personal pilgrimage is aligned with the Indian and French political struggles in Canada, Morag manages to establish her own form of sovereignty-association with society. While remaining independent, she interacts with a wide international, generational and cultural assortment of people. *The Diviners* develops Ethel Wilson's identity-in-community theme.

A corollary of this theme is Morag's exploration of a diversity of lifestyles and opinion. Morag lives in "a log house nearly a century old, built by a great pioneering couple," much like the home of her long-dead parents; but with humor and a sense of irony, Morag lives there on her own terms, in a garden of wildflowers and unmowed grass. Very much a new woman of the 1970s, she exorcises the ghost of the Old Woman in the New World who figures in her imagination as the nineteenth-century pioneer and writer, Catharine Parr Traill: "I'm going to stop feeling guilty that I'll never be as hardworking or knowledgeable or all-round terrific as you were. . . . I'm not built like you, Saint C." (p. 332). Angelika Maeser rightly points out that "Morag rejects the model of domestic industriousness . . . ; instead, she cultivates 'a wise passiveness' to balance inner functions of intuition and activity."[21] Morag has developed *"the power and the second sight and the good eye and the strength of conviction"* which long ago Christie had established as worthy values in his tales of Piper Gunn's wife, Morag (p. 42). Living in the century-farmhouse, adopting the Currie ancestors, aligning herself with the Metis heritage, she bears witness to Laurence's statement to Cameron that beyond one's grandparents, "the ancestors are everybody's ancestors" (p. 113). "I stand somewhere in between" the nineteenth-century pioneers and the generation of Canadian youth, muses Morag (p. 332). She divines the process of "meditation" and "assimilation" (p. 343) necessary for her well-being and that of the Canadian global community in the 1970s.

"*Look ahead into the past, and back into the future*" (p. 370). These final words stand as a thematic and structural epigraph for *The Diviners*; they specify the primary thrust of Morag's pilgrimage and explain why so much of the novel deals with the past. The process of Morag's liberation has necessitated coming to terms with her ancestors, a process Laurence deems necessary for everyone. But the time present of the novel is not quite as successful, except for Morag's inner monologues in which she is "still fighting the same bloody battles as always, inside the skull" (p. 239). Her struggles with her lifestyle continue and her roles as mother to an eighteen-year-old daughter and as a writer continue. Having accepted that she has "worked out my major dilemmas as much as I'm likely to do in this life" (pp. 238–39), Morag struggles to "let go" of her daughter as well as of unresolvable emotions from her own past and present (p. 358).

Laurence's treatment of Pique, entering the adult world, is far from confident. But while Pique's voice is not fully realized, her symbolic function as "*harbinger of [Morag's] death, continuer of life*" (p. 239) is clear. The product of the three ethnic groups—Scots, French and Indian—is central to the novel as well as to Canadian history. She is the inheritor, but resolution of the disparate parts is left for her, as well as for Canada's, future. The offspring of a liberated woman, she experiences independence of movement and freedom to love whomever she pleases; at the same time, she searches for her own way, struggling against exploitation by her lovers, trying to assimilate her heritage. Pique's problems are Canada's problems in the seventies, as Indian land claims proceeded to the Supreme Court of Canada and French Canada elected a provincial government dedicated to the principle of separation. Canadians at large were as unsure as Laurence of the future character of their country. But Laurence is hopeful. As Jules, who "never managed to do [a song] for myself" (p. 350), was able, after ten years, to "get a song about Lazarus," his father (p. 348), by the novel's end Pique has written her first song about "the valley [that] holds my name . . . [where] my fathers . . . lived . . . long ago" (p. 360). Her quest, Morag notes, "might feel to her unique, [but] was not unique" (p. 360), implying that, like Morag and Jules, Pique will someday discover her ancestors, write a song about her father and thus become, herself, a more clearly defined woman. But Pique's voice, for Laurence's reader, is never clearly heard.

Laurence and Morag have certainly discovered their respective voices; the reader suspects that as Morag goes "to write the remaining private and fictional words, and to set down her title" (p. 370), the book she is writing is *The Diviners*. Just as the novel is a resolution of the themes of Laurence's earlier Manawaka novels, so too the style of *The Diviners* is both a combination of and a development beyond that of her previous works. It continues the experimental style of *The Fire-Dwellers*, slipping easily from third-person narration to interior monologue, but adding the film techniques of Memory-bank Movies and Innerfilms to recall past events. These flashbacks, which make up the bulk of the novel, are arranged in chronological order, as the memories of Hagar were in *The Stone Angel*. *The Diviners* is the assimilation of Laurence's own literary past.

Finally, the style of *The Diviners* is a culmination of qualities reflective of contemporary Canadian society. Laurence mirrors Morag's androgynous character through the eclectic style, for the ordering principle of the flash-backs allows for the masculine artistic principle of distance from material, while the interior monologues and Innerfilms convey the immediacy of experience typical of the feminine. Furthermore, Morag's humor and self-irony convey her maturity, and in a subtle way Laurence suggests that both women and Canada have come of age in the 1970s, for Morag now has the security to laugh at herself, whereas when she struggled to find her creative voice while married to Brooke she could not "bear not to be taken seriously" (p. 211). Moreover, the influence of film, the modern medium of the electronic age, is quite fitting for an "international" novel. Characterization, theme and technique fuse in *The Diviners* to reflect both continuity and openness, characteristics felt necessary, despite Trudeau, by Canadians in the 1970s.

Margaret Atwood continues her literary dialogue with Laurence through her allusions, in *Lady Oracle* (1976), to *The Diviners*. Joan Foster, like Morag, moves to London in the early 1960s, but whereas Morag is a published writer of serious fiction, Joan learns to write Costume Gothics. When her book of poetry is well received by both critics and readers, however, Morag is echoed in Joan's admission that "it was much better than not being taken seriously."[22] Like Morag also, Joan's chief personality crisis concerns her growing awareness of the disparity between her outward appearance and her inner sense of identity; she hides her past from her lovers and her husband, as Morag hid her past from Brooke. *Lady Oracle*, too, has an international setting: Toronto, London and Terremoto (Italy). And Joan has affairs with men from several different backgrounds but, rather than learning from, and assimilating her experiences of them, as does Morag, Joan tries to escape the tangled web of her relationships. When she travels to Italy, she discovers to her consternation that "all the time my own country was embedded in my brain" (p. 310); Morag, on the other hand, accepts with serenity that "the town where I grew up . . . was inside my head, for as long as I live" (p. 290). While Joan shares Morag's sense of humor and self-irony, she does not develop Morag's "wise passiveness"; instead, her "whole life was a tangent" (p. 311). In many respects, it would seem, Atwood has deliberately characterized her heroine as a failed version of Laurence's.

Most critics agree that the novel's central theme is the resolution of multiple personalities. Joan Foster learns, in the end, to acknowledge the various personalities she has always kept separate and also to see the dual or multiple personalities in others, particularly the men in her life. Perhaps her preoccupation with multiplicity accounts for the diversity of styles in the work. Clara Thomas observes that the novel was not "what readers and critics expected from Margaret Atwood . . . nor of a major Canadian novel at this time. . . . *Lady Oracle* has not been compatible with our contemporary mood of urgent and self-conscious literary nationalism."[23] Despite the dismayed reactions of literary nationalists, this comic novel does contribute to the subject of national and feminine identity quests through the protagonist's search for integration in her sense of self and also in her style of writing.

The key to this connection lies in the brief reference, in the novel, to Canadian prime ministers. Twice, within four pages, Joan describes a photograph of the spiritualist Leda Sprott "shaking hands with Mackenzie King" (pp. 203, 207). The picture evokes King's involvement in spiritualism, his devotion to his mother, and his long political hold on the country. The crucial fact about King is that much of his personality—reflected in his interest in spiritualism and women of the night—was well hidden from the Canadian people while he held public office and has been revealed only recently, upon publication of his diaries. His public image as a solid, competent and trustworthy leader disguised many facets of his personality. As Wilfred Cude notes, "Atwood draws our attention to our respectable Prime Minister with the bizarre secret life [as if to say] 'if you think my characters are whirlybirds . . . what do you think of the ones you can find in your history books?' "[24] Atwood explicitly connects her writing style, specifically her characterization, with Canadians', if not Canada's, multiple identities.

The parallels between Atwood's characters and Canadian historical figures do not stop with the references to King. When Joan fakes her suicide in order to escape to Italy, she soon receives, from the friends who helped her, a telegram consisting of "a single word: BETHUNE. That was the code word for success" (p. 185). Norman Bethune was a Canadian hero, of sorts, a doctor who left his family and a lucrative practice in Montreal to assist in the Spanish Civil War and the Chinese Revolution. Official Canadian reaction to his altruism was one of embarrassment, partly because Bethune's communist affiliations made it expedient for Canada, during the cold war, to downplay Bethune's contributions to communist causes, but also because Bethune's unorthodox lifestyle challenged, as Cude notes that King's interest in spiritualism did, "the Canadian self-image of staid conventionality" (p. 152). Bethune acted out his inner compulsions in ways distressing to his public.

Joan goes on to describe her friends' message: "if there had been a fiasco, the letter would have said TRUDEAU." Sherrill Grace discusses Atwood's treatment of the complexities of identity with reference to the role of Trudeau in her works. Analyzing Atwood's *Two-Headed Poems* (1978), Grace notices its thematic focus on "the human tendency to polarize experience, to affirm one perspective while denying the other . . . [which] makes choosing to live with duality very difficult."[25] In the title sequence, Grace concludes, "Atwood portrays the contemporary national dilemma, Quebec separatism, in terms of violent duality." Trudeau "reflects this duality with his two voices . . . but he is accepted and trusted by neither" (p. 133). "What *Lady Oracle* implies," continues Grace, "is . . . that we are all double, perhaps multiple. This condition becomes immoral or psychologically untenable when the desire to be one is reduced to the need to be 'single-minded, single-hearted, single-bodied' (*LO*, p. 211). The oracle tells us that she is 'one and three,' a multiplicity with unity. It is learning how to live, practically, with this knowledge that is difficult" (p. 126). The references in *Lady Oracle* to Trudeau and King, while certainly suggesting that the two prime ministers who remained longest in power have done so through their ability "to live practically" with their dualities, may also be claiming that the insistence by these men on national unity and public propriety, respectively, was "immoral or psychologically untenable."

Atwood is not the only artist or citizen to notice Trudeau's multiple personality. Linda Griffiths has written a "fantasy of love, politics and the media," *Maggie and Pierre* (1980), in which the character of Trudeau comments on his relationship with the Canadian electorate: "As Heraclites said, 'You never walk in the same river twice,' and that's what being Prime Minister of Canada is like. The only way to stay alive is to avoid their wish to define you. Am I a millionaire who's never worked a day in his life, or a dangerous Communist? Québecois or a sellout? They'll never find out."[26] The image of Trudeau as an actor, enjoying the "fluctuations in his performance," is the metaphor Jim Coutts, Trudeau's one-time principal secretary, uses to describe his boss in George Radwanski's biography *Trudeau* (1978): "He's the best actor I've ever seen. He's got more moves than Bobby Orr. You know, in the House one day he's baiting the Opposition, the next he's doing the mumbling number so you can hardly hear him, another he's doing the professor and giving a lecture. He does it to keep everybody off balance. The greatest weapon in a prime minister's arsenal is surprise."[27] In a more sober assessment of Trudeau's political longevity, Radwanski credits his "remarkable ability to keep presenting himself in new guises. . . . Voters . . . have been given the opportunity in each recent election to 'change leaders' by voting for a new Trudeau" (p. 24).

Radwanski also notes Trudeau's "political . . . luck which has made his changing life-style the very embodiment of the changing times":

In 1968, when the New Morality was all the rage and open sexuality was a new adventure, there was Trudeau the swinging bachelor, dating a dazzling succession of beautiful young women. . . . By the early 1970s, the times were settling down, and so was Trudeau; now he was the stable family man, with an adoring young wife and

charming little children. And if there has been a social phenomenon which characterizes the closing years of this decade, it has been the erosion of marriage as an
institution . . . and there, in 1977, was Trudeau the single father, abandoned by a
flighty wife and coping bravely with the demands of his job and three small children.

(pp. 24–25)

Trudeau expresses his multifaceted personality in his political philosophy as
well. Claude Bissell notes, "Trudeau gladly accepted the concept of multi-
cultural mosaic; his insistence that the French language should have equality
with English went along with the encouragement of ethnic variety" (p. 5).
Trudeau embodied, in his political and his private lives, the complexity and
change his voters experienced. George Woodcock, in *The Canadians* (1979),
has concluded that because the "confederation of former colonies . . . [was]
a compact of limited unification," regionalism is a geographic and historical
factor in the Canadian nation, necessitating "a presentation of Canada as a
country whose very nature is contained in the fact that it has as many faces
as a Buddhist deity. An identity can in real life be many-faceted; a unity can
find its reality in diversity."[28] This optimistic belief in integration, paralleled
both by the success of the chameleon Trudeau and by the affirmation of
unity and complexity in *The Diviners*, was typical of the early 1970s.

Midway through the decade, however, national unity seemed more difficult to achieve, and Canadians accepted the need for greater governmental
controls. Such a mood was foreshadowed when the decade began with the
declaration of the War Measures Act which curtailed all civil liberties. By
1974 the phenomenal rise in interest rates and correspondingly high wage
settlements led Trudeau to reverse his election promise and impose wage
and price controls for two years. Federal-provincial conferences demonstrated that relations among the regions were so strained that unity was an
almost impossible dream; Trudeau threatened to repatriate the constitution
unilaterally if the provinces could not reach an agreement on an amending
formula. Threats to the country's unity climaxed in 1976 with the election
of the Parti Québecois in response to its central platform, separatism. By
1976, the hope for unity in diversity had given way to the fear of imminent
fragmentation which could be resisted only by enforced centralization.

Atwood portrays the fragmentation of Canadian identity in the mosaic of
roles which threaten to tear her heroine apart. Joan grows up in English-
speaking Toronto and yet her surname suggests French ancestry; her childhood is influenced, like Atwood's, by American culture; like Morag, she
tries to find herself by living in England; her first lover is European; her
husband is a maritimer running from his roots and trying to find an identity
in American causes; like Atwood too, Joan becomes a literary cult figure on
the Canadian scene. Atwood in *Lady Oracle* is not just reflecting the trends
of Canadian social history but rather is exploring the psychological implications of all these cultural cross-currents which lead, almost inevitably, to

split personality. "If I let [my country] get out of control," cries Joan, "it would take over my head" (p. 310). During her talk in 1976 at York University, Atwood referred to the images of herself which have been created by the media: "I could tell you about Margaret the Magician, Margaret the Medusa, Margaret the Man-Eater . . . Margaret the powerhungry Hitler, with her megalomaniac plans to take over the entire field of Canadian Literature."[29] And during a speech in 1972 at the Empire Club she humorously explained how she had become "a thing" in Canadian society.[30] Both in her public statements and in *Lady Oracle*, Atwood addresses the often contradictory identities required of Canadian public figures.

From the evidence of *Chatelaine* and *Maclean's* magazines in 1975 and 1976, Canadians seemed to want colorful "personalities," perhaps to rival the stars of the American film and television industries, perhaps to satisfy the curiosity and need for vicarious glamor for which the British use the Royal Family. Both magazines in these two years profiled prominent Canadian women such as Margaret Trudeau, Maureen McTeer, Flora Macdonald, Laura Sabia, focusing on the differences between the women's public images and personal identities.[31] If the magazines reflect public tastes, then there developed in the mid–1970s a compulsion to discover the "real woman" beneath the media hype; the irony, which betrays another typically Canadian contradiction, is that this search is conducted in articles which are themselves "media hype."

Lady Oracle, which examines a colorful personality—her public masks and the "real woman" beneath these disguises—is as flamboyant and difficult as its subject. Clara Thomas emphasizes in "The Narrative of a Fool-Heroine" the problem of undertaking critical analysis of this "mixture of comedy, satire and parody" (p. 173); Grace remarks that Atwood "pokes fun at traditions in Canadian writing including her own" (p. 123). For instance, when Joan explains during her first television interview the process of automatic writing which spawned her poetry collection, "Lady Oracle," she parodies Atwood's own comments about the voice of Susanna Moodie inspiring her to compose *The Journals of Susanna Moodie* (1970).[32] Also, self-consciously nationalistic literature is spoofed as Joan considers putting the nationalist's "message into a form that people could understand": "*Terror at Casa Loma*, I'd call it, I would get in the evils of the Family Compact, the martyrdom of Louis Riel, the horrors of colonialism, both English and American, the struggle of the workers, the Winnipeg General Strike" (pp. 246–47). Joan's lover, the concreate poet, the Royal Porcupine, denounces the "beaver . . . as a national symbol. . . . A dull animal and too nineteenth-century; all that industry" (p. 240). Nowhere in the novel does Atwood propose a viable Canadian poetics; instead, she shows, in her style and her comments on Canadian writing, that Canada, colorful and complex as it is, lacks a coherent poetics in much the same way that Joan lacks a coherent personality.

If the inadequate and ridiculous symbol of the beaver and the outline of

"Terror at Casa Loma" connect Canadian art and Canadian history, this novel, which criticizes Canadian art to the point of self-parody, likewise mocks so many Canadian political and social institutions that it frustrates any discovery of a statement of positive alternatives. This is a satire without that genre's traditional moral stance which implies the possibility of a better world. Bilingualism, the cornerstone of Trudeau's political leadership, is spoofed in Joan's reference to her "Weekend Set" of underwear: "I had *Friday* and *Saturday* too, all bilingual" (p. 29). The Canadian National Exhibition, the Queen, the Royal Canadian Mounted Police, all are objects of Joan's—and Atwood's—ridicule. Nothing in Canadian history or society is valued and no social alternative is proposed.

The range of this novel's humor recalls the sense of inadequacy typical of Canadians in the 1950s and 1960s; Atwood draws attention to this inferiority when Joan, falling in love with Arthur Foster, comments: "unfortunately he was only a Canadian, like me, but I over-looked this defect" (p. 165). Arthur had been "absorbed . . . for two years" in the "ban-the-bomb movement" in London, "but somehow he was still on the fringes, a leaflet man." "Perhaps," adds Joan, "it was because he was a Canadian." At the same time, however, that the novel mocks the Canadian need for self-deprecation, its humor demonstrates great vitality and wit, qualities which Atwood's Canadian readers obviously value. The most positive reading of this novel's humor could argue that by 1976 Canadians had become secure enough in their sense of identity as a nation that they could begin to laugh at themselves, at their former inadequacies and unresolved complexities. In this vein, Joan's personality could be seen as spontaneous, creative in a way similar to the broadcaster Barbara Frum as she is portrayed in a 1976 *Chatelaine* profile which presents Frum's compulsive and hectic manner as the source of her success.[33] But such an optimistic reading of the humor and the heroine of *Lady Oracle* is belied by the pervasively cynical tone of the work.

Unlike Atwood's two previous novels, *Lady Oracle* makes specific references to dates which coincide with important phases in Canada's development. Joan says she is seven when she joins the Miss Flegg school of dance in 1949 and later mentions she is thirteen in 1955; to these dates, which establish that she was born in 1942, she later adds that her birthday is in the summer (p. 162). Her formative years are those of wartime, when her father is absent for five years, and her birthdate corresponds most notably with the time of the Dieppe raid in which so many Canadians lost their lives in fighting the Germans. This battle may have demonstrated to the world the strength and courage of Canadian men, but it also, as Wilson's *Hetty Dorval* (1947) suggests, indicated the destructiveness of which Canadians were capable. In this light, then, Cude's psychological assessment in "Bravo Mothball! An Essay on *Lady Oracle*" that "because [Joan] takes her past to be ugly, she lies constantly to conceal what she cannot contemplate,"[34] takes on a political perspective; "her past" is also Canada's.

If by associating Morag with phases of Canada's historical evolution Laurence meant to record the positive effects of the "de-colonization of a psyche," Atwood presents in Joan the confusion and destructiveness of a postcolonial vacuum. Cude attributes Joan's unhappy life to the cruelty of the Miss Flegg School of Dance and to her ensuing conflict with her mother. What one must also note is that the date of these experiences, 1949, corresponds with numerous governmental steps, witness the Canadian Citizenship Act and the Royal Commission on Arts and Letters, to disassociate Canada formally from the mother country. Joan begins her struggle for independence from her mother at the same time that Canada did.

But while Canada began moving away from the trappings of British colonialism, she was also welcoming American culture and investment. Before the country had time to establish its own cultural identity, or even to implement the recommendations of the Massey Commission, its citizens, encouraged by government policy, had assimilated American goods and values. Joan's teen years begin in 1955—the date is mentioned twice—and like most North American youngsters in the mid–1950s, she listens to Elvis Presley singing some such song as "Heartbreak Hotel" (p. 71). This typical teenager plans to name her goldfish after Susan Hayward, the movie star, because "the odds were stacked against this goldfish and I wanted it to have a courageous name" (p. 80); during the 1950s, Hayward starred in three biographical pictures about brave women who struggled against overwhelming personal agonies. But the point is that, as for so many Canadian teenagers in the 1950s, the reigning cultural models were the American which had simply replaced the British.

Atwood indicates American domination of postcolonial Canadians by the direct derivation of Joan's name from the American silver screen; her mother named her after actress Joan Crawford as confidently as she herself named her goldfish after Susan Hayward. The result, for the girl if not for the fish, is the traumatic sense of having no identity: "did she give me someone else's name because she wanted me never to have a name of my own?" (p. 42). The choice of Crawford symbolizes much more than the beauty and alien identity recognized, respectively, by Mrs. Delacourt and her daughter. If *Mommie Dearest* (1978) had been published before 1976, we could speculate about its influence on Atwood's characterization in *Lady Oracle*; as it is, the novelist was certainly prophetic, for Crawford's daughter Christina dramatizes that underneath the glamorous public image of the movie star existed a neurotic, sadistic woman. More likely, Atwood had in mind Joan Crawford's Academy Award–winning performance in *Mildred Pierce* (1945), a film which depicts the emotional battle between an overprotective mother and her vindictive daughter. As well, the actress herself contains a blend of multiple personalities, for Joan Crawford is the stage name of Lucille LeSueur, and she acted the roles of so many "screen characters," all of whom are "beautiful, ambitious, ruthless, destructive to men" (p. 42), that they were perceived as various masks of her own femme-fatale qualities. Joan's name, then, introduces not only the themes of multiple personality and cultural imperialism, but also the models of female identity implicit in the conflict between mother and daughter.

The political ramifications of the conflict between Joan and her mother center on the latter's attempts to shape Joan into her notion of female identity and her refusal to let Joan develop her own. That female image corresponds to society's mold which is clearly stamped "made in America." Mrs. Delacourt makes herself up in the mirror to look "like Bette Davis" (p. 68), but the new face is never complete; she is left "sadder, as if she saw behind or within the mirror some fleeting image she was unable to capture or duplicate" (p. 66). Joan's mother is characterized as a woman unfulfilled by the roles of wife and mother yet unable to graft movie glamor into her life. She redecorates a succession of homes to reflect upward social mobility and throws dinner parties "to help [her husband] with his career" as anesthetist, a career for which "he had studied . . . at my mother's urging" (pp. 72–73). Mrs. Delacourt is frustrated by her failure to remodel her family and home according to American images which, distorted, create only a lack of meaning.

Atwood describes the politics, within this family, of the creation and resistance to American images as that of warfare. In adolescence Joan resists her mother's efforts to "make me over in her image, thin and beautiful" (p. 88) simply by gorging herself on sweets and becoming fat. "To think that I named you after Joan Crawford," muses her mother (p. 42). The "battleground was my body" (p. 69). Obesity in women is the topic of Judy Kopinka's *Fat Is a Feminist Issue*, which asserts that "being fat represents an attempt to break free of society's sex stereotypes. For many women, being fat says 'screw you' to all who want me to be the perfect mom, sweetheart, maid and whore."[35] From enrollment at the age of seven in dancing class to a year in Brownies, Joan discovers the socially accepted cruelty inflicted on girls who do not fit into the "sugar-and-spice" image. Whereas Marian, in *The Edible Woman*, conforms to the "thin and beautiful" prescription through her anorexia, Joan's rebellious obesity is a "refutation" of her mother, a "victory" (p. 74).

Cude's extensive discussion of *Lady Oracle* in *A Due Sense of Differences* (1980) presents Joan, the deliberate "consumer," as an object lesson for Western society. He may be right to point out, as does the novel, that "a nation of shop-keepers" (p. 147) is to be found in Britain as well as North America, that the social values criticized in the novel are common to all Western nations, but in so doing he underestimates the extent to which the novel pins the American label to such consumer values. Atwood's characterization specifies that the formative influence on Joan is American. The satirical target of *Lady Oracle* is ultimately the same as that of *The Edible Woman*: the takeover of Canadian identity by American consumerism and the acceptance by women, such as Joan's mother and Marian McAlpin, of the "sexual sell" of North American advertising. Both protagonists rebel, finally, but whereas Marian tries to stop the process of consumption, the adolescent Joan of the earlier decade gives in to it. Joan's gluttony provides a humorous and grotesque analogy of the 1950s glut of American products on the Canadian market. In the tension between Joan and her mother, Atwood subtly reflects the guilt of a nation which not only turned from her motherland but also betrayed her in favor of "the fat cat" closer to home.

In *Lady Oracle*, then, Atwood continues to argue the overriding similarities of the societies of the United States and Canada. Joan becomes involved with a European whose inability to distinguish between a Canadian and an American specifies the political implications of her characterization. But Joan's decision to escape to England, because "living in a rented room in Albany would be the same, finally, as living in a rented room in Toronto" (p. 141), suggests another political fact; the one consistent difference between the American and Canadian traditions has always been Canada's loyalty to the monarchical system. To continue to note the dating of events, Joan flees from home to England in 1961, in other words, at about the same time as did Morag, a time when, as indicated in the discussion of *The Diviners*, Canadians still widely accepted the British component of their identity.

For Atwood, however, unlike Laurence, the British connection is not easily maintained or severed. And Atwood's more accurately reflects Canada's experience in the early 1960s. "In [Pearson's] view," state Bothwell, Drummond and English, "Canada could not remain a nation if it continued to dwell upon its past" (p. 270). Pearson continued, in the Liberal policy of Mackenzie King and Louis St. Laurent, to move Canada away from the outward signs and symbols of her colonial ties to England, adopting, to mention his most obvious and controversial effort to this end, a distinctively Canadian flag. The confusion which resulted, instead of the positive sense of identity Pearson promised, is mirrored in Joan's growing sense of nonentity. Joan is aware that she is "a different person" in England, having slimmed down to "the right shape" (p. 141) but her new image has "the wrong past." Whereas Morag's stay in England brought her increased maturity, stability and the recognition that her true identity lay in the past she had so long denied, Joan simply grows "narrower" (p. 145). And while earlier she had at least felt herself to be "an exception, with the limitations that imposed, now [she] was average" (p. 144). Unlike Morag who grows beyond her colonial attitude, Joan remains "provincial" in the face of imperial standards; England, she discovers, is "a message in code which I didn't know how to decipher" (p. 145). Morag initiates a love relationship with a Scotsman on the basis of their common past while Joan becomes entangled with two "patronizing" men; from both she, typically, hides her true identity (p. 146).

That Joan falls in love with Arthur Foster in 1963 serves to further Atwood's satire of the Canadian search for identity. In *A Due Sense of Differences*, Cude, interpreting both the Polish count and Arthur Foster as models of courage and idealism for Joan to emulate, overlooks Atwood's more pessimistic intent (pp. 145–46). Arthur mirrors both the drift toward "being on the American team" as Pearson proposed and the tendency of Canadian youths and intellectuals in the 1960s to involve themselves in American socio-political issues. Arthur's emotional fulfillment derives primarily from his championship of American causes: "This time it was civil rights: he went down to the States and almost got shot. . . . In quick succession he went through Vietnam and sheltering draft dodgers, student revolt" (p. 211). In 1968, Joan and Arthur take a belated honeymoon to Quebec because "it was Arthur's Quebec separatist incarnation," but even as Arthur adopts this radical Canadian political stance, they spend the first night there watching "the funeral of Robert Kennedy" (p. 208) on television. The date, therefore, is June 8, 1968, and one might think it strange that there is no mention in the book of the Trudeau campaign which culminated on June 22 with the election of the first majority government in Canada since 1958. The point is that Arthur, caught up by the issues and personalities of the American stage, is oblivious to the political phenomenon of his own country. For him as for Joan, vicarious American identity overshadows a viable Canadian role.

Moreover, "the absence of a sense of purpose" (p. 196) in Arthur's political energies echoes Joan's sexual politics. When they first meet, she believes "the right man had come along, complete with a cause I could devote myself to. My life had significance" (p. 171). Frank Davey, analyzing Joan's difficulties in male-female relationships, rightly concludes that she "relives her parents' drama of the unfulfilled, isolated, and dependent woman linked to an aloof and undemonstrative man."[36] Joan's greatest role is that of Mrs. Arthur Foster. And like Mrs. Brooke Skelton, Joan adopts the image of a self-effacing, supportive wife; but where Morag grows increasingly restive within the restrictions of her role of housewife, Joan desires to preserve the security marriage provides. Cude argues that Joan uses Arthur as an excuse for her failings, a reason for not trying to improve herself as a person in her own right (p. 161). To this end, she serves inedible food because "Arthur enjoyed my defeats. . . . My failure was a performance and Arthur was the audience. His applause kept me going" (p. 210). Just as Brooke insisted that Morag conform to his notion of femininity, so too, Joan strives "to turn into what Arthur thought I was, or what he thought I should be" (p. 210). Moreover, Arthur's "expectations . . . were [not] confined to cooking"; with every change in Arthur's social concerns, Joan had to adjust her views, despite the fact that she "found it so hard to read theories" (p. 211). Joan, unlike Morag, willingly remains in her colonized marital role because she lacks the strong sense of identity necessary for assuming responsibility for the direction of her own life.

Atwood has her narrator describe her childhood and adolescence in Parts

One and Two, respectively, so that the reader might have some understanding of Joan's confusion and inadequacy as an adult. And certainly some degree of compassion is evoked for both Joan and her mother because of the few creative outlets provided them in the subservient role prescribed for women. But Atwood does not allow a simple, one-sided sympathy for her heroine. Throughout adulthood, Joan is haunted by the image of her former fat self, "wearing pink tights with spangles, a short fluffy pink skirt, satin ballet slippers and, on her head, a sparkling tiara" (p. 102). Joan "knew how Arthur would analyze this fantasy": his simplistic interpretation would see "the attitudes of society, forcing me into a mold of femininity that I could never fit. . . . How much better for me if I'd been accepted for what I was and had learned to accept myself, too" (p. 103). Neither Joan nor Atwood allows the reader to accept this view of Joan as victim of social conditioning for, as she adds, the feminist analysis is "very true, very right, very pious. But it's still not so simple. I wanted those things, that fluffy skirt, that glittering tiara. I liked them" (p. 103). Joan wills her own colonization.

The narrator in *Surfacing*, Marian in *The Edible Woman* and Morag in *The Diviners* all discover the extent to which they inculcate their society's image of femininity, but the difference between them and the heroine of *Lady Oracle* is that Joan never breaks out of her repressed state. Joan would rather "dance as a ballerina, though faultily, than as a flawless clown" (p. 286). Despite her adolescent rebellion against the ballerina image, she harbors the desire to conform to the feminine qualities of slim gracefulness. That her social initiation took place in 1949 corresponds to Canada's attempts to fit imperial cultural standards, exemplified by the formation of the National Ballet Company by Celia Franca and Betty Oliphant. Although no nation or individual wants to be considered a clown, Joan's use of the term "flawless" suggests that she, and Canada, could achieve a distinctive, if conventionally odd, perfection by establishing their own standards instead of trying to live up to imported ideals.

Unfortunately, Joan does not, and her self-destructive habits of imitation in the roles of "dancer" and housewife carry over into her artistic expression. Whereas Morag finds her own literary voice, Joan merely learns to write derivative "historical romances" in order to "make money faster" (p. 155). Joan defends her books on feminist grounds, pointing out that while the "great escapes" such as "war, politics and explorations up the Amazon . . . hockey or football" of the masculine world are "by and large denied" to her female readers, she offers them "hope . . . a vision of a better world, however preposterous" (p. 35). Certainly Joan offers a "preposterous" "vision": romance fictions rely on stereotyped sex roles and, according to one study of Harlequin romances, Margaret Ann Jensen's *Love's Sweet Return* (1984), affirm the notion that "heroines are still helpless, politically unconscious individuals who want to be dominated by heroes."[37] Indeed, during the years of her marriage to Arthur, Joan's "work at [her] current Costume

Gothic" provides a fantasy release which allows her to remain "patient and forbearing, warm, a sympathetic listener" (p. 213). In other words, her "vision of a better world," which promises highly questionable improvement, keeps her enslaved in an otherwise untenable existence.

In her portrayal of this author of romance fiction, Atwood develops her satire of Canadian women. Harlequin, which began in Winnipeg, developed into the world's largest publisher of romance fiction and by 1977 accounted for 28 percent of all paperback sales in Canada. Joan's justification is consistent with the comments made by Harlequin readers to Janice Radway in her exploration of the attraction of romance fiction, that romance fiction offers an escape from and a means of coping with the demands of their roles as wives and mothers.[38] Although Harlequin editors defend the Harlequin formula on the grounds that it is simply giving its female readers what they want, romance fiction, by reinforcing stereotyped sex roles, is a modern method of keeping women in their place as surely as Catharine Parr Traill did in the nineteenth century with her handbook on good housewifery. The enormous popularity of Harlequin is symptomatic of the reactionary mood in the 1970s among the many women who rejected the concepts of women's liberation and followed instead the advice of the Angelin Institute which counselled women to maintain their marriages by cultivating their positions of subservience.[39] It is no surprise that during the rise of feminism such strong opposition, deriving perhaps from Jerry Falwell's very popular Moral Majority, also developed. Like Joan, many Canadian women prefer male dominance to female liberation, romance fiction to artistic expression of personal voices.

Such "innocence has its hazards," Joan discovers (p. 149), as did the narrator of *Surfacing*. Twice Joan is told by Leda Sprott that she has "great powers" which, if not developed, "will make use of [her] in any case, though perhaps in a less desirable way" (p. 206). Joan is "afraid to develop them" (p. 286) but Leda Sprott's prophecy is realized when Joan's unacknowledged feelings finally "go public" (p. 216). She publishes a sequence of poems which both her friends and the literary community read as an attack on marriage, "a very angry book" (p. 237). She fails to see this hostility, claiming that she is happy in her marriage. Joan's refusal to act upon, or even recognize, her growing impatience with Arthur is indicative of her failure to rebel against male domination. If one can compare her to the more successful writer and woman, Morag Gunn, one must also consider her misuse of her "great powers" of psychic complexity as a criticism of those other public chameleons, Mackenzie King and Pierre Trudeau.

Joan's lack of self-knowledge, which so limits her experience of marriage, prevents her from growing beyond destructive behavior. Unlike the liberated Morag who finds both independence and relatedness, "reaching out to hold others," Joan is constricted by her need for dependence, for someone to "hold" her. The childish haze through which she views the world constantly causes her to see men in such romantic guises that she reshapes facts to fit her fantasies. Gisella Konopka, in *The Adolescent Girl in Conflict*, observes that "the gap between this feminine ideal and her own reality can motivate her to seek an outlet for aggression that is linked to her feelings of acceptance as a woman. Sexual misconduct is the logical result."[40] When Joan tires of serving Arthur, rather than taking steps to redefine their marriage, she has an affair with the Royal Porcupine; they stay together only as long as he conforms to her bizarre fantasy-image. Likewise, although she insists that she never treats Arthur as one of her heroes, all the while she is in Terremoto, she imagines him "coming to retrieve" her (p. 8). It is such consistently misguided femininity, such pathetic immaturity, which, contrary to her assertions, makes her a very flawed clown.

Joan, ignoring in adolescence her high-school teacher's lesson on Canada's "natural resources" (p. 102) as well as her own "great powers" in adulthood, resembles the "fiasco" both of Trudeau's enforced centralization of the country and that of the women's movement. The "fiasco" of International Women's Year, according to Greer, was that "feminism is a revolutionary movement and cannot reasonably expect to find its interest served by governments which have come to power in the traditional masculine ways." "Discussion of the . . . phenomenon of sexism would have to wait," it seems, "on economic redistribution" between the developed and undeveloped countries of the world.[41] Examining the impact of *International Women's Year* on Canada, Michele Landsberg strikes a similar note when she concludes that "government ballyhoo in honour of women fell flat . . . [and] official funds were dribbled away" on programs designed to change "people's attitudes" rather than "the painful but necessary laws enforcing equal rights."[42] *Lady Oracle* reflects the confusion in 1976 when so many conflicting voices were telling women how to live: be a mother and/or have a career; enter a traditional marriage and/or be promiscuous. Like women, Canada found it extremely difficult to find her way. Trudeau was forced in mid-decade to turn from his isolationist tendencies of the early 1970s and back to the traditional markets of the United States for investment and growth. Bothwell, Drummond and English emphasize that many of Trudeau's desires in the early 1970s could not be implemented because of external factors such as the worldwide recession and the escalation in the world price of oil; in the end, they conclude, "Trudeau's attempt to create long-range plans had produced mainly ambiguity; with ambiguity comes confusion and even paranoia" (p. 355). *Lady Oracle* conveys this national mood in the face of hard economic facts by the telling parallel of the confusion of a Canadian woman.

In conclusion, it is apparent that Laurence and Atwood present two contrasting perspectives on the future, one basically optimistic and the other pessimistic. Laurence's portrait of liberation radically conflicts with the selfish aggression of Germaine Greer and Helen Gurley Brown; Morag may exercise her strength of character, but she remains responsible to those who

care for her. And while Pique, representative of future womanhood, remains
confused, her quest is presented with compassionate hope. Although Atwood's characterization of Joan seems to imply that the reader should, as
Atwood says, "go . . . and do unlikewise,"[43] a positive alternative is not offered. Perhaps this character is best approached in the spirit of Atwood's
injunction at the end of her Gerstein Lecture: she hopes that a female
character like Joan with "the emotions all human beings have" will not be
"pronounced a monster, a slur, or a bad example." "Men in literature,"
continues Atwood, "have been seen as individuals, women merely as examples of a gender; perhaps it is time to take the capital W off Woman"
(p. 26). Canadians, after the midpoint of the decade, must read Morag and
Joan, characters of this time in Canadian history, as individuals, not just as
women typical of their time. This perspective leads to discovery of the saving
humor of the novels and the affirmation in both of the vitality, however
misdirected, of the heroines. One might, finally, extend this point of view
to a perception of Canada as a country at long last like other independent
nations: paradoxical, complex, in short, adult at last. Analysis of fictional
Canadian women of the years after the mid–1970s as "examples of a gender"
may be as inappropriate as analysis of Canada after the mid–1970s as an
example of a colonized country.

NOTES

1. Margaret Laurence, *The Diviners* (Toronto, 1974), p. 343.
2. Donald Cameron, *Conversations with Canadian Novelists* (Toronto, 1973),
pp. 102–5.
3. Margaret Laurence, "Ten Years' Sentences," *Canadian Literature* 41 (Summer 1969): 10.
4. Margaret Atwood, "Face to Face," *Maclean's* (May 1974): 38.
5. Margaret Laurence, Public Forum, Mohawk College, Hamilton, May 10,
1975.
6. Jane Leney, "Prospero and Caliban in Laurence's African Fiction," *Journal
of Canadian Fiction* 27 (1980): 63–80.
7. Margaret Laurence, *The Prophet's Camel Bell* (Toronto, 1963), p. 227.
8. Ken Hughes, "Divining the Past, Present, Future," *Canadian Dimension*
(March 1975): 43.
9. Susan Brownmiller, *Femininity* (New York, 1983), p. 139.
10. Desmond Morton, *A Short History of Canada* (Edmonton, 1983), p. 221.
11. Leslie Monkman, "The Tonnerre Family: Mirrors of Suffering," *Journal of
Canadian Fiction* 27 (1980): 143, 148.
12. Clara Thomas, "Myth and Manitoba in *The Diviners*," in *The Canadian Novel:
Here and Now*, ed. John Moss (Toronto, 1978), p. 107.
13. Harold Cardinal, *The Unjust Society* (Edmonton, 1969).
14. Germaine Greer, *The Female Eunuch* (London, 1970), p. 320.
15. Dickens' "misery in his marriage" is recounted in Edgar Johnson, *Charles*

Dickens: His Tragedy and Triumph (New York, 1952), pp. 904–26, and in Edward Wagenknecht, *The Man Charles Dickens* (Norman, Oklahoma, 1966), pp. 155–71.

16. Woolf echoes her famous prescription for the woman writer in *A Writer's Diary*, ed. Leonard Woolf (London, 1953), p. 119: "I don't like the physicalness of having children of one's own. . . . I can dramatise myself a parent, it is true. And perhaps I have killed the feeling instinctively." Yet in another entry she anguishes, "I want to appear a success even to myself. Yet I don't. . . . It's having no children . . . failing to write well" (p. 29).

17. John Ripley, "Drama and Theatre," in *Literary History of Canada*, gen. ed. Carl F. Klinck, 3 vols. (Toronto, 1976), 3: 212.

18. Claude Bissell, "Politics and Literature in Canada in the 1960s," in *Literary History of Canada*, ed. Klinck, 3: 9; W. H. New, "Fiction," in *Literary History of Canada*, ed. Klinck, 3: 234.

19. Elizabeth Waterston, *Survey: A Short History of Canadian Literature* (Toronto, 1973), p. 139.

20. Robert Bothwell, Ian Drummond and John English, *Canada since 1945: Power, Politics, and Provincialism* (Toronto, 1981), p. 371.

21. Angelika Maeser, "Finding the Mother: The Individuation of Laurence's Heroines," *Journal of Canadian Fiction* 27 (1980): 163.

22. Margaret Atwood, *Lady Oracle* (Toronto, 1976), p. 286.

23. Clara Thomas, "*Lady Oracle*: The Narrative of a Fool-Heroine," in *The Art of Margaret Atwood*, ed. Arnold E. Davidson and Cathy N. Davidson (Toronto, 1981), p. 174.

24. Wilfred Cude, *A Due Sense of Differences: An Evaluative Approach to Canadian Literature* (Lanham, Md., 1980), p. 152.

25. Sherrill Grace, "More Than a Very Double Life," in her *Violent Duality* (Montreal, 1980), p. 133.

26. Linda Griffiths, *Maggie and Pierre* (Vancouver, 1980), pp. 64, 66.

27. George Radwanski, *Trudeau* (Toronto, 1978), p. 14.

28. George Woodcock, *The Canadians* (Don Mills, 1979), p. 292.

29. Margaret Atwood, "The Curse of Eve—Or, What I Learned in School," in *Women on Women*, ed. Ann B. Shteir (Toronto, 1978), p. 25.

30. Margaret Atwood, "Getting Out from Under," *Empire Club Addresses 1972–73* (Toronto, 1973), pp. 356–57.

31. See Bobbie Turcotte and Mary Hemlow, "Searching for the Real Margaret Trudeau," *Chatelaine* (October 1975): 64–65, 127–32; Susan Swan, "Barbara Ann Scott, Are You Still Happy, Happy?" *Chatelaine* (November 1975): 50, 74–86; Bonnie Buxton, "Meet Maureen McTeer," *Chatelaine* (October 1976): 52–53, 117–23. In light of her thesis in *Survival*, Atwood would appreciate the focus of Sheena Paterson and Mary C. McEwan's article, "Margaret Trudeau's Struggle for Identity: Victor or Victim?" *Chatelaine* (August 1977): 32–33, 91–93.

32. Atwood explained to David Arnason and Dennis Cooley during a radio interview at the University of Manitoba, in November 1975, how a dream about Susanna Moodie spawned a few poems which she set aside, until a few months later Moodie's voice began to speak to her and she created *The Journals of Susanna Moodie* (1970).

33. Heather Robertson, "Keep Plugging, Barbara Frum," *Maclean's* (June 1975): 32–35.

34. Wilfred Cude, "Bravo Mothball! An Essay on *Lady Oracle*," in *The Canadian Novel: Here and Now*, ed. Moss, p. 48.

35. As quoted in John Haslett Cuff, "Too Fat to Make the Grade?" *The Globe and Mail*, July 16, 1983, Fanfare, p. 2.

36. Frank Davey, "Atwood's Comic Novels," *Studies in Canadian Literature* 5 (1980): 214.

37. Margaret Ann Jensen, *Love's Sweet Return* (Toronto, 1984), p. 97.

38. Janice Radway, *Reading the Romance: Women, Patriarchy and Popular Literature* (University of North Carolina Press, 1984).

39. Valerie Ross, "She Stoops—Grovels!—to Conquer," *Maclean's* (December 15, 1975): 67.

40. As quoted in Judith Finlayson, "More to Birth Control Than Mere Education," *The Globe and Mail*, August 6, 1983, Fanfare, p. 4.

41. Germaine Greer, "On Women's Year," *Chatelaine* (September 1975): 101, 103.

42. Michele Landsberg, "Has Women's Year Laid an Egg?," *Chatelaine* (November 1975): 53.

43. Margaret Atwood, "What's So Funny?: Notes on Canadian Humour," in her *Second Words: Selected Critical Prose* (Toronto, 1982), p. 183.

7

"Welcome to the 1980s!": A Conservative Conclusion

On October 18, 1929, the Privy Council of Great Britain decreed that women are persons. Up to this date, the only persons appointed to the Canadian Senate were male because the British North America (BNA) Act, in defining the constitution of the Senate, took legal precedent from an 1876 British court ruling: "women are persons in matters of pains and penalties, but are not persons in matters of rights and privileges."[1] Led by Emily Murphy, Nellie McClung and three other women appealed to the Privy Council for a clarification of the word "persons" in the BNA Act; the Council explained that its verdict, calling for recognition of women as "persons," conformed to the spirit of the BNA Act in that it was conceived, not as a static document, but as the law which would enable Canada to evolve, to become "mistress in her own house." Again and again in Canadian history, as this statement from the Persons Case illustrates, feminism has been connected with nationalism. The preceding chapters focused on the formative struggle of Canada and women for equality, recognition and status. This chapter continues that examination with focus on the 1980s, the decade of the repatriation of the Canadian Constitution with a Charter of Rights and Freedoms which guarantees equal rights for the women of Canada.

Ever since Frances Brooke's *The History of Emily Montague* (1769), women writers have recognized the close connection between the personal and the political. Women, throughout Canadian history, used feminine forms of writing to reflect, and to reflect on, the issues of their times. They perceived, as did Nellie McClung, that "the home . . . include[s] the whole state." In the 1980s, the relation of the personal and the political, implicit in and central to an understanding of the history of Canadian women's literature, is quite explicit, no longer "sub/versive," as Lorna Irvine main-

tains in her 1986 study *Sub/Version: Canadian Fiction by Women*.[2] On the
contrary, as this chapter will briefly demonstrate, the fiction published by
Margaret Atwood in the 1980s is as overtly political as Atwood herself is
socially active during the decade. Atwood was editor of and contributor to
This Magazine, a left-wing journal of social and cultural commentary; she
appeared on the Canadian Broadcasting Corporation's *Journal* from time to
time encouraging viewers to write their members of Parliament. She was
spokesperson for Amnesty International and president of PEN International.
In 1988 she spoke before a Commons committee against the government's
proposed Bill 101, the Censorship Law. Likewise her friend and colleague,
Margaret Laurence, was socially active right up until her death in 1986.
Although there was no fiction after *The Diviners* in 1972, Laurence was
heavily involved as chancellor of Trent University, often engaging in dialogue
with staff and students there. She made numerous speaking engagements
on peace and ecology, her stance perhaps best summed up in her oft-quoted
"My Final Hour."[3] These major women writers moved, in the 1980s, from
fiction, which can be read politically, into political action, and, in Atwood's
case, overtly political fiction.

Moreover, in an address to a world meeting of Amnesty International in
1981, Atwood commented that readers and critics of books "are good at
measuring an author's production in terms of his craft. [But] we are not good
at analyzing it in terms of his politics, and by and large we do not do so."[4]
As Margaret Laurence did with her essay "Ivory Tower or Grassroots,"
Atwood here invites a political reading of her work. Certainly her involvement with Amnesty International and her tenure as president of PEN International provided material for *Bodily Harm* and *The Handmaid's Tale*.
In fact, Atwood's three novels of the 1980s coincide with three political
periods in this decade: the publication of *Bodily Harm* in 1981 with Pierre
Trudeau's last term of office, 1980–84; the publication of *The Handmaid's
Tale* in 1985 with the first term of Brian Mulroney's Conservative government, 1984–88; and the publication of *Cat's Eye* in 1988 with the reelection
of the Mulroney government that same year. Atwood's writing in the 1980s
develops quite explicitly her political observations.

When Trudeau's Liberals were defeated by Joe Clark's Conservatives in
the 1979 election, many political analysts would have labelled the Trudeau
years the "fiasco" suggested in *Lady Oracle* (1976). But when Trudeau stood
before television cameras and his victorious fellow Liberals on election night
in February 1980 and announced, "Well, welcome to the 1980s," he seemed
to suggest that his vision of Canada would prevail throughout the decade.
Such prophecy was not to be fulfilled, yet during his last term in office
Trudeau certainly succeeded in implementing many of his policies. After
the defeat of the Parti Québécois's referendum on sovereignty-association,
Trudeau turned his attention to repatriation of the Constitution. In April
1982, the Canadian Constitution with an attached Charter of Rights and

Freedoms was signed in Ottawa by the Queen; after 115 years, Canada had its own made-in-Canada constitution. Trudeau responded to the rise in international oil prices by forming PetroCanada and the Canada Development Corporation, nationalistic measures designed to protect the supply of oil and natural gas for future Canadians. Near the close of his last term Trudeau travelled the globe on a personal peace mission and took an active role in encouraging greater North-South dialogue between the have and have-not countries. Trudeau's last term was one of active, national and international politics.

The international setting and the political plot and themes of Atwood's *Bodily Harm* echo these larger concerns. The novel dramatizes human rights issues such as the treatment of political prisoners, North-South relations, Canadian ignorance of and unwitting complicity in Third World poverty and politics, and the complacency of northern people in the face of repression. The book seems to reprise *Surfacing*'s theme of culpable innocence as the heroine discovers that "no one is exempt"[5] from brutality by reason of race or nationality. As the title, the legal term for rape, suggests, the novel explores male dominance of and violence to the female body and female complicity in this violent act. As in *Surfacing* (1972), the two types of violence, political and sexual, are connected, but *Bodily Harm* is much more explicit in this theme, and the violence which illustrates this message is much more widespread and brutal.

The protagonist, Rennie Wilford, a lifestyles journalist for a Toronto magazine, travels as tourist to a Caribbean island nation, ostensibly to write a travel piece but actually to rest and recover after her mastectomy and subsequent separation from her lover, Jake. Because she is suspected of being a CIA operative using the cover of a journalist, she gets caught up in a political election, the first since the ruling British left, and a revolution. Rennie becomes an accomplice when she unwittingly smuggles a machine gun through Customs for one of the opposition political parties. In similarly helpful fashion, "the sweet Canadians"—the ironic label given by one of the island politicians—send hurricane relief aid which is used by the corrupt incumbent to bribe the people during the election. Jailed because of her association with people on the losing side, Rennie realizes that torture and terror can touch her, "no one is exempt," that the "lifestyles" value of decency which she learned in her Canadian childhood does not guarantee her immunity; in fact, her Canadian "niceness," hiding truth as it does, has led to naïve complicity. Her island lover, Paul, for example, always corrects her middle-class views with the reality of the needs of the Third World: when Rennie quips that "sugar is bad for you," he responds, "that depends on what else you have to eat" (p. 223). Released from prison at novel's end, she agrees when the Canadian diplomat asks her not to write about what she has observed, but then her final thoughts imply that she will, that over the course of the novel she has been politicized beyond the traditionally

Canadian stance: "she is a subversive. She was not one once but now she is. A reporter" (p. 301).

Rennie learns the truth of Paul's statement: "There's only people with power and people without power" (p. 240). But the reader recognizes that all the power in the novel is in the hands of men: men have it, women don't, as the novel's epigraph implies: "A man's presence suggests what he is capable of doing to you or for you. By contrast, a woman's presence . . . defines what can and cannot be done to her." Jake is a sadist, playing out sexual rape fantasies with Rennie. She is haunted by the memory of a Canadian police exhibit on pornography, the climactic image being that of a live rat poking from a woman's vagina. The guards of her island jail manipulate sexual favors from Lora, a girlfriend of one of the political leaders, and then beat her senseless when she asks too many questions. Caught in the cross-fire of revolution, Rennie watches Paul's energy during their attempted escape and ponders: "we get into these messes because they [men] love it" (p. 256). But her complicity here is evident too: just as she took part in the sexual games with Jake, she also, as "tourist," does not see things as they are and gets herself hurt through her passive involvement with Paul. She finally acknowledges her fear of men when she witnesses the torture of prisoners in the courtyard of the prison: "she's afraid of men and it's simple, it's rational, she's afraid of men because men are frightening" (p. 290). Political and sexual images coincide at this point as Rennie goes on to connect "here and there," for "she's seen the man with the rope," the "faceless stranger" who, at novel's opening, broke into her apartment and left a coil of rope on her bed, his intention, according to the police, rape. As Coral Ann Howells notes, "the power struggle has . . . expanded from a personal to an impersonal political struggle where oppression and victimization have no sexual focus; dictatorships, whether colonial or post-colonial, do not distinguish between women and men."[6] Men everywhere, Rennie learns, have the power to inflict "bodily harm," and women, representing all victims of oppression, although they have very little power to defend themselves, can at least refuse to abdicate.

Rape may seem too much a women's issue by which to develop such a broad political perspective, but not for the reader familiar with Susan Brownmiller's analysis of the history of male-female relations, *Against Our Will* (1975). Rape, she says, is "a political act," for it "imposes humiliation and oppression on the victim."[7] In the same year that women's equality rights were guaranteed in the new Canadian Charter of Rights and Freedoms, the incidence of rape in Canada was high enough that Michele Landsberg called it a "national disgrace."[8] Equally disgraceful was the battle Canadian women were forced to wage against male politicians to get the rights of women enshrined in the Charter. In light of Rennie's occupation, it is ironic that the historic struggle focused on a journalist, Doris Anderson, for twenty years editor of *Chatelaine*. Appointed by the Liberal government as president of the Advisory Council on the Status of Women, Anderson spearheaded plans for a conference on women and the constitution. Asked by the minister responsible to postpone the conference because it would be embarrassing to the government in the midst of constitutional negotiations, Anderson resigned, formed the Ad Hoc Committee of Canadian Women, and proceeded with the conference. When the provincial premiers and federal ministers reached agreement on the Constitution and the Charter of Rights in November of 1981, they omitted the guarantee of sexual equality for women, along with native rights. Women, led by the Ad Hoc Committee, lobbied all the premiers and finally succeeded in reversing the decision, gaining equality rights in the Charter. "Canadian feminism had come of age" (p. 47), declared Landsberg, but the point was reinforced that it is still a man's world: power is elsewhere, not in the hands of women. Moreover, statistics on women in the labor force from the Canadian Advisory Council on the Status of Women reveal that, despite the guarantee of equality on the parchment signed by Elizabeth Regina, "in 1984, the wages of women who worked full time for a full year averaged only 64% of the average earnings of men who worked on the same basis."[9] "Rape" is a relevant term.

Other critics besides Howells have noticed the national dimensions of Rennie's vulnerability in both sexual and political relations. Lorna Irvine, for example, notes that Rennie, "like the narrator of *Surfacing*, seems often to represent the country in which she lives. Like Canada, Rennie is perceived by many different characters as naïve, politically shallow" (p. 43). But beyond a generalized connection of female and national definitions, Irvine makes no extensive exploration of the parallel. Atwood herself is not so reticent. In a 1981 address delivered to the Harvard Consortium in Inter-American Relations, "Canadian-American Relations: Surviving the Eighties," Atwood made a deliberate connection between feminism and nationalism: "The cultural nationalism of the early '70s was not aggressive in nature. It was a simple statement: we exist. Such movements become militant only when the other side replies, in effect, No, you don't. Witness feminism."[10] She then continued with specific reference to the Trudeau government's National Energy Policy of the early 1980s: "Canada, it seems, was going to get back its own oil. It would have cost less if they'd done it earlier or never sold it in the first place, but why quibble? 'Canada comes of age,' someone predictably announced, and the United States reacted as though someone had just seduced its sister" (p. 388). It was Canadians who were legitimately concerned about the rape of their natural resources. Ron Graham, in his 1986 examination of the turbulent politics of the early 1980s, *One-Eyed Kings*, reports the extent to which power in Canada was elsewhere: "By 1980 seventeen of Canada's top twenty-five oil companies were foreign-controlled. They accounted for 72 per cent of Canadian oil and gas sales. By the same year, Canada had moved to first place on the United Nations' list of countries with high foreign ownership."[11] The formation of the National

Energy Program to protect Canadian national interests against rising OPEC oil prices and foreign ownership, however, failed because before long the world price of oil in the early 1980s went down. The Liberal government's efforts were overwhelmed by worldwide recession. Read in the context of such specific international developments, *Bodily Harm* reflects the increase in a global perspective which all Canadians were learning once again, that their lifestyle was extremely vulnerable to the whims of power elsewhere.

The chief power-broker affecting Canadian life, the United States, had in the 1980s shifted to the political right under Republican Ronald Reagan. Canadians followed this political wind in the election of 1984 when they gave Brian Mulroney's Conservatives their first majority government since the John George Diefenbaker landslide of 1958, and, in 1988, the first consecutive majorities in over forty years of Canadian history. What typifies the Mulroney era is the economic conditioning of women's and the nation's identities; free trade and the rising deficit dominated the national agenda throughout the latter years of the decade and will continue to do so well into the 1990s. One recalls the effect of economic factors in Laurence's *The Stone Angel* (1964) when Hagar asserted "the money's the main concern" to justify her negative actions. While the Mulroney government has been successful in implementing its economic agenda, it has failed on two key issues of concern to women: abortion and childcare. In the dying days of its first mandate, the Conservative government was unable to pass needed abortion legislation; immediately following reelection in 1988, the Conservatives reneged on their election promise to establish a National Childcare Program because of a lack of money. Yet the Conservative government found the money in 1988 to fund a conference organized by REAL Women, an anti-feminist lobby group, thereby angering many women's organizations. As in the United States, conservative policies could be damaging to women's lifestyles. One might recall Jerry Falwell's announcement, through the media on June 11, 1989, that the Moral Majority was to be disbanded because it was no longer necessary now that the religious right was firmly in power. Perhaps no event was more symbolic of the danger of right-wing policies than the loss by American women in their decade-long struggle for ratification of the Equal Rights Amendment to the American Constitution, ironically in the same year that Canadian women fought and won equality rights in the repatriated Constitution.

Atwood's *The Handmaid's Tale* (1985) reflects upon, and even foreshadows, the international conservative backlash of the late 1980s. Dubbed "speculative fiction" by Atwood,[12] *The Handmaid's Tale* presents a dystopia, a satire, about how the United States could become a right-wing totalitarian state in which politics are explicitly sexual. Several references in the novel suggest that the "Republic of Gilead" practices South African *apartheid* on an expanded scale: not only are the "Children of Ham" resettled in "National

Homeland One,"[13] but also "Unwomen" and other political undesirables such as feminists are sent to "the Colonies." A right-wing theocracy, compared in the "Historical Notes" at the end of the novel to the "monotheocracy" of present-day Iran (p. 312), rules the United States. If that seems an outrageous comparison, Atwood is not the first to make it: Betty Friedan in *The Second Stage* (1981) warned that Nazi anti-feminism is "rising again, in the resurgent religious fundamentalism of Moslem nations—and in the United States" (p. 326). Her description of Germany under Hitler describes the historical precedent for Atwood's novel:

One of Hitler's first acts after he came to power was to disband feminist organizations and to close down feminist publications. In 1933, feminists were removed from teaching and other public posts by the same law that removed "non-Aryans" from such jobs. All women were banned from the Reichstag, from judgeships and from other decision-making posts. Married women were to stay at home and leave paid jobs to men. Birth-control clinics were padlocked . . . abortion became sabotage. . . . "The right of personal freedom," Hitler told women in *Mein Kampf,* "recedes before the duty to preserve the race. . . . The sacrifice of personal existence is necessary to secure the preservation of the species."[14]

The first acts of the new order in the Republic of Gilead were to disallow women from holding jobs, from having money or possessions of their own. A complex series of disasters has made procreation a difficult and rare achievement and, hence, some women in the Republic of Gilead are prized for their demonstrated ability to procreate. These "handmaids" are "saved by childbearing" (p. 233), for, as before in the history of many paternalistic societies, it is the women who are deemed to have the problem: "There is no such thing as a sterile man . . . not officially. There are only women who are fruitful and women who are barren, that's the law" (p. 71). The rationale for such action, as in Fascist Germany, is the survival of the state; this connection is made explicit when, during the impregnation "Ceremony," the narrator recalls "Queen Victoria's advice to her daughter. *Close your eyes and think of England*" (p. 105). Recalling the past—"think of England"—Atwood projects a future scenario based on very present political prejudices.

Gilead has a paternalistic culture which "reveres" women. Men have power—"there's no doubt about who holds the real power" (p. 146)—symbolized by the reference to the head of the protagonist's household as "Commander"; she, in contrast, is not allowed her real name but must use the patronymic indicating possession by the man, "Offred." She is aware that a male doctor has the power to "fake the tests, report [the handmaids] for cancer, for infertility, [to] have [them] shipped off to the Colonies, with the Unwomen" (p. 71). Whereas once, "in the days of anarchy," there were "rules that were never spelled out but that every woman knew" to protect her from male violence, now there were laws to ensure that "no man shouts

obscenities at us, speaks to us, touches us. No one whistles" (p. 34). And
in this paternalistic society, it is women, the Aunts, who train and police
the handmaids, using religious piety and ritual to keep them subservient.
At a "Testifying" session, as one of the handmaids-in-training tells "about
how she was gang-raped at fourteen and had an abortion," the other handmaids are led to catechize her for her sins:

But *whose* fault was it? Aunt Helena says, holding up one plump finger.
Her fault, *her* fault, *her* fault, we chant in unison.
Who led them on? Aunt Helena beams, pleased with us.
She did. *She* did. *She* did.
Why did God allow such a terrible thing to happen?
Teach her a *lesson*. Teach her a *lesson*. Teach her a *lesson*. (pp. 81–82)

Offred thinks ruefully of her liberated mother: "You wanted a women's
culture. Well, now there is one. It isn't what you meant, but it exists"
(p. 137). Atwood suggests how matriarchal values can be absorbed into the
social fabric and perverted to ensure that traditional power groups maintain
their hold.

The novel makes only one reference to Canada, in a distorted television
news report of a smuggling operation of "natural resources" (p. 93). When
one considers the reversal of the usual North-South flow of resources, one
realizes that the reference is to handmaids. The "Historical Notes" confirm
that Canada during the time of the Republic of Gilead was a place of escape;
the Underground Femaleroad smuggled women "into what was *then* Canada" (p. 323, emphasis mine), implying that in the year 2195, Canada does
not exist in the same form as in 1985. Indeed, the "International Historical
Association Convention" takes place in the Arctic at the University of Denay,
Nunavit, a pun based on the present Inuit claims for a Dene nation; in the
twenty-second century, land claims settlements seem to have produced a
separate nation. In what could be considered an ironic gibe by Atwood at
Canada's tendency to follow Americans in the formulation of foreign policy,
the speaker notes that "Canada at that time did not wish to antagonize its
powerful neighbour"; consequently, "there were roundups and extraditions
of such refugees" (p. 323). The ultimate fate of the novel's nameless protagonist remains unknown, as does Canada's; however, the fictional Canada at
least seems to provide a thin lifeline to freedom, as in the past Canada has
for people from United Empire Loyalists to Vietnam draft dodgers. In face
of the southern direction of Canada's economic future under the Free Trade
Agreement, it remains to be seen whether Canada in the future will still
exist—in the sense that George Grant meant—as a conservative alternative
to the republic south of the forty-ninth parallel.

However, as Atwood suggests in "Canadian-American Relations," there
are "values beyond national ones," such as "political repression, torture and

mass murder. . . . The most important field of study at the moment is not Canadian literature or . . . American . . . [but] the study of human aggression" (p. 391). Like Orwell's *1984* (1949), *The Handmaid's Tale* reflects on current issues, besides those of women, which have global consequences for the future: ecology, nuclear holocaust, toxic waste, AIDS, racism are all brought into play to explain the origin of the Republic of Gilead (pp. 316–17). Atwood has written a "modest proposal" for the future in the form of a sexual-political satire: in contrast to Professor Pieixoto's caution about "passing moral judgement" on the Gileadeans (p. 314), Atwood invites her readers to judge a state by its treatment of minorities. And in case Canadians and Americans are tempted to believe that political repression "can't happen here," Atwood reminds her listeners at the Amnesty International conference that the American and Canadian "record on civil rights issues [especially since World War II] is less than pristine" (p. 395). Like the satire of *Lady Oracle*, *The Handmaid's Tale* suggests that individuals and nations should "Go, and do unlikewise."

Atwood's novels of the 1980s also reveal that her literary dialogue with Margaret Laurence, noted in earlier chapters, continues, even after the death of the senior writer. The epigraph from Genesis, upon which the impregnation ceremony of *The Handmaid's Tale* is based, recalls the biblical handmaid, Hagar, whose tale influenced so much of Laurence's writing of *The Stone Angel*. Luke is the name of Offred's husband in *The Handmaid's Tale* and of Stacey's lover in *The Fire-Dwellers*. In both *The Handmaid's Tale* and *A Jest of God* the protagonist's lover's name is Nick. All of these male characters, moreover, are positive "help-mates" to the heroines. The Laurence-Atwood dialogue seems to carry on in the publication of *Cat's Eye* (1988) as well. The protagonist, Elaine Risley, like Morag in Laurence's *The Diviners*, is an "eminent artist"[15] who takes her daughter to Vancouver when she leaves her husband. Like Morag in the time present of *The Diviners*, the mature Elaine has come to terms with herself and her life, including all her imperfections and irresolutions. Furthermore, the narrative structure of each novel is similar: chronological scenes from the time present are interspersed with a chronological retrospective of the narrator's maturation into an artist. Just as *The Diviners* was acknowledged to be Laurence's "spiritual autobiography," *Cat's Eye* seems to be the most personal of Atwood's work to date, drawing heavily as it does on the details of her own life.[16] Both novels present a summing up of a life, of a career, of an era.

Cat's Eye, this close examination of childhood influences, presents characters, situations, images and themes common to Atwood's novels, notably *Surfacing* and *Lady Oracle*. The heroines in each of these books, for example, struggle with their awkwardness in the face of feminine social conventions. In Elaine's childhood friendship with Cordelia, we witness women policing women as Cordelia tries to "improve" Elaine: "I worry about what I've said today, the expression on my face, how I walk, what I wear, because all of these things need improvement. I am not normal, I am not like other girls. Cordelia tells me so, but she will help me" (p. 118). Although there is some social criticism of the 1980s, *Cat's Eye* mostly chronicles the 1940s and 1950s in "dowdy" Toronto (p. 8) through the eyes of a Canadian girl for whom material possessions, feminine games, urban life and the British Empire are foreign. The female world offers "no end to imperfection" (p. 138) and the narrator feels far more comfortable among the northern woods of Ontario, as do her parents and brother. The difference she notices is that her father and brother carry their northern behavior into the urban setting, whereas she and her mother are expected to act differently. But like her mother, Elaine develops in adulthood "fine, irreverent carelessness" (p. 214) about feminine conventions; as a woman who does not fit into any feminist or artistic niches, she rejects labels, makes independent judgements and paints in her own unique style. The novel implies that the essential Canadianness of the protagonist—northern, natural and free—enables her eventually to balance with humor the demands of her art and family, while keeping society's demands for feminine conventions at bay.

The novel presents a challenge to literary critics in Elaine's denigration of the predictable criticisms of her retrospective: "the inevitable *eclectic*, the obligatory *post-feminist*, a *however* and a *despite*. . . . Bet-hedging and qualification" (p. 226). It is important, while avoiding empty labels, to point out the political dimensions, in this personal history, of concern to women and Canada. Most significantly, Elaine uses both feminist and national points of reference to define herself as woman and artist. Asked by a young interviewer to "say something about . . . [her] generation of woman artists . . . the seventies," Elaine states that her generation is "the forties. . . . The war. There are people who remember the war and people who don't." "You mean the Viet Nam War?" asks the interviewer. "No," responds Elaine. "The Second World War" (p. 89). In this humorous exchange the artist ignores the feminist label and insists on a historical reference, not to the American war, but to the war from which Canada truly emerged as a nation, to define her generation and herself. Again, Elaine refuses the label of "feminist painter" (p. 90) and explains her own clear-headed assessment of her work, its value and impact: "I'm a painter. Painters paint women. Rubens painted women, Renoir painted women, Picasso painted women. Everyone paints women. . . . Anyway, why should my women be the same as everyone else's women?" (pp. 90–91). By placing Elaine within an artistic heritage which is both masculine and international, Atwood suggests that the vision of a Canadian artist is unique and mature enough to be judged on its artistic merits, just as the nation must be judged by its contribution to the international struggle.

Elaine's "refusals" to follow any feminist "party lines" suggest she is more modern than the young interviewer; the generation gap evokes the state of the women's movement at the end of the decade. A recent profile of the twenty-one female Progressive Conservative members of Parliament, one-third of whom were born after World War II, revealed "distaste for anything that smacked of 'feminism'... [yet] real concern about... a major revision of social programmes—of which women are the chief users."[17] Feminists have certainly been reevaluating their former stances; Germaine Greer in *Sex and Destiny* (1984) and Susan Brownmiller in *Femininity* (1983) explained that women were in the process of reexamining the meaning of femininity and the goals of modern women, questioning whether in gaining equal opportunity with men, they have simply entered a male world where, to achieve success, they must conform to a lifestyle devised by and for males.[18] *The Bassett Report: Career Success and Canadian Women* (1985) by Isabel Bassett revealed that career women are concerned with the sacrifices they must make in their personal lives and relationships in order to reach the top of their chosen fields.[19] Betty Friedan has labelled this period of soul-searching "the Second Stage" and, on a positive note, imagines her own daughter and her spiritual daughters "can say 'no' to superwoman stan-dards—in their work or their homes—because they already feel good enough about themselves as women to trust themselves. Sure, they will have prob-lems, putting it all together, but they won't have as many problems and guilts as we did."[20] As the 1980s came to a close, there seemed to be a retrospective nature to the feminist movement as it documented the history of the women's movement, collating significant texts in such compendiums as *Outrageous Acts and Everyday Rebellions* (1983) by Gloria Steinem and *The Sisterhood: The True Story of the Women who Changed the World* (1988) by Marcia Cohen, and as it sought to discover not only how to preserve the gains of the first stage, but also how to apply feminist values to the changing situations of the coming decades.

Moreover, as the women's movement seems to be searching for the next stage, Canada ponders its shape for the 1990s. The conservative political mandates have been renewed in the United States and Canada well into the 1990s. Canadians aligned themselves even more to this international political direction in the 1988 election when they decided to do what they have refused throughout this century, to open the borders to freer trade with the United States; yet, at the same time, Canadians also expressed the desire to preserve the social programs which distinguish them from American en-trepreneurial society. The resulting mood is one of watchfulness and careful reassessment. As Peter C. Newman noted in his 1988 essay, "Sometimes a Great Nation," Canadians "must devise a new and more contemporary way of seeing our country and ourselves. Canada must be re-invented."[21] Perhaps symbolic of this mood of reflectiveness is the renewed search for the meaning of liberalism in Canada. The leaderships of the Liberal party under former Trudeau lieutenant, Jean Chretien, and of the New Democratic party under parliamentary newcomer, Audrey McLaughlin—the first female leader of a federal political party in Canadian history—poses an intriguing choice for the Canadian electorate; they will in great part define new directions for the left in Canada for the 1990s, directions which will, in turn, have their influence on the identity of the nation. Finally, the growing international movements for peace and ecology, advocating as they do such "feminine" values as preserving and nurturing, may yet have their impact on the destructive, exploitive "masculine" attitudes which have for so long produced profits, pollution and international conflict. As in her history, the Canada of the future may be forced by domestic and international concerns to alter her political course.

"Welcome to the 1990s!" The decade of the 1980s, which began with such optimism under Trudeau's leadership, ended with cautious, conservative hope for the future. But many decisions face Canadians in the early years of the 1990s: constitutional realignment after the failure of the Meech Lake accord, full implementation of the Free Trade Agreement, Native land claims, and legislation governing abortion. The process of defining independence, not only for women and for Canada, but also for other "distinct societies" within Canada will continue. Atwood concludes her address to the Amnesty International conference by quoting the American writer Flannery O'Connor: "people without hope do not write novels" (p. 397). The hope in both Laurence's *Diviners* and Atwood's *Cat's Eye*, as in Friedan's *Second Stage*, is embodied in the daughters: Morag's Pique will find her "unique [but] . . . not unique" way, while Elaine's two "sane" daughters, who "take everything in, look at it straight, accept everything," will be, she hopes, "the happy end, of my story" (p. 115). But when Elaine adds, "of course they are not the end of their own," she acknowledges, perhaps for us all, the continuum of life itself. Part of that story for Canadians is to be found in the writings of the daughters of all the women examined in this study; Alice Munro, Carol Shields, Audrey Thomas are only a few of the excellent writers charting the "lives" of contemporary Canadian "girls and women." Others explore national-international experiences: Mavis Gallant writes brilliant stories from Paris; Australian-born Janette Turner Hospital's Canadian heroines struggle to understand themselves in many international settings; Bharati Mukarjee's Indian-born immigrants seek homes in North American society; Joy Kogawa's Japanese Canadians want acceptance and understanding.[22] To understand the process of Canada's political and social evolution, it would be advisable, this study suggests, to continue to look as much at what contemporary Canadian women writers *say* as at what *historians* record.

NOTES

1. Canada, Department of Justice, *Decisions of the Judicial Committee of the Privy Council Relating to the BNA Act (full), 1867, and the Canadian Constitution, 1867–1954* (Ottawa, Imprint 1973), pp. 641–42.

2. "*Bodily Harm* reveals, subversively, certain characteristics of Canada." Lorna Irvine, *Sub/Version: Canadian Fiction by Women* (Toronto, 1986), p. 40.

3. Margaret Laurence, "My Final Hour," *Canadian Literature* 100 (Spring 1984): 187–97.

4. Margaret Atwood, "Amnesty International," in her *Second Words: Selected Critical Prose* (Toronto, 1982), p. 394.

5. Margaret Atwood, *Bodily Harm* (Toronto, 1981), p. 290.

6. Coral Ann Howells, *Private and Fictional Words: Canadian Women Novelists of the 1970s and 1980s* (London, 1987), p. 61.

7. Susan Brownmiller, *Against Our Will: Men, Women and Rape* (New York, 1975).

8. Michele Landsberg, *Women and Children First* (Toronto, 1982), p. 97.

9. Canadian Advisory Council on the Status of Women, *Fine Balances: Equal Status for Women in Canada in the 1990s* (Ottawa, March 1987), p. 8.

10. Margaret Atwood, "Canadian-American Relations: Surviving the Eighties," in her *Second Words*, p. 385.

11. Ron Graham, *One-Eyed Kings: Promise and Illusion in Canadian Politics* (Toronto, 1986), p. 86.

12. See Mary McCarthy, "Breeders, Wives and Unwomen," *The Book Review* 7 (February 9, 1986): 1, 35.

13. Margaret Atwood, *The Handmaid's Tale* (Toronto, 1985), p. 93.

14. Betty Friedan, *The Second Stage* (New York, 1981), p. 326.

15. Margaret Atwood, *Cat's Eye* (Toronto, 1988), p. 226.

16. Judith Timson, "Atwood's Triumph," *Maclean's* (October 3, 1988): 56–61.

17. "Charlotte Gray, "The New F-Word," *Chatelaine* (April 1989): 17–18.

18. Germaine Greer, *Sex and Destiny* (New York, 1984), and Susan Brownmiller, *Femininity* (New York, 1983).

19. Isabel Bassett, *The Bassett Report: Career Success and Canadian Women* (Toronto, 1985).

20. Friedan, *The Second Stage*, p. 340.

21. Peter C. Newman, "Sometimes a Great Nation," in his *Sometimes a Great Nation: Will Canada Belong to the 21st Century?* (Toronto, 1988), p. 17.

22. See Alice Munro, *Lives of Girls and Women* (Toronto, 1971), Carol Shields, *Small Ceremonies* (Toronto, 1976), Audrey Thomas, *Mrs. Blood* (Vancouver, 1970), Mavis Gallant, *Home Truths* (New York, 1981), Janette Turner Hospital, *The Ivory Swing* (Toronto, 1982), Bharati Mukarjee, *The Tiger's Daughter* (Toronto, 1971) and Joy Kogawa, *Obasan* (Toronto, 1981).

Bibliography

PRIMARY SOURCES

Atwood, Margaret. *Bodily Harm*. Toronto, 1981.
———. *Cat's Eye*. Toronto, 1988.
———. *The Edible Woman*. Toronto, 1969.
———. *The Handmaid's Tale*. Toronto, 1985.
———. *Lady Oracle*. Toronto, 1976.
———. *Surfacing*. 1972; Don Mills, 1973.
Brooke, Frances. *The History of Emily Montague*. 1769; Toronto, 1961.
Duncan, Sara Jeannette. *The Imperialist*. 1904; Toronto, 1971.
Jameson, Anna. *Winter Studies and Summer Rambles in Canada*. 1838; Toronto: Coles facsimile ed., 1972.
Laurence, Margaret. *The Diviners*. Toronto, 1974.
———. *The Fire-Dwellers*. Toronto, 1969.
———. *The Stone Angel*. 1964; Toronto, 1968.
McClung, Nellie. *Purple Springs*. Toronto, 1921.
Moodie, Susanna. *Roughing It in the Bush*. 1852; Toronto: Coles facsimile ed., 1980.
Ostenso, Martha. *Wild Geese*. Toronto, 1925.
Traill, Catharine Parr. *The Backwoods of Canada*. 1836; Toronto: Coles facsimile ed., 1980.
Wilson, Ethel. *Hetty Dorval*. 1947; Toronto, 1967.
———. *The Innocent Traveller*. Toronto, 1949.
———. *Swamp Angel*. 1954; Toronto, 1962.

SECONDARY SOURCES

Aitken, Hugh G. J. *American Capital and Canadian Resources*. Cambridge, 1961.
Allen, Peter. "Narrative Uncertainty in Sara Jeannette Duncan's *The Imperialist*." *Studies in Canadian Literature* 9, no. 1 (1984): 41–60.
Atwood, Margaret. "Face to Face." *Maclean's* (May 1974): 38–39, 43–46.

———. "Getting Out from Under." *Empire Club Addresses 1972–73*. Toronto, 1973, pp. 356–57.

———. *Power Politics*. Toronto, 1971.

———. *Second Words: Selected Critical Prose*. Toronto, 1982.

———. *Survival*. Toronto, 1972.

———. "Travels Back: Refusing to acknowledge where you come from is an act of amputation." *MacLean's* (January 1973): 28, 31, 48.

Ballstadt, Carl P. A. "Secure in Conscious Worth: Susanna Moodie and the Rebellion of 1837." *Canadian Poetry* 18 (Spring-Summer 1986): 88–98.

Bassett, Isabel. *The Bassett Report: Career Success and Canadian Women*. Toronto, 1985.

Berger, Carl. *Sense of Power: Studies in the Ideas of Canadian Imperialism 1867–1914*. Toronto, 1970.

Bothwell, Robert, Ian Drummond, and John English. *Canada since 1945: Power, Politics, and Provincialism*. Toronto, 1981.

Boutelle, Ann Edwards. "Brooke's Emily Montague: Canada and Woman's Rights." *Women's Studies* 12 (Winter 1986): 7–16.

Brown, Robert Craig, and Ramsay Cook. *Canada 1896–1921: A Nation Transformed*. Toronto, 1974.

Brownmiller, Susan. *Against Our Will: Men, Women and Rape*. New York, 1975.

———. *Femininity*. New York, 1983.

Buss, Helen M. "Margaret Laurence—a Bibliographical Essay." *American Review of Canadian Studies* 11, no. 5 (Autumn 1981): 1–14.

Buxton, Bonnie. "Meet Maureen McTeer," *Chatelaine* (October 1976): 52–53, 117–23.

Cameron, Donald. *Conversations with Canadian Novelists*. Toronto, 1973.

Canada, Department of Justice, *Decisions of the Judicial Committee of the Privy Council Relating to the BNA Act (full), 1867, and the Canadian Constitution, 1867–1954*. Ottawa, Imprint 1973.

Canadian Advisory Council on the Status of Women. *Fine Balances: Equal Status for Women in the 1990s*. Ottawa, March 1987.

Cardinal, Harold. *The Unjust Society*. Edmonton, 1969.

Chase, Richard. *The American Novel and Its Tradition*. New York, 1957.

Cleverdon, Catherine L. *The Woman Suffrage Movement in Canada*. Toronto, 1950.

Cobban, William. "Dealing Out Death Discreetly: The Traffic in Canadian Arms." *Saturday Night* 86 (November 1971): 23–26.

Cohen, Marcia. *The Sisterhood: The True Story of the Women Who Changed the World*. New York, 1988.

Cooley, Dennis. "Antimacassared in the Wilderness: Art and Nature in *The Stone Angel*." *Mosaic* 11 (Spring 1978): 29–46.

Creighton, Donald. *Dominion of the North*. Toronto, 1957.

———. *The Forked Road: Canada 1939–1957*. Toronto, 1976.

Cude, Wilfred. *A Due Sense of Differences: An Evaluative Approach to Canadian Literature*. Lanham, Md., 1980.

Dahlie, Hallvard. "Self-conscious Canadians." *Canadian Literature* 62 (Fall 1974): 6–16.

Daly, Mary. *Beyond God the Father: Toward a Philosophy of Women's Liberation*. Boston, 1973.

Davey, Frank. "Atwood's Comic Novels." *Studies in Canadian Literature* 5 (1980): 209–21.

Davidson, Arnold E., and Cathy N. Davidson, eds. *The Art of Margaret Atwood*. Toronto, 1981.

Dean, Misao, "The Process of Definition: Nationality in Sara Jeannette Duncan's Early International Novels." *Journal of Canadian Studies* 20 (Summer 1985): 132–49.

Denham, Paul, ed. *The Evolution of Canadian Literature in English: 1945–1970*. Vol. 4. Toronto, 1973.

Djwa, Sandra. "Canadian Poets and the Great Tradition." *Canadian Literature* 65 (Summer 1975): 42–52.

Duncan, Sara Jeannette. *Sara Jeannette Duncan: Selected Journalism*. Ed. Thomas E. Tausky. Ottawa, 1978.

———. *A Social Departure. How Orthodocia and I Went Round the World by Ourselves*. New York, 1890.

Edwards, Mary Jane, Paul Denham and George Parker, eds. *The Evolution of Canadian Literature in English: Beginnings to 1867*. Vol. 1. Toronto, 1973.

———. *The Evolution of Canadian Literature in English: 1867–1914*. Vol. 2. Toronto, 1973.

Fiedler, Leslie. *Love and Death in the American Novel*. New York, 1975.

Fowler, Marian. *The Embroidered Tent*. Toronto, 1982.

———. *Redney: A Life of Sara Jeannette Duncan*. Toronto, 1983.

Fraser, Blair. *The Search for Identity: Canada, 1945–1967*. Toronto, 1967.

Friedan, Betty. *The Feminine Mystique*. New York, 1963.

———. *The Second Stage*. New York, 1981.

Frye, Northrop. *The Bush Garden*. 1943; Toronto, 1971.

Gairdner, William D. "Traill and Moodie: The Two Realities." *Journal of Canadian Fiction* 1 (Spring 1972): 35–42.

Gallant, Mavis. *Home Truths*. New York, 1981.

Garebian, Keith. "*Surfacing*: Apocalyptic Ghost Story." *Mosaic* 9 (Spring 1976): 1–9.

Gibson, Graeme. *Eleven Canadian Novelists*. Toronto, 1972.

Giltrow, Janet. " 'Painful Experience in a Distant Land' : Mrs. Moodie and Mrs. Trollope in America." *Mosaic* 14 (Spring 1981): 131–44.

Gotlieb, Phyllis. "On Margaret Laurence." *Tamarack Review* 52 (1969): 76–80.

Grace, Sherrill. *Violent Duality*. Montreal, 1980.

Graham, Ron. *One-Eyed Kings: Promise and Illusion in Canadian Politics*. Toronto, 1986.

Grant, George. *Lament for a Nation*. Toronto, 1965.

Gray, Charlotte. "The New F-Word." *Chatelaine* (April 1989): 17–18.

Greer, Germaine. *The Female Eunuch*. London, 1970.

———. "On Women's Year." *Chatelaine* (September 1975): 4, 101–3.

———. *Sex and Destiny*. New York, 1984.

Griffiths, Linda. *Maggie and Pierre*. Vancouver, 1980.

Harding, M. Esther. *Woman's Mysteries*. New York, 1976.

Heath, Jeffrey M., ed. *Profiles in Canadian Literature 1*. Toronto, 1980.

———. *Profiles in Canadian Literature 3*. Toronto, 1982.

Hewlett, Sylvia Ann. *A Lesser Life: The Myth of Women's Liberation in America.* New York, 1986.

Hinz, Evelyn J. "The Masculine/Feminine Psychology of American/Canadian Primitivism: *Deliverance* and *Surfacing.*" In *Other Voices/Other Views: a Collection of Essays from the Bi-centennial.* Ed. Robin W. Winks. New York, 1978, pp. 75–96.

Hinz, Evelyn J., and John J. Teunissen. "*Surfacing*: Margaret Atwood's 'Nymph Complaining.'" *Contemporary Literature* 20, no. 2 (1979): 221–36.

Hite, Shere. *Women and Love: A Cultural Revolution in Progress.* New York, 1987.

Hole, Judith, and Ellen Levine. *Rebirth of Feminism.* New York, 1971.

Horn, Michael, ed. *The Dirty Thirties.* Toronto, 1972.

Horney, Karen. *Feminine Psychology.* New York, 1967.

Hospital, Janette Turner. *The Ivory Swing.* Toronto, 1982.

Howard, Irene. "Shockable and Unshockable Methodists in Ethel Wilson's *The Innocent Traveller.*" *Essays in Canadian Writing* 23 (Spring 1982): 107–34.

Howells, Coral Ann. *Private and Fictional Words: Canadian Women Novelists of the 1970s and 1980s.* London, 1987.

Hughes, Ken. "Divining the Past, Present, Future." *Canadian Dimension* (March 1975): 41–45.

———. "Politics and *A Jest of God.*" *Journal of Canadian Studies* 13 (Fall 1978): 40–54.

Hutchison, Bruce. "The Canadian Personality." In *Man and His World.* Ed. Malcolm Ross and John Stevens. Toronto, 1961, pp. 185–92.

Innis, Mary Quayle, ed. *The Clear Spirit: Twenty Canadian Women and Their Times.* Toronto, 1966.

Irvine, Lorna. *Sub/Version: Canadian Fiction by Women.* Toronto, 1986.

Jackel, David. "Mrs. Moodie and Mrs. Traill, and the Fabrication of a Canadian Tradition." *The Compass* 6 (Spring 1979): 1–22.

James, Henry. "The Art of Fiction." In *The American Tradition in Literature.* Ed. Sculley Bradley, Richard Croom Beatty and E. Hudson Long. New York, 1967, pp. 1263–80.

Jameson, Anna. *Winter Studies and Summer Rambles in Canada.* Ed. James Talman and Elsie Murray. Toronto, 1943.

Jardine, Alice, and Paul Smith, eds. *Men in Feminism.* New York, 1987.

Jensen, Margaret Ann. *Love's Sweet Return.* Toronto, 1984.

Johnson, Edgar. *Charles Dickens: His Tragedy and Triumph.* New York, 1952.

Kaminski, Margaret. "Interview with Margaret Atwood." *Waves* 4 (Autumn 1975): 8–13.

Keirstead, B. S. *Canada in World Affairs, September, 1951 to October, 1953.* Toronto, 1956.

Klinck, Carl F., gen. ed. *Literary History of Canada: Canadian Literature in English.* 2d ed. 4 vols. Toronto, 1976.

Kogawa, Joy, *Obasan.* Toronto, 1981.

Kostash, Myrna. *Long Way from Home.* Toronto, 1980.

Landsberg, Michele. "Has Women's Year Laid an Egg?" *Chatelaine* (November 1975): 53, 113–18.

———. *Women and Children First.* Toronto, 1982.

Laurence, Margaret. *A Bird in the House.* 1971; Toronto, 1974.

————. "My Final Hour." *Canadian Literature* 100 (Spring 1984): 187–97.

————. *The Prophet's Camel Bell*. Toronto, 1963.

————. "Sources." *Mosaic* 3 (Spring 1970): 80–84.

————. "Ten Years' Sentences." *Canadian Literature* 41 (Summer 1969): 10–16.

Lecker, Robert, Jack David and Ellen Quigley, eds. *Canadian Writers and Their Works*. Toronto, 1983.

Leney, Jane. "Prospero and Caliban in Laurence's African Fiction." *Journal of Canadian Fiction* 27 (1980): 63–80.

Lever, Bernice. "An Interview with Margaret Laurence." *Waves* 3 (Winter 1975): 4–12.

Light, Beth, and Alison Prentice, eds. *Pioneer and Gentlewomen of British North America 1713–1867*. Toronto, 1980.

McCarthy, Mary, "Breeders, Wives and Unwomen." *The Book Review* 7 (February 9, 1986): 1, 35.

McClung, Nellie. *Clearing in the West*. Toronto, 1935.

————. *In Times Like These*. 1915; Toronto, 1975.

McCombs, Judith, ed. *Critical Essays on Margaret Atwood*. Boston, 1988.

McDonald, R. D. "Serious Whimsey." *Canadian Literature* 63 (Winter 1975): 40–51.

McGregor, Gaile. *The Wacousta Syndrome: Explorations in the Canadian Landscape*. Toronto, 1985.

Mackail, J. W. *Virgil and His Meaning to the World of Today*. New York, 1963.

Mackenzie, William Lyon. *The Selected Writings of William Lyon Mackenzie*. Ed. Margaret Fairley. Toronto, 1960.

MacLulich, T. D. "Crusoe in the Backwoods: A Canadian Fable?" *Mosaic* 9 (Winter 1976): 115–26.

McMullen, Lorraine. *An Odd Attempt in a Woman: The Literary Life of Frances Brooke*. Vancouver, 1983.

————, ed. *The Ethel Wilson Symposium*. Ottawa, 1982.

Maeser, Angelika. "Finding the Mother: The Individuation of Laurence's Heroines." *Journal of Canadian Fiction* 27 (1980): 151–66.

Martin, Ged. "Queen Victoria and Canada." *American Review of Canadian Studies* 13 (Spring 1983): 215–33.

Mathews, Robin. "Margaret Atwood: Survivalism." In *Canadian Literature: Surrender or Revolution*. Toronto, 1978, pp. 119–30.

————. "Susanna Moodie, Pink Toryism, and Nineteenth Century Ideas of Canadian Identity." *Journal of Canadian Studies* 10 (August 1975): 3–14.

May, Henry F. *The Enlightenment in America*. New York, 1976.

Mews, Hazel. *Frail Vessels*. London, 1969.

Miles, Rosalind. *The Female Form*. London, 1987.

————. *Fiction of Sex*. London, 1974.

————. *The Women's History of the World*. London, 1988.

Miner, Valerie. "The Many Facets of Margaret Atwood." *Chatelaine* (June 1975): 33, 66–69.

Monkman, Leslie. "The Tonnerre Family: Mirrors of Suffering." *Journal of Canadian Fiction* 27 (1980): 143–50.

Moodie, Susanna. *Roughing It in the Bush*. Toronto, 1966.

————. *Life in the Clearings*. 1853; Toronto, 1959.

———. *Susanna Moodie: Letters of a Lifetime*. Ed. Carl Ballstadt, Elizabeth Hopkins and Michael Peterman. Toronto, 1985.

Morton, Desmond, *A Short History of Canada*. Edmonton, 1983.

Morton, W. L. *The Canadian Identity*. Toronto, 1961.

———. *The Kingdom of Canada*. Toronto, 1963.

Moss, John. *Sex and Violence in the Canadian Novel*. Toronto, 1977.

———, ed. *The Canadian Novel: Beginnings*. Toronto, 1980.

———. *The Canadian Novel: Here and Now*. Toronto, 1978.

———. *The Canadian Novel: Modern Times*. Toronto, 1982.

Mukarjee, Bharati. *The Tiger's Daughter*. 1971; Toronto, 1987.

Munro, Alice. *Lives of Girls and Women*. Toronto, 1971.

Neuman, Shirley, and Smaro Kamboureli. *A Mazing Space: Writing Canadian Women Writing*. Edmonton, 1986.

New, W. H. "Frances Brooke's Chequered Gardens." *Canadian Literature* 52 (Spring 1972): 24–38.

———. "The 'Genius' of Place and Time: The Fiction of Ethel Wilson." *Journal of Canadian Studies* 3 (February 1968): 39–48.

———, ed. *Margaret Laurence: The Writer and Her Critics*. Toronto, 1977.

———. "*The Old Maid*: Frances Brooke's Apprentice Feminism." *Journal of Canadian Fiction* 2 (Summer 1973): 9–12.

———. "Rhythms of Discovery." *Canadian Literature* 100 (Spring 1984): 8–10.

———. ed. *A Political Art*. Vancouver, 1978.

Newman, Peter C. *Sometimes a Great Nation: Will Canada Belong to the 21st Century?* Toronto, 1988.

Nin, Anais. *The Novel of the Future*. New York, 1968.

Northey, Margot. *The Haunted Wilderness*. Toronto, 1976.

Onley, Gloria. "Power Politics in Bluebeard's Castle." *Canadian Literature* 60 (Spring 1974): 21–42.

Pacey, Desmond. *Ethel Wilson*. New York, 1968.

Parker, George L., ed. *The Evolution of Canadian Literature in English: 1914–1945*. Vol. 3. Toronto, 1973.

Paterson, Sheena, and Mary C. McEwan. "Margaret Trudeau's Struggle for Identity: Victor or Victim?" *Chatelaine* (August 1977): 32–33, 91–93.

Perret, Jacques. "*The Georgics*." In *Virgil: A Collection of Critical Essays*. Ed. Steele Commager. Englewood Cliffs, 1966, 28–40.

Porter, John. *The Vertical Mosaic*. Toronto, 1965.

Radwanski, George. *Trudeau*. Toronto, 1978.

Radway, Janice. *Reading the Romance: Women, Patriarchy and Popular Literature*. Chapel Hill, N.C., 1984.

Record of the Roblin Government, 1900–1914. Winnipeg, 1914.

Reid, J. H. Stewart, Kenneth McNaught and Harry S. Crowe, eds. *A Source-book of Canadian History: Selected Documents and Personal Papers*. Toronto, 1959.

Rigney, Barbara Hill. *Madness and Sexual Politics in the Feminist Novel*. Madison, 1978.

Robertson, Heather. "Keep Plugging, Barbara Frum." *Maclean's* (June 1975): 32–35.

Ross, Valerie. "She Stoops—Grovels!—to Conquer." *Maclean's* (December 15, 1975): 67.

Royds, T. F., trans. *The Eclogues and Georgics of Virgil*. London, 1907.

Rubin, Jerry. *We Are Everywhere*. New York, 1971.

Russell, Peter, ed. *Nationalism in Canada*. Toronto, 1966.

Sandler, Linda. "Interview with Margaret Atwood." *Malahat Review* 41 (January 1977): 7–27.

Savage, Candace. *Our Nell: A Scrapbook Biography*. Saskatoon, 1979.

Shields, Carol. *Small Ceremonies*. Toronto, 1976.

Showalter, Elaine. "Critical Cross-Dressing: Male Feminists and the Woman of the Year," in Alice Jardine and Paul Smith, eds., *Men in Feminism* (New York: Methuen, 1987), 116–32.

Shteir, Ann B., ed. *Women on Women*. Toronto, 1978.

Smith, A.J.M., ed. *The Masks of Fiction*. Toronto, 1961.

Sonthoff, H. W. "The Novels of Ethel Wilson." *Canadian Literature* 26 (Fall 1965): 33–42.

Springer, Marlene. *What Manner of Woman*. New York, 1973.

Staines, David, ed. *The Canadian Imagination: Dimensions of a Literary Culture*. Cambridge, 1977.

Steele, James. "The Literary Criticism of Margaret Atwood." In *In Our Own House: Social Perspectives on Canadian Literature*. Ed. Paul Cappon. Toronto, 1978, pp. 73–81.

Steinem, Gloria. *Outrageous Acts and Everyday Rebellions*. New York, 1983.

Stephens, D. G., ed. *Writers of the Prairies*. Vancouver, 1973.

Stern, Karl. *The Flight from Woman*. New York, 1965.

Strong-Boag, Veronica. "Cousin Cinderella: A Guide to Historical Literature Pertaining to Canadian Women." In *Women in Canada*. Ed. Marylee Stephenson. Don Mills, 1973.

Stursberg, Peter. *Lester Pearson and the American Dilemma*. Toronto, 1980.

Sullivan, Rosemary. "*Surfacing* and *Deliverance*." *Canadian Literature* 67 (Winter 1976): 6–20.

Swan, Susan. "Barbara Ann Scott, Are You Still Happy, Happy?" *Chatelaine* (November 1975): 50, 74–86.

Tausky, Thomas E. *Sara Jeannette Duncan: Novelist of Empire*. Port Credit, 1980.

Thomas, Audrey. *Mrs. Blood*. Vancouver, 1970.

Thomas, Clara. "A Conversation about Literature: An Interview with Margaret Laurence and Irving Layton." *Journal of Canadian Fiction* 1 (Winter 1972): 65–69.

———. "Journeys to Freedom." *Canadian Literature* 51 (Winter 1972): 9–11.

———. *Love and Work Enough*. Toronto, 1967.

———. *Our Nature, Our Voices*. Toronto, 1972.

———. "Proud Lineage: Cather and Laurence." *Canadian Review of American Studies* 2 (Spring 1971): 1–12.

Timson, Judith. "Atwood's Triumph." *Maclean's* (October 3, 1988): 56–61.

Traill, Catharine Parr. *The Backwoods of Canada*. 1842; Toronto, 1929.

———. *The Backwoods of Canada*. Toronto, 1966.

———. *The Canadian Settler's Guide*. 1854; Toronto, 1969.

———. *Lost in the Backwoods: A Tale of the Canadian Forest*. London, 1886.

———. *Studies of Plant Life in Canada*. Ottawa, 1885.

Trofimenkoff, Susan Mann. "Henri Bourassa and 'the Woman Question.' " *Journal of Canadian Studies* 10 (November 1975): 3–11.

———. "Nationalism, Feminism and Canadian Intellectual History." *Canadian Literature* 83 (Winter 1969): 7–20.

Turcotte, Bobbie, and Mary Hemlow. "Searching for the Real Margaret Trudeau." *Chatelaine* (October 1975): 64–65, 127–32.

Verduyn, Christl, ed. *Margaret Laurence: An Appreciation.* Toronto, 1988.

Wagenknecht, Edward. *The Man Charles Dickens.* Norman, Oklahoma, 1966.

Waite, P. B., ed. *Pre-Confederation: Canadian Historical Documents Series.* Scarborough, 1965.

Wasserstrom, William. *Heiress of All the Ages.* Minneapolis, 1959.

Waterston, Elizabeth. *Survey: A Short History of Canadian Literature.* Toronto, 1973.

Weaver, Mrs. Rix. *The Old Wise Woman.* New York, 1973.

Woodcock, George. *Canada and the Canadians.* London, 1973.

———. *The Canadian Novel in the Twentieth Century.* Toronto, 1975.

———. *The Canadians.* Don Mills, 1979.

Woolf, Virginia. *A Writer's Diary.* Ed. Leonard Woolf. London, 1953.

Index

ABOUT THE AUTHOR

WAYNE FRASER, Ph.D., presently teaches English full-time at Ridley College, St. Catharines, Ontario, where he was, for the past decade, job-sharing with his wife, Dr. Eleanor Johnston, and raising their three children. He is, as well, a lay-reader in the Anglican Chapel there.